Trade, Investment, Migration and Labour Market Adjustment

This is IEA Conference volume no. 135

Trade, Investment, Migration and Labour Market Adjustment

Edited by

David Greenaway, Richard Upward and Katharine Wakelin
Leverhulme Centre for Research on Globalisation and Economic Policy,
University of Nottingham, UK

in association with
International Economic Association

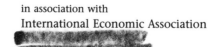

First published 2002 by
PALGRAVE MACMILLAN
Houndmills, Basingstoke, Hampshire RG21 6XS and
175 Fifth Avenue, New York, N.Y. 10010
Companies and representatives throughout the world

PALGRAVE MACMILLAN is the global academic imprint of the Palgrave
Macmillan division of St. Martin's Press, LLC and of Palgrave Macmillan Ltd.
Macmillan® is a registered trademark in the United States, United Kingdom
and other countries. Palgrave is a registered trademark in the European
Union and other countries.

ISBN 0-333-96922-7

This book is printed on paper suitable for recycling and made from fully
managed and sustained forest sources.

A catalogue record for this book is available from the British Library.

A catalogue record for this book is available from the Library of Congress

10   9   8   7   6   5   4   3   2   1
11   10   09   08   07   06   05   04   03   02

Typeset by Aarontype Limited Easton, Bristol, England
Printed and bound in Great Britain by
Antony Rowe Ltd, Chippenham and Eastbourne

Contents

The International Economic Association

A non-profit organisation with purely scientific aims, the International Economic Association (IEA) was founded in 1950. It is a federation of some 60 national economic associations in all parts of the world. Its basic purpose is the development of economics as an intellectual discipline, recognising a diversity of problems, systems and values in the world and taking note of methodological diversities.

The IEA has, since its creation, sought to fulfil that purpose by promoting mutual understanding among economists through the organisation of scientific meetings and common research programmes, and by means of publications on problems of fundamental as well as current importance. Deriving from its long concern to assure professional contacts between East and West and North and South, the IEA pays special attention to issues of economies in systemic transition and in the course of development. During more than 50 years of existence, it has organised 110 round-table conferences for specialists on topics ranging from fundamental theories to methods and tools of analysis and major problems of the present-day world. Participation in round tables is at the invitation of a specialist programme committee, but 13 triennial World Congresses have regularly attracted the participation of individual economists from all over the world.

The Association is governed by a Council, comprising representatives of all member associations, and by a 15-member Executive Committee which is elected by the Council. The Executive Committee (1999–2002) at the time of the Nottingham Conference was:

President:	Professor Robert M. Solow, USA
Vice-President:	Professor Vittorio Corbo, Chile
Treasurer:	Professor Jacob Frenkel, Israel
Other members:	Professor Bina Agarwal, India
	Professor Maria Augusztinovics, Hungary
	Professor Eliana Cardoso, Brazil
	Professor Jacques Drèze, Belgium
	Professor Gene M. Grossman, USA
	Professor Seppo Honkapohja, Finland
	Professor Valery Makarov, Russia
	Professor Andreu Mas Colell, Spain
	Professor Mustapha Nabli, Tunisia
	Professor Adrian Pagan, Australia

Professor Hans Werner Sinn, Germany
Professor Kotaro Suzumura, Japan
Secretary-General: Professor Jean-Paul Fitoussi, France
General Editor: Professor Michael Kaser, UK

Sir Austin Robinson was an active Adviser on the publication of IEA Conference proceedings from 1954 until his final short illness in 1993.

The Association has also been fortunate in having secured many outstanding economists to serve as President:

Gottfried Haberler (1950–53), Howard S. Ellis (1953–56), Erik Lindahl (1956–59), E.A.G. Robinson (1959–62), Ugo Papi (1962–65), Paul A. Samuelson (1965–68), Erik Lundberg (1968–71), Fritz Machlup (1971–74), Edmund Malinvaud (1974–77), Shigeto Tsuru (1977–80), Victor L. Urquidi (1980–83), Kenneth J. Arrow (1983–86), Amartya Sen (1986–89), Anthony B. Atkinson (1989–1992), Michael Bruno (1992–95) and Jacques Drèze (1995–99).

The activities of the Association are mainly funded from the subscriptions of members and grants from a number of organisations, including continuing support from UNESCO, through the International Social Science Council.

Acknowledgements

The chapters in this volume were initially presented as papers at an IEA Conference on 'Globalisation and Labour Markets' held at the University of Nottingham, 7–9 July 2000.

The Conference programme was developed by a Steering Group comprising:

David Greenaway, University of Nottingham, UK (chair)
Jagdish Bhagwati, Columbia University, USA
Alan Deardorff, University of Michigan, USA
André Sapir, University of Brussels, Belgium
Matthew J. Slaughter, Dartmouth College, USA
Rod Tyers, Australian National University, Australia.

The Editors are grateful for the support of this Group. We would like to acknowledge financial support from the Leverhulme Trust under Programme Grant F114/BF and from the International Social Science Council.

We also wish to acknowledge editorial support from Susan Berry in the preparation of this volume.

List of Contributors

Olivier Bontout, Ministry of Labour and Social Affairs, Paris, France
Michael Burda, Humboldt University, Berlin, Germany
Carl Davidson, Michigan State University, USA
Donald R. Davis, Columbia University and National Bureau for Economic Research, USA
Barbara Dluhosch, University of the Federal Armed Forces, Hamburg, Germany
Nigel Driffield, University of Birmingham, UK
Augustin Fosu, African Economic Research Consortium, Nairobi, Kenya
Noel Gaston, Bond University, Australia
Sourafel Girma, University of Nottingham, UK
David Greenaway, University of Nottingham, UK
Keith Head, University of British Columbia, Canada
Sébastien Jean, Centre d'Etudes Prospectives et d'Informations Internationales (CEPII)
Steve Matusz, Michigan State University, USA
J. Peter Neary, University College, Dublin, Ireland
Douglas Nelson, Tulane University, USA
Trevor A. Reeve, Board of Governors of the Federal Reserve System, USA
John Ries, University of British Columbia, Canada
Karl Taylor, University of Leicester, UK
Richard Upward, University of Nottingham, UK
Katharine Wakelin, University of Nottingham, UK
Peter Wright, University of Nottingham, UK

List of Abbreviations and Acronyms

AA	Assisted Area (UK)
CEEC	Central and Eastern European countries
CEPII	Centre d'Etudes Prospectives et d'Informations Internationales (France)
CEPR	Centre for Economic Policy Research (UK)
CES	constant elasticity of supply
CGE	computable general equilibrium
EEA	European Economic Association
EP	export-promoting
ES	export supply
ESRC	Economic and Social Research Council (UK)
EU	European Union
FDI	foreign direct investment
FPE	factor price equalisation
FRBNY	Federal Reserve Bank of New York
GDP	gross domestic product
GNP	gross national product
HIC	high-income country
HO	Heckscher-Ohlin
HOS	Heckscher-Ohlin-Samuelson
I/O	input/output
IS	import-substituting
IV	instrumental variables
LFS	Labour Force Survey (UK)
LIC	low-income country
MENA	Middle East–North Africa
MNE	multinational enterprise
NBER	National Bureau of Economic Research (US)
NIC	newly industrialised country
NIESR	National Institute of Economic and Social Research (UK)
NILF	not in the labour force
OECD	Organisation for Economic Cooperation and Development
OLS	ordinary least squares
ONS	Office for National Statistics (UK)
PPP	purchasing power parity
R&D	research and development
SDI	supply-demand-institutions
SGA	selling, general and administration
SIC	Standard Industrial Classification

SITC   Standard International Trade Classification
SMSA   standard metropolitan statistical area
SSA   Sub-Saharan Africa
UNCTAD   United Nations Conference on Trade and Development
VA   value added
WTO   World Trade Organization

1
Introduction

David Greenaway, Richard Upward and Katharine Wakelin
University of Nottingham, UK

One of the most celebrated and widely cited theorems in the international trade literature is the Stolper-Samuelson theorem. In fact the theorem is so celebrated that a special volume of papers honouring its fiftieth anniversary was published (Deardorff and Stern (1994)). As any student of international trade knows, this is a theorem about the relationship between trade and relative factor rewards. Given its centrality and longevity, it is remarkable that for so long the links between trade and factor rewards received so little attention, either from trade economists or labour economists.

Over the last decade or so all of that has changed and a major literature has developed on the links between various dimensions of openness – trade, cross-border investment, migration – and various dimensions of labour market adjustment, including wage dispersion, employment patterns and job turnover. This volume adds a range of original contributions to that literature in the form of a series of papers presented at an IEA Conference held at the Leverhulme Centre for Research on Globalisation and Economic Policy at the University of Nottingham.

In Chapter 2, Donald Davis and Trevor Reeve begin from the observation that over the past 20 years both American and European labour markets have experienced serious but different problems. Europe has suffered high and persistent unemployment, reaching double digits in many countries, while America has seen the skilled to unskilled wage premium rise sharply. The authors consider these disparate labour market developments within a common framework based on an augmented Heckscher-Ohlin model. This is a full general equilibrium model with trade among two countries with divergent factor market institutions – America is taken to be a flexible wage economy while Europe is viewed as an economy with institutionalised wage rigidity. The central analytical contribution is that the human capital accumulation decision is included endogenously, based on the model by Findlay and Kierzkowski (1983). A variety of comparative static exercises are examined, including changes in educational capital and population, entry of new countries to the trading world, technical change and a productivity slowdown. The evolution of relative wages, unemployment and the skill composition of the labour force are considered. No single cause accounting for recent factor market developments is advanced. The results from the comparative statics suggest that one or more forces may, in combination, have contributed to the differences in experience between America and Europe, including a decline in demand for unskilled workers.

The decline in demand for unskilled workers in the OECD is regarded by many as a stylised fact. The decline has manifested itself either in lower relative wages and/or higher unemployment on the part of the less skilled. In turn, this has stimulated a major debate on whether it is globalisation or skill-biased technical change which is responsible for the shift in demand, with the balance of evidence favouring the latter. In Chapter 3, Peter Neary argues that although it appears to 'fit the facts', the skill-biased technical change explanation does not provide a coherent account of all aspects of labour market developments and he offers an alternative framework which does. The framework is one in which firms compete strategically. The key result from his model is that with increased competition, domestic and foreign firms invest more aggressively, thereby increasing demand for skilled labour. He argues that not only is this result consistent with the stylised facts, it also points out the importance of recognising interactions between trade and technology, rather than treating them as entirely separable exogenous forces.

In Chapter 4 Michael Burda and Barbara Dluhosch continue on the same theme. They argue that firms' production processes are affected by the increased openness of economies, and therefore the impact of trade on labour markets may be underestimated by studies which consider technological change and trade to be separate phenomena. Two observations motivate this idea. First, globalisation has been occurring not only in the production of final goods, but also in the production process itself: trade in intermediate goods has been increasing faster than trade in final goods. Second, the production process has become increasingly *fragmented*, as firms extend production across national boundaries via outsourcing and international mergers. Burda and Dluhosch develop a model which asks whether this observed increase in the globalisation and fragmentation of production can explain current labour market developments in OECD countries. The removal of barriers to trade and factor mobility cause firms to change their production processes, which in turn affects the demand for different types of labour. In particular, the fragmentation of production requires an increase in the demand for highly skilled labour in the service sector to manage the production process. This helps to explain the fact that the demand for skilled labour has increased not only in traded but also in non-traded sectors, and the fact that the service sector has witnessed a bimodal increase in demand for high and low skill workers.

In the next chapter Carl Davidson and Steve Matusz begin with the striking contrast between the textbook case of increased trade liberalisation and the view of many policy makers and journalists. In the former, factors of production can move costlessly from one sector to another, and so while trade results in winners and losers, factors are never unemployed and so the net aggregate result is always positive. In the latter, there are potentially large costs of adjustment: workers may become unemployed as a result of changing patterns of demand, and find it difficult, or even impossible, to find work in expanding sectors of the economy. If the adjustment costs are large enough they could even outweigh the benefits of liberalisation. Davidson and Matusz therefore develop a dynamic model of trade liberalisation which accounts for the costs of labour market adjustment. The model includes both search frictions and training costs. If a worker becomes unemployed it takes time to find another job, even if s/he is suitably trained. If a worker needs to find a job in a different sector s/he must first undertake a period of training. The least-skilled workers may even find that the costs of retraining are too high, and leave the labour market altogether. Because of these frictions, trade liberalisation initially causes an increase in the level of unemployment as workers try to move from the declining to the expanding sector. Simulations from the model show that although in the long run the benefits of liberalisation outweigh the adjustment costs, these adjustment costs can be considerable. In addition, the model gives clear predictions about the winners and losers from liberalisation. Those workers who find it most difficult to retrain and thus to switch into the expanding sectors are those with most to lose.

Of course most trade models make extreme assumptions concerning the reallocation of factors of production between sectors, which subsequently affect how economies respond to external shocks. Assumptions include that factor reallocation is frictionless (as in the Heckscher-Ohlin model) or very slow (as in the specific factors model). In Chapter 6 David Greenaway, Richard Upward and Peter Wright draw together evidence on two important questions. First, has the speed of labour reallocation actually increased? Second, what are the costs of worker reallocation in terms of wages and unemployment? There is some evidence that the rate of sectoral transformation was particularly high in the UK in the 1970s and 1980s, but that it has now returned to post-war levels. A large proportion of the required net flows of workers occurred by movements between employment and non-employment. However, changes in employment shares disguise large flows in and out of sectors. These gross flows in the UK appear to be procyclical with no secular trend. A survey of the evidence suggests that sectoral reallocation is costly, particularly in terms of aggregate unemployment and unemployment duration. Microeconometric evidence suggests that movements between sectors are associated with longer unemployment spells than movements within sectors. Possible policies to address this process of adjustment are considered in the conclusions.

The five most frequently cited causes of the increase in the wage gap between skilled and unskilled workers in many industrialised countries are: changes in factor supplies, modifications of consumption patterns, institutional changes, technological change and international trade. Despite a large literature investigating each of these, it remains difficult to measure their relative importance. This is partly because each cause is often investigated separately, making it impossible to account for interactions between them. In Chapter 7 Sébastien Jean and Olivier Bontout construct a computable general equilibrium (CGE) model of the French economy between 1970 and 1992. The model allows the structural change of the economy over this time period to be summarised in terms of four components: technological change, changes in factor supplies, shifts in consumption patterns, and international trade. Jean and Bontout compare the effect of these shocks assuming initially that each operates independently, but then go on to analyse the case where technological change itself is affected by trade intensities. In fact, the ratio of skilled to unskilled wages changed very little in France between 1970 and 1992. However, the decomposition analysis allows us to see that technological change and the increasing supply of skilled labour operated in opposite directions, and effectively cancelled each other out. These two effects appear to be by far the most important influences on relative wages, and the role of international trade is relatively minor. However, if technological change is partly driven by international trade, then the role of trade in explaining increasing wage inequality is increased.

The literature on trade and labour market adjustment overwhelmingly relates to developed rather than developing countries, despite the fact that trade shocks have probably been more pervasive in the latter over the last 20 years given the pervasiveness of structural adjustment. In Chapter 8 Augustin Fosu evaluates the applicability of standard models and tools, routinely used for evaluating trade-induced adjustment, to a developing economy context. He takes as the standard framework the two-sector Heckscher-Ohlin-Samuelson model and a widely used modification, the three-sector specific factors model. He argues that neither is entirely satisfactory as a vehicle for thinking about adjustment in developing countries because of the special characteristics of labour markets. He emphasises in particular the role of rural/urban divisions, formal/informal markets, wage rigidities and the pervasive role of the public sector. He concludes by arguing that theoretical models need to be refined to acknowledge the presence of such characteristics if they are to provide useful insights.

As noted above, cross-border investment has increased dramatically, especially where the location of Japanese manufacturing firms in concerned. There has been a large increase in foreign production by Japanese firms and a corresponding rise in the share of non-production workers in the wage bill in Japan. This has led to the suggestion that the rise in international activities of Japanese firms has shifted the demand for labour in Japan towards non-production workers. One consequence of this could be to increase wage inequality in Japan. In Chapter 9 Keith Head and John Ries outline different strategies for multinational enterprises and model the effect of each alternative on demand for production and non-production workers at home. Using firm-level data on Japanese manufacturing firms they measure the impact of the scale of foreign activity, and the share of foreign to total activity, on the ratio of production to non-production workers in Japan. They find that investment in both low- and high-income countries is associated with skill upgrading at home. Increases in overseas employment appear to be a small but significant factor in observed skill upgrading in Japan.

Government subventions to attract inward investment are of course very common. The existence of such subventions reflects a belief on the part of governments in the presence of spillovers of one form or another from multinationals. One important dimension which is neglected is the possibility of regional spillovers and that is what Sourafel Girma and Katharine Wakelin focus upon in Chapter 10. The authors address a series of questions relating to the magnitude of spillovers and the likelihood of these being related to regional dimensions. They find that spillovers do appear to have a regional dimension, with domestic firms gaining when foreign firms locate in the same sector and region as them. Interestingly, however, this effect is mitigated in the case of regions with Assisted Area status, suggesting that using regional incentives to attract FDI may actually reduce the level of spillovers from their presence. The magnitude of any technology gap between domestic and foreign firms also appears to be relevant: lower gaps are associated with bigger gains from spillovers, suggesting that some threshold level of absorptive capacity may be necessary for domestic firms to benefit from spillovers.

In Chapter 11 Karl Taylor and Nigel Driffield investigate how technology, trade and multinational activity may have influenced total employment in the domestic sector. The analysis is based on sector-level data for the UK over the period 1983–1992. Rather than focusing on relative outcomes such as skilled employment relative to unskilled employment as much of the literature does, the emphasis is on aggregate total employment. The chapter overviews the changes in employment and skills in the UK over the period, and corresponding changes in FDI, technology and trade. The authors develop a theoretical model, based on a Cobb-Douglas production function approach and an empirical model that is subsequently tested. The results indicate that technology intensity, import penetration and multinational activity have all contributed to the job losses witnessed in the manufacturing sector. Given the well documented shift in demand towards skilled labour the authors suggest that any employment gains made by skilled workers have been outweighed by job losses amongst the lower skilled; this is consistent with a reduction in the aggregate number of jobs.

In the final chapter, Noel Gaston and Douglas Nelson begin from the observation that we are living in a period of rising immigration of unskilled workers. Politically this is a sensitive issue in many parts of the world. Since much of the migration is from developing to developed countries, it is especially sensitive in the latter. But in reality what kind of impact do migrants actually have on host labour markets? The authors review the alternative approaches which labour and trade economists have used to try to answer this question. They then review the empirical findings that emerge from this literature. They show that there is in fact a very considerable consensus: short of major migrations which lead to fundamental shifts in production structure, immigration has no significant impact on long-run labour market conditions. This in turn raises an interesting paradox: if immigration has a minimal impact on labour markets in host countries, why is it such a politically sensitive issue? The authors go on to argue that it has much more to do with perceptions about race and governance than about distribution.

The purpose of the Conference at which the chapters of this volume were presented was to give new insights into, and evidence on, the links between openness and labour market adjustment. We believe that the IEA Conference achieved that objective and hope that readers will also find that to be the case from the chapters selected for this volume.

References

Deardorff, A. and R. Stern (1994) *The Stolper-Samuelson Theorem: A Golden Jubilee* (Ann Arbor, MI: University of Michigan Press).

Findlay, Ronald and Kierzkowski (1983) 'International Trade and Human Capital: A Simple General Equilibrium Model', *Journal of Political Economy*, vol. 91(6), pp. 957–78.

2
Human Capital, Unemployment and Relative Wages in a Global Economy*

Donald R. Davis
Columbia University and NBER, USA

Trevor A. Reeve
Board of Governors of the Federal Reserve System, USA

1 Human capital and the global economy

Over the past 20 years both the American and the European labour markets have experienced serious problems. Yet the manifestations have been distinct. Europe has suffered high and persistent unemployment, reaching double digits in many countries. America has seen the skilled to unskilled wage premium rise sharply. From 1979 to 1989 the relative wage of a worker in the 90th percentile to one in the 10th percentile rose by 20 per cent (Freeman and Katz (1995)).

There are good reasons for considering these developments in a common framework. America and Europe are part of a single global economy. The web of trade, bilaterally and with third parties, links their goods markets and thus their prices. The goods prices in turn link their factor markets. Also, many of the shocks contributing to these developments are global shocks that affect both America and Europe. One suspects, for example, that an important component of technological shocks in recent years is global. Finally, consideration of the cases in a common framework may be valuable in enforcing consistency among the accounts we provide for each.

Consideration of these disparate labour market developments within a common framework must confront a crucial fact: labour market institutions differ across countries. This observation plays an important role in interpretations of the recent comparative labour market experience of America and Europe (Freeman and Katz (1995), Krugman (1995), Bertola and Ichino (1995)). Much of this work has examined the role of institutions one country at a time. This has proved valuable, as it allows a rich examination of local institutions. Yet it also misses an important part of the story, as the consequences of institutional choices differ markedly depending on whether the economies are closed or in a global trading world. This point is developed in the recent work of Davis (1998a, b).

* Donald Davis is grateful for support for this project from the Harvard Institute for International Development (HIID), and Trevor Reeve acknowledges the support of the National Science Foundation. The views expressed in this chapter are those of the authors and do not necessarily reflect those of the Federal Reserve.

Freeman and Katz (1995) emphasise that within this institutional matrix one wants to consider the consequences of a range of shocks to both relative demand for and supply of factors. For good reasons, much of the attention has focused on the sources of shocks to relative demand, such as technology and trade (Katz and Murphy (1992)). Yet insofar as many of these shocks are global, they may not help to explain cross-country differences in experience.

An alternative perspective for understanding the diversity of the cross-country experience has emphasised cross-country differences in the evolution of relative supplies of the factors. In particular, Katz, Loveman and Blanchflower (1995) note that there was a marked deceleration of the growth rate of relative skill supply in the US, UK and Japan, countries where skill premia grew, while no such deceleration was evident in France, where the wage premium was more stable. The analytic framework that they employ makes local relative wages depend on *local* relative supplies of factors, and takes changes in these relative supplies as exogenous. Within their framework, if substitutability across skill categories is at the low end of the preferred range, then changes in the growth rate of relative supplies may account for much or all of the changes in relative wages in the relevant period.

This apparent dependence of local relative wages on local relative factor supplies is at odds with the preferred framework within the international trade literature for thinking about long-run changes in relative factor returns, that of Heckscher-Ohlin (HO).[1] The culprit in this regard may appear to be factor price equalisation, which implies that factor returns depend on global rather than local relative factor supplies (Leamer (1995)).

There are modifications to the HO theory that could help to provide an account. These include trade barriers, sectoral factor immobility, and imperfect substitutability of American and European goods. However, each of these accounts has undesirable features. Trade barriers among these countries are not high, sectoral factor immobility should not be such a great problem over the stretch of decades under discussion, and (as should be evident from the Dixit and Stiglitz (1977) framework) it is not sufficient to believe that individual goods are imperfect substitutes – one must believe at a deep level that American and European labour of the various classes are different.

However, there is one shortcoming common to both the trade and labour literature in this area. The division of new entrants into skilled and unskilled is treated as an exogenous shock to the economy. When we are thinking about evolution of the labour force over decades, with substantial changes in relative wages, this is not really satisfactory. Moreover, when factor supplies are allowed to adjust endogenously, there may well be alternative accounts one can provide of the Katz, Loveman and Blanchflower (1995) observation of the wedge between American and European experience. A full accounting of these relative supply changes and their consequences requires careful attention to historical conditions (e.g. baby boom and bust). But the interpretation one places on these findings will be seen to depend crucially on the analytic structure.

Accordingly, the central analytic contribution of this chapter is that it endogenises the human capital accumulation decision. This has a number of important advantages. The first is that we provide a simple and unified analytic framework in which researchers can consider the interplay of unemployment, relative wages and relative factor supplies where all are determined endogenously. An interesting analytic feature that emerges is that within this augmented Heckscher-Ohlin framework there are non-factor-supply-based shocks that replicate the correlations between movements in relative wages and (endogenous) relative factor supplies. This suggests the possibility of an upward bias in the Katz, Loveman and Blanchflower (1995) estimates of the role of relative supply in explaining relative wage movements.

A second advantage of endogenising the human capital accumulation decision is that it provides a richer framework for considering cross-country differences in the evolution of relative wages. As noted, the workhorse for international analysis of these events has been the Heckscher-Ohlin model. In this framework, many of the shocks under consideration (e.g. global technology shocks) move the world from one equilibrium to another, both featuring factor price equalisation. Hence they obviously cannot explain the divergence across America and Europe in the evolution of relative wages. This shortcoming has been evident even in the models that allow for unemployment. When we make the human capital accumulation decision explicit, changes in unemployment will have feedback effects on this decision, hence giving rise to differences across countries in observed wages and their changes. Thus this provides an opportunity to explain not only changes in unemployment, but also in the evolution of relative wages across countries. And it does so without the necessity of appealing to country-specific policy or technology shocks.

In the present work, America is taken to be a flexible wage economy while Europe is viewed as an economy in which a variety of institutions make wages rigid.[2] This highly stylised representation of the world is borrowed from Davis (1998a), which, in turn, built on Brecher (1974) and Krugman (1995). Endogenising the skill composition of the labour force is accomplished with the model of human capital accumulation developed in Findlay and Kierzkowski (1983). The introduction of a minimum wage and unemployment into the Findlay-Kierzkowski model is in the same spirit as Flug and Galor (1986).[3]

When we examine comparative statics, it will prove useful to characterise the impacts in terms of three *wedges* separating the experience of America from that of Europe. From above, these are: (a) a rise in unemployment in Europe, but not America; (b) a rise in the skill premium in America, but not in Europe; and (c) a slowdown in the growth rate of relative skill abundance in America, but not in Europe. These characterisations are not meant to substitute for a careful empirical inquiry. Our aim is and must be more modest. The approach developed here is highly stylised. The model is simple and the institutional characterisation is very sharp. We do not propose a single-cause explanation for the recent factor market maladies on both sides of the Atlantic.

We hope only to provide a framework for thinking about these problems that empirical researchers can exploit in a closer examination of these issues.

This chapter contains six parts. Section 2 sets up the basic model in the case of flexible wages and develops an approach to the Findlay and Kierzkowski model focused on factor markets. In Section 3 we begin by introducing a minimum wage in a closed economy. Then we consider this rigidity in the central case of interest, that of global trade between countries with differing labour market institutions. Section 4 uses these models to consider various comparative statics of particular relevance to American and European labour market experience. Section 5 gathers the principal results and relates them to the three wedges between the experience of America and Europe noted above. Section 6 concludes.

2   The flexible wage world

The seminal model of Findlay and Kierzkowski (1983) provides the basic structure for the analysis in this section. We provide a simple representation of equilibrium that focuses on factor markets. This will be particularly useful when we consider an economy with a minimum wage. We consider the model in a closed economy and then in an open economy.

The closed economy

We begin by describing the point in time equilibrium. This is a conventional two-by-two general equilibrium model. Skill, measured in efficiency units, is available in quantity H. Unskilled labour in natural (equals efficiency) units is available in quantity L. These factors are used to produce two goods under constant returns to scale and perfect competition. Good Y will serve as numeraire, so $P \equiv P_X/P_Y$. Good X is assumed to be the relatively skill-intensive good at any common factor prices. The production functions for the two goods are thus:

$$X = X(H, L) \qquad Y = Y(H, L). \tag{1}$$

Preferences of agents are assumed identical and homothetic, so that the composition of goods demand depends on relative prices, and is independent of income. With all income devoted to final demand, goods market clearing may be represented by the equality of relative supply and demand.

We now turn to describe the dynamic economy for which this is the stationary steady state. There are N identical individuals born in every period, each with lifespan T. At birth they make an irrevocable choice between two career paths. E of the newborns seek an education, while the remaining $(N - E)$ enter immediately and for their entire lifespan into unskilled employment. Each of the E students will spend θ periods in school, and will then work as a skilled worker for the remaining $(T - \theta)$ periods of life. While in school, the E students have access to K units of educational capital, which allows them to accumulate $Q = F(K, E; \theta)$ efficiency units of skill over the period θ. The educational production function is assumed to be constant returns to scale in (K, E) for fixed θ. In the intensive form this is $Q = qE = f(k)E$, where $k \equiv K/E$ is the amount of educational capital per student, and $q = f(k)$ indicates the number of efficiency units of skill per worker, hence the quality of skilled labour.

Because this is a stationary steady state, the cross-section and time series look alike. At any point in time the population may be divided as follows: $NT = E\theta + E(T - \theta) + (N - E)T =$ Students $+$ Skilled Workers $+$ Unskilled Workers. The stocks of skilled and unskilled workers that serve as inputs are thus $H = qE(T - \theta)$ and $L = (N - E)T$.

It is necessary to make several distinctions in our characterisation of factor returns. The simple case is that of unskilled labour, which receives the per-period wage w_L. We must be more careful when we discuss the returns to skilled labour. Producers focus on the wage that they pay per efficiency unit of skill, denoted $\tilde{w}_H$. The observed (gross) wage adjusts this for the quality of skill, so that $w_H = q\tilde{w}_H$. Finally, it is assumed that tuition is paid for the use of the educational capital K equivalent to a competitive factor return. Thus the net return to skilled labour is $\tilde{w}_H \, \partial Q/\partial E$. Often it will be convenient to refer to the relative wage (implicitly the skill premium) with reference to one or more of these concepts of the skilled wage. Define $\omega \equiv w_H/w_L$, and $\tilde{\omega} \equiv \tilde{w}_H/w_L$.

The stock of educational capital K that serves as an input to the educational process is determined exogenously. However the number of students E is endogenous. Since all individuals are identical *ex ante*, and capital markets are assumed perfect, an arbitrage condition assures that the present discounted value of the alternate career paths must be equal. The rate of interest r in equilibrium will equal the constant rate of time preference. Thus the arbitrage condition can be written as:

$$\int_\theta^T \tilde{w}_H f(k) \, e^{-rt} \, dt - \int_\theta^T \tilde{w}_H k f'(k) \, e^{-rt} \, dt = \int_0^T w_L \, e^{-rt} \, dt. \tag{2}$$

Noting that $\partial Q/\partial E = f(k) - kf'(k)$, and defining the discount factor $\Delta \equiv [1 - e^{-rT}]/[e^{-r\theta} - e^{-rT}]$, this fundamental arbitrage condition can be written more compactly as:

$$\frac{\tilde{\omega}}{\Delta} = \frac{1}{\partial Q/\partial E}. \tag{3}$$

Sometimes it is more convenient to refer to observed wages. Letting $\eta_{Q,E}$ be the elasticity of Q with respect to E (at fixed K), this condition becomes:

$$\frac{\omega}{\Delta} = \frac{1}{\eta_{Q,E}}. \tag{4}$$

We now turn to the determination of the full equilibrium. Note that for fixed technology, and assuming diversified production, the relative price P stands in a one-to-one increasing relation with the relative efficiency wages $\tilde{\omega}$, in accord

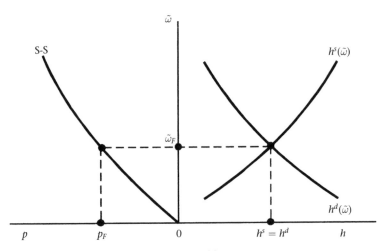

Figure 2.1   Flexible wage closed economy equilibrium

with the conventional Stolper-Samuelson relation. The price also determines the levels of the wages, w_L and $\tilde{w}_H$. Let the ratio $h \equiv H/L$.

A first key relation describes the general equilibrium structure of relative factor demand. This is summarised in the decreasing relation $h^D(\tilde{\omega})$ in Figure 2.1. A decline in P (so $\tilde{\omega}$) shifts the composition of goods demand from Y towards X. Also, the decline in $\tilde{\omega}$ leads both sectors to adopt more skill intensive techniques. Both elements imply that the structure of relative factor demand has shifted toward relatively skilled labour.

The second key relation describes the endogenous response of steady state relative factor supplies to changes in relative rewards, as indicated in the arbitrage equations above. With r, T and θ fixed, Δ is fixed. Hence for fixed K, a rise in $\tilde{\omega}$ requires a rise in E to satisfy the arbitrage condition. This raises the stock of skill while reducing the stock of unskilled labour, raising skill abundance. The full equilibrium of our dynamic system can then be described as $h^D(\tilde{\omega}) = h^S(\tilde{\omega})$ as in Figure 2.1. The market clearing goods prices are then read off of the Stolper-Samuelson relation.

The trading equilibrium in a flexible wage world

The modern framework for thinking about the Heckscher-Ohlin model under factor price equalisation is what Dixit and Norman (1980) have termed the 'integrated equilibrium'. It states conditions under which a world with trade in goods alone (but no international factor mobility) replicates the equilibrium that would exist in a fully integrated world. The usual approach is to start with the fully integrated world and ask what partitions of endowments among the countries are consistent with full employment in all countries, goods being produced under the integrated equilibrium techniques, and non-negative quantities of the goods being produced in all countries. The set of such partitions is then termed the Factor Price Equalisation (FPE) set.

A similar approach would show that with a mild alteration in restrictions, trade in this world again will replicate the integrated equilibrium. If trade is free and costless, then goods prices will be common. If final goods technologies across the countries are common, and production diversified, then wages in efficiency units will be equalised. If the countries share common structural parameters affecting discounting (r, T, θ), and a common educational production function $F(\cdot, \cdot)$, then they likewise have a common arbitrage condition. Because of the constant returns to scale property of $F(\cdot, \cdot)$, $\partial Q/\partial E$ depends only on the ratio $k = K/E$. This implies that the quality of skilled labour q will be common across the countries, so that observed (not only efficiency) wages will be common. This is true in spite of differences in the relative availability of educational capital, K/N. Thus the availability of skilled labour in each country c is $H^c = qE^c(T - \theta)$, where $E^c = K^c/k$, and this also provides the stock of unskilled labour as $(N^c - E^c)$. With these definitions in hand, we can use the conventional restrictions on the FPE set (see Helpman and Krugman (1985)). Using these definitions it is straightforward to show that for countries c and c':

$$\frac{L^c}{H^c} - \frac{L^{c'}}{H^{c'}} = \frac{kT}{q(T - \theta)} \left[\frac{N^c}{K^c} - \frac{N^{c'}}{K^{c'}} \right]. \tag{5}$$

Thus the country which is abundant in population N relative to educational capital will likewise be abundant in unskilled relative to skilled labour, so will be the exporter of the labour-intensive good Y. In terms of Figure 2.1, the relative labour demand curve is entirely unchanged, and so also the world

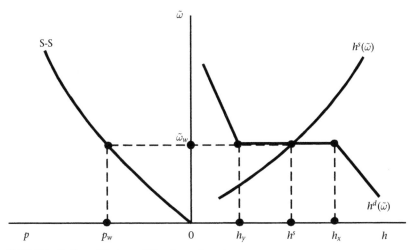

Figure 2.2   Full equilibrium of the dynamic system

relative supply curve that determines equilibrium. However the population-abundant country will have a relative supply curve that is less skill-abundant than the world, and vice versa for the other country.

Although our work on trade and unemployment will concern countries of the same order of magnitude in terms of income, we will see that institutions in one country will leave the other country facing an infinitely elastic export supply curve. Accordingly, it will prove useful to develop a small open-economy version of our model. In a diagram reminiscent of Leamer (1995), relative factor demand becomes infinitely elastic at relative wages $\tilde{\omega}_W$, so long as we are in the range of diversified production. As illustrated in Figure 2.2, this determines the structure of relative factor supply, production, income and absorption.

3   Minimum wages, unemployment, and labour force composition

The closed economy

We here consider the same model, but now with rigid labour market institutions in the form of an exogenously specified binding minimum wage in terms of the numeraire.[4] We consider this first for a closed economy before turning to our central project of considering this for a global trading world. A schematic view of the model is given in Figure 2.3.

With no minimum set for skilled labour, it must always be fully employed. However, if the flexible wage equilibrium delivers an unskilled wage below the minimum, unemployment must arise. The new equilibrium is determined by

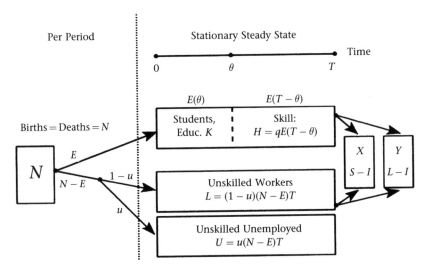

Figure 2.3   Schematic view of the model with unemployment

two fundamental relations. One reflects arbitrage in the choice whether to be skilled or unskilled, and the other reflects market clearing.

Let $(1 - u)$ be the employment rate for unskilled. Then for our risk neutral unskilled, $(1 - u)w_L$ is the expected unskilled wage. Our arbitrage condition (3) thus must be revised to:

$$\frac{\tilde{\omega}_M}{\Delta} = \frac{1 - u}{\partial Q/\partial E}. \tag{6}$$

With $\tilde{\omega}$ fixed at $\tilde{\omega}_M$ by the minimum wage, this defines a relation between E and u that satisfies the arbitrage condition. We will label this curve AA, and define it as $E = \phi(u)$, where $\phi' > 0$.

Equilibrium also requires that goods markets clear. The minimum wage fixes $\tilde{\omega}$, so also P. This in turn determines the structure of relative goods demand. But the structure of relative goods supply, at fixed $\tilde{\omega}$ and P, depends on employment, hence on E and u. We will label this relation MM, and define it as $E = \sigma(u)$. We easily verify that $\sigma' < 0$. A rise in u at fixed E implies a fall in unskilled labour, hence by Rybczynski a decline in output of Y and increase in output of X. Equilibrium with the initial ratio of X to Y can only be restored if E falls. The full equilibrium is at the intersection of the AA and MM curves, as depicted in Figure 2.4.

An alternative perspective comes from looking at the impact of the minimum wage on the structure of relative factor demand and supply. The functional relationship $h^D(\tilde{\omega})$ is not affected by the choice of a minimum wage, so we need only look at the implications for $h^S(\tilde{\omega})$. As in Flug and Galor (1986), we can

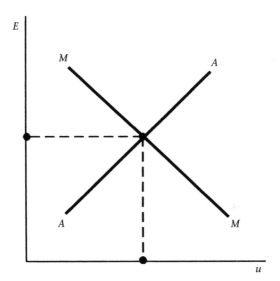

Figure 2.4 Equilibrium in the minimum wage economy

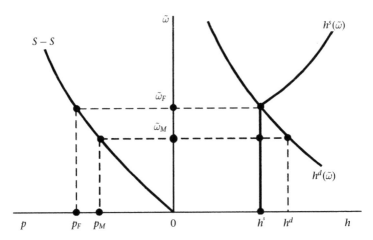

Figure 2.5   Equilibrium with Cobb-Douglas demand and technology in the minimum wage economy

consider a special case in which both goods demand and production technologies are Cobb-Douglas. The former assures that the division of spending between the two goods is fixed. The latter insures that the factor shares of income within each sector are fixed. These remain true even in the presence of unemployment. Thus in this case the rise in relative income to the unskilled implied by the minimum wage is exactly offset by the reduced probability of employment at the initial E. The minimum wage has no impact in this boundary case on the division between skilled and unskilled. The level of unemployment is thus determined implicitly as that required to bridge the gap between the fixed labour force composition and the relative demand at the minimum wage. At $\tilde{\omega}_M$, unskilled wages are higher than at the flexible $\tilde{\omega}_F$. This situation is depicted in Figure 2.5.

The global economy with unemployment

We now turn to consider a global economy. As in Davis (1998a), we assume that our two countries differ in one important respect. The country we will refer to as America has perfectly flexible wages for skilled and unskilled alike. The country we will call Europe has a rigid minimum wage for the unskilled set at the level $\tilde{\omega}^*$.

We consider first the cross-country links in factor prices. Free trade with zero transport costs insures that goods prices will be common for our countries. Common technologies and diversified production ensure that factor prices in efficiency units will likewise be common. Since for unskilled labour, efficiency and natural units are the same, this implies that employed unskilled in both Europe and America receive the same wage. However, the unemployment that will arise in Europe means that the expected wage of the unskilled is lower there. To compare the position of the skilled across the two countries, it is convenient to examine the arbitrage conditions. In America, they are those of the flexible wage economy, given by equation (3), while in Europe they are those of the minimum wage economy, given by equation (6). From above, the left-hand side is common, $\tilde{\omega}/\Delta$. With $u > 0$, this requires that Europe have a lower $\partial Q/\partial E$, so lower $k = K/E$. This in turn implies a wedge in the labour quality, so $q^E < q^A$ Finally, this implies a larger observed wedge between the skilled and unskilled in America than in Europe, $\omega^A > \omega^E$.

We will consider the implications of trade for the evolution of employment and the composition of the labour force in our countries. We begin as in Davis (1998a) with a benchmark in which Europe and America are identical in every respect except for the labour market institutions. If both had flexible labour markets, the composition of their labour forces would be identical, as would all factor prices in efficiency and natural units. If instead Europe in autarky instituted a binding minimum wage while America did not, Europe would enjoy the higher unskilled wage, but would also suffer the consequences of unemployment. In the double Cobb-Douglas case discussed above, they would continue to have the same division between skilled and unskilled. For the moment, hold their labour forces fixed at this initial composition. Davis (1998a) showed that with exogenous factor supplies, a move from autarky to free trade for these two countries would exactly double the European unemployment rate, while raising the American unskilled wage to the European level.

The trading equilibrium is illustrated in Figure 2.6. This is an import demand (MD), export supply (ES) diagram, with the twist that the minimum wage implies that the equilibrating variable is not the global goods price but rather unemployment in Europe. The fixed wage fixes the goods price, which in turn fixes American import demand. Higher unemployment rates in Europe imply a

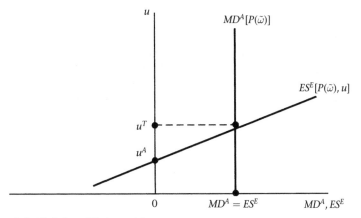

Figure 2.6 Global equilibrium with a minimum wage in Europe

reduction in Europe's supply of unskilled labour both directly and via the incentives for schooling. With a fixed relative composition of demand at P, this reduction in European unskilled labour, and consequent increase in skilled labour creates greater export supply of the skill-intensive good X. The case illustrated is the benchmark in which America and Europe are identical except for their labour market institutions, and so in which trade raises European unemployment.

Opening to trade raises European unemployment from the autarky level u^A to u^T (see Figure 2.6). In this benchmark, this may be more or less than the doubling of unemployment that occurs in the case of inelastic factor supplies. The reason is that the opening to trade places opposing pressures on the labour force composition, and so correspondingly on employment, in Europe. The rise in the unskilled wage in America reduces the incentives to accumulate skill. This will lead to a decline in the skill abundance of the work force relative to the autarky level. This implies increasing relative supply of the unskilled good Y as America's labour force adjusts, putting downward pressure on the relative price of Y (rise in P). This alone places additional pressure for a rise in European unemployment. This is offset by the fact that the sharply higher u has reduced the expected unskilled wage at fixed $\tilde{\omega}$, which is leading the European labour force to seek greater education to escape unemployment. Adjustment in Europe is thus leading to reduced unemployment relative to that without adjustment.

4 Comparative statics

Section 3 developed our principal model, that of trade between a flexible wage America and a minimum wage Europe. We consider here selected comparative statics of interest for the salient factor market developments. We also contrast these results with the counterparts in the closed and/or flexible wage world.

Primary factor accumulation

An increase in educational capital K in the flexible world economy shifts the relative labour supply curve (see Figure 2.1). Equilibrium is characterised by a higher skill abundance, a lower relative skilled wage in efficiency terms, and a reduced relative price of the skill-intensive good. From the arbitrage condition (3), the decline in the relative efficiency wage $\tilde{\omega}$ requires that $\partial Q/\partial E$ rise, so k rise. This means that the quality of skilled labour q must likewise rise. From the arbitrage condition (4), the impact on the observed skill premium depends on how $\eta_{Q,E}$ depends on k. Nevertheless, the rise in the unskilled wage w_L with a falling P suffices to show that in welfare terms the unskilled are better off. But then because they are *ex ante* identical, the skilled are better off as well.

An increase in educational capital K in the closed minimum wage economy leaves goods prices and efficiency unit wages unaltered. However it raises the equilibrium skill abundance of the labour force, even as the skill abundance of the employed is unchanged. From the arbitrage condition (6), the consequent fall in the unemployment rate u implies a required rise in $\partial Q/\partial E$ and so also k and q. Thus the observed skill premium rises even as unemployment declines. A key insight coming here is that with relative efficiency wages $\tilde{\omega}$ and prices P fixed, the unemployment rate u becomes a sufficient statistic for the welfare of the unskilled, so also of the skilled.

Let us return now to our two-country model of flexible wage America and minimum wage Europe. An increase in educational capital in America shifts its relative factor supply curve. But it does not affect $\tilde{\omega}$ or P. From the arbitrage condition (3), we see that k must remain unchanged, so also America's skill quality q^A. While the composition of the labour force in America is changed, nothing happens to the skill premium in America. In terms of Figure 2.6, this implies a leftward shift of the American import demand curve. Now we turn to the effects on Europe. The arbitrage condition (6) in Europe, summarised by AA in Figure 2.4, is unaffected. However the market clearing conditions, MM in Figure 2.4, shift so that equilibrium occurs with a lower u and E. Thus educational capital accumulation in America has decreased the supply of skill in Europe, while raising its quality. The observed skill premium in Europe rises, although there was no change in this premium in America. Unemployment likewise falls in Europe.

Consider instead if there had been an increment of educational capital in minimum wage Europe. America would have been wholly unaffected. In Europe, both the arbitrage and market clearing (AA and MM) curves in Figure 2.4 would have shifted left. Both imply a decline in unemployment, although the impact on E is ambiguous. Nevertheless, from the arbitrage condition (6), the fall in u in equilibrium requires a rise in k^E, so labour quality q^E. Thus the observed skill premium in America is unaffected, and Europe's rises, with educational capital accumulation, irrespective of the site of accumulation.

Now consider an increase in the population in America. At fixed K and $\tilde{\omega}$, E is fixed, so all of the additional population becomes unskilled. In America there are no changes in the skill premium. In terms of Figure 2.6, this implies a rightward shift of the import demand curve. This increment in N^A leaves the European arbitrage condition unchanged, but shifts the MM curve out in Figure 2.4, leading to higher u and E. This implies a fall in q^E, so a fall in the skill premium in Europe, although that in America was unaffected.

An increase in the population in Europe leaves America wholly unaffected. Since K and $\tilde{\omega}$, remain fixed, the European arbitrage condition remains unchanged. The MM curve will shift out, reflecting the need to shift relative production toward the skill-intensive good in order to satisfy local demand with American import demand unchanged. Workers will be worse off in Europe as reflected by the fall in q (increase in E) and the increase in u at fixed $\tilde{\omega}$. Thus, increases in population, regardless of location, increase unemployment in Europe.

NICs shock

The entry of new countries to the world trading economy is frequently advanced as a possible explanation of recent adverse labour market developments.[5] We assume the new countries' comparative advantage lies in the unskilled-labour-intensive sector. Their emergence can then be modelled as an increase in import demand for good X. If prices were fully flexible, this demand would put upward pressure on the relative price of X. Europe's commitment to the minimum wage prevents such a price movement. With no change in relative prices, relative efficiency unit wages remain unchanged. Hence, America is fully insulated from the demand shock. In terms of Figure 2.6, this would be a rightward shift of a joint American–NICs import demand curve for Europe (with no change in America).

Europe, on the other hand, must fully accommodate the increase in demand for X by shifting its production toward the X sector. In terms of Figure 2.4, the demand shock generates an outward shift in the MM curve. The AA curve is unaffected, as there is no change in $\tilde{\omega}$. Both u and E^E increase but q falls, reducing the wage differential in Europe. Thus Europe bears the full cost of adjustment to the shock while America is wholly unaffected.

Technological change

Example: Neutral technical progress in the skill-intensive sector

We now consider the implications of global technical progress for factor returns, employment, and skill composition of the labour force. A detailed consideration of the many possible cases is beyond the scope of this chapter (see Davis (1998b)). We consider here only the example of global neutral technical progress in the X sector. We assume that the minimum wage in Europe binds both before the technical progress and in the full equilibrium. This makes analysis of the effect on America simple. While the impact effect (i.e. at fixed goods prices) of the technical progress in X raises the skilled wage and reduces that of the unskilled, the full equilibrium must see the relative price of X fall so that the unskilled wage in terms of the numeraire is unchanged. This implies that America does not change. Hence neither is there a change in labour quality in America, q^A, so the observed skilled wage w_H.

Analysing the situation in Europe is a bit more complex. We know that in equilibrium, E^A does not change. For the moment, hold E^E and u fixed as well. Then at the initial goods prices, we know that the neutral technical progress in X must give rise to an excess supply of X, so downward pressure on its price. The case of interest here is what Davis (1998b) terms the *elastic* case – that in which these induced price effects do not suffice to restore the initial unskilled wage. In this case, the equilibrium unemployment rate must rise to make unskilled labour sufficiently scarce to again support the initial wage. In terms of Figure 2.4, this represents a rightward shift of the MM curve, with the AA curve fixed. In equilibrium, E^E rises, and the quality of European labour q^E falls.

Summarising, global technical progress in the X sector in the elastic case leaves the skilled wage premium unchanged in America, while reducing it in Europe. The skill composition of the labour force in America is unchanged, while that in Europe rises. Unemployment in Europe rises.

Productivity slowdown

While the story that we have told is explicitly dynamic, two important features of evolution through time have been set to the side. First, we have considered technical change only as a once-and-for-all event, rather than as a continual evolution of productive ability. Second, we have ignored the fact that the level at which wages are rigid likewise evolves over time. Consideration of both of these facts is straightforward, and allows us to consider the consequences of a global productivity slowdown. Assume, then, that productivity in the two sectors grows at a common rate γ, as indicated by:

$$X(t) = e^{\gamma t} X(H, L) \qquad Y(t) = e^{\gamma t} Y(H, L). \tag{7}$$

The only modification this introduces into the equilibrium conditions (3) and (6) is through the Δ parameter, which will now equal $[1 - e^{(\gamma-r)T}] / [e^{(\gamma-r)\theta} - e^{(\gamma-r)T}]$. This term is decreasing in the growth rate of total factor productivity, γ. Absent other shocks, this allows the European minimum wage to rise at the rate γ without inducing any changes in unemployment. We assume that European institutions are such that the actual European minimum wage does in fact grow at this rate.

A productivity slowdown will be represented by a discrete fall in the rate of total factor productivity growth, from γ_0 to $\gamma_1 < \gamma_0$, leading to a rise in Δ. From the arbitrage condition (3) for America, it is clear that $\partial Q / \partial E$ must rise, so E must fall. Since earnings will grow at a slower rate as a result of the slowdown, it is not as attractive to go to school since this choice involves postponing income.

Thus, in America, E will fall, reducing the skill intensity of the labour force and increasing the observed skill premium ω. In Europe, the change in the arbitrage condition (6) implies an outward shift of the AA schedule. Moreover, America's production shift toward Y causes the MM schedule to shift outward as well. Overall, Europe experiences higher unemployment, but observed relative wages will depend on what happens to the quality of skilled labour in Europe. This, in turn, will depend on the relative strengths of the disincentive to become educated through the rise in Δ and the incentive to become educated through the rise in u.

5 The three wedges

Unifying elements

We will provide a discussion of the analytic elements that unify the comparative static results, and then relate them to the three wedges. We collect our principal results in Table 2.1. We start with a heuristic description of the role of European unemployment. If the European unskilled wage is to attain the minimum, this must be supported by an appropriate relative goods price sufficiently high for the unskilled-intensive good. Such a goods price will be an equilibrium only if the unskilled-intensive good is sufficiently scarce in relative terms. And this will be true only if employed unskilled labour is itself sufficiently scarce. For given educational capital and population, this determines the required European unemployment rate. This also indicates simply many of the shocks that will induce a rise in the European unemployment rate: they are ones that present incipient excess supply – hence downward pressure on the price – of the unskilled-intensive good. These include direct increases in the relative availability in the world of people relative to educational capital, as well as indirect increases in this relative availability via opening to trade with countries that feature a lower relative price for the unskilled good. A distinct, though related, process is at work in the case of neutral technical change in the skill-intensive sector. The direct impact of this change depresses the unskilled wage; however, these are at least partly offset by a rise in the relative price of the unskilled good. When demand is sufficiently elastic, the magnitude of the price movement is insufficient to compensate unskilled labour. The minimum wage is met only if the unemployment rate rises. Finally, the productivity slowdown works through yet another channel. With growth proceeding at a slower pace, students find smaller compensation for postponing entry to the workforce. This in turn creates a rise in the relative supply of unskilled labour at the initial relative wages, so downward pressure on the unskilled wage. This can be staunched only with a rise in the unemployment rate.

Analysis of relative wage changes for America is straightforward. The high relative skilled wage for America compared with Europe under trade reflects two simple facts, that there is FPE in efficiency units, and that Europeans crowd the available educational capital to escape unemployment, thereby lowering the quality of skill in Europe. The impact of opening trade with Europe on the observed American skill premium is uncertain because the decline in the efficiency unit skill premium is offset by a rise in the quality of American skill. Through most of the comparative statics, including endowment changes in either country, entry of the NICs, or the case of technical progress considered, the American skill premium is unaffected. In all but the last, this is because equilibrium relative goods prices are unaffected by the comparative static, and (conditional on r, T, and θ) this suffices to determine the observed American skill premium. In the case of technical progress considered, a similar result arises because the equilibrium price movements exactly offset the initial disturbance to the zero profit conditions that establish the efficiency unit wages. Finally, in the case of the productivity slowdown, the rise in the American skill premium is required to compensate skilled workers for the reduced incentive to take income in later years relative to the present due to the reduced income gradient.

The analysis of the evolution of American skill abundance is likewise straightforward. Europe's commitment to maintain the minimum wage and associated goods price shield America from the relative wage shocks which would induce adjustments in skill composition. Hence primary endowment shocks in Europe, entry of the NICs, and even the case of technical progress considered leave the American skill composition unaffected. Local primary factor supply shocks do have an impact on American skill composition, as does the productivity slowdown for the reason noted in discussing the movement in the relative wage.

With the exception of the productivity slowdown, all of the comparative statics that we consider that raise unemployment in Europe also reduce the skill premium there. The reason is simply the rebalancing of incentives, with higher unemployment making unskilled employment less attractive, there has to be a reduced skill premium as compensation. The case of the productivity slowdown differs because there are already two competing elements. The slowdown makes postponement of entry to the labour force less attractive, so making it more attractive to be unskilled, while the higher unemployment by contrast makes being unskilled more attractive. Accordingly it is uncertain which way the relative wages need to move in Europe to rebalance the incentives.

Finally, a large set of external shocks – opening to trade with America or the NICs, increases in American relative unskilled abundance – all lead the skill abundance of European labour to rise. This may be looked on as the labour force composition consequences of the rise in unemployment required to sustain the minimum wage. Essentially similar forces are at work in the case of technical progress considered, where the equilibrium rise in unemployment forces the rise in skill abundance in Europe. A contrary story emerges when the rise in population or decline in educational capital occurs in Europe.

The three wedges

Earlier we suggested that in considering the results of the model it would be convenient to focus on three stylised wedges in experience between America and Europe. These are: (a) a rise in unemployment in Europe, but not America; (b) a rise in the skill premium in America, but not in Europe; and (c) a slowdown in the growth rate of relative skill abundance in America, but not in Europe. Since much of our work, for simplicity, has abstracted from trend changes in the economy, we will interpret these broadly in terms of differences in experience rather than focusing on levels.

The second column of Table 2.1 illustrates that a broad variety of shocks – European, American, and Global – could in principle have been the source of the rising unemployment affecting Europe but not America. The third and fourth columns of Table 2.1 make an important point not evident in the simpler framework of Davis (1998a, b). The wedge between European and American relative wage evolution can also be accounted for by a wide variety of shocks. Such an account need not rely on idiosyncratic national technology or policy

Table 2.1

Benchmark Trade Equilibrium					
Levels	$u^E > 0$	$\omega^E < \omega^A$		$h^E > h^A$	
Comparative Statics					
Changes	du^E	$d\omega^A$	$d\omega^E$	dh^A	dh^E
Opening to trade	+	+/−	−	−	+
Fall in K^A	+	0	−	−	+
Fall in K^E	+	0	−	0	−
Rise in N^A	+	0	−	−	+
Rise in N^E	+	0	−	0	−
NICs shock	+	0	−	0	+
Tech progress in X	+	0	−	0	+
Prod slowdown	+	+	+/−	−	+/−

shocks. The final two columns show that many, though not all, of the shocks could have accounted for the wedge between European and American relative skill evolution. This holds an important lesson. In combination with the earlier results, it shows that the correlations between the contrasting experience of America and Europe in relative wage evolution need not be the consequence of differences in the evolution of relative skill availability, but instead that they may both have a common cause that may be quite independent of direct links to factor availability (e.g. technical progress in X). This suggests, for example, some caution in reading the results of Katz, Loveman and Blanchflower (1995) on the contribution of factor supplies to the relative wage movements.

6   Conclusion

Factor market developments in recent years in America and Europe have been a source of great concern, though for distinct reasons. In America, the focus has been on a growing skilled-to-unskilled wage gap, while in Europe the focus has been on high and persistent unemployment. A large literature has addressed these problems, including both detailed studies of individual countries, as well as comparative analyses across countries. The country studies have emphasised the importance of local institutional structure in understanding these developments, while the cross-country studies have searched for common themes. Davis (1998a, b) developed a framework which allowed for differences across countries in institutional structure, but which also allowed a complete and rigorous description of the general equilibrium comparative statics in a world in which these countries trade with one another. The results from this approach diverged significantly from those one would obtain considering the cases one at a time.

   Previous work in this area has taken the skill composition of the labour force to be exogenous. Yet given that we are considering developments over the course of decades, this is clearly inadequate. Thus a central thrust of this chapter has been to endogenise the accumulation of human capital. This has a number of advantages. The first is that if we are to distinguish the candidate theories in accounting for these factor market developments, we need to be able to bring new sources of evidence to bear on the problem. This chapter suggests that empirical researchers may do well to consider the relative evolution of the skill composition of the labour force in the two regions as an additional basis on which to separate the theories. Moreover, allowing for cross-country differences in the quality of skilled labour provides an alternative framework for thinking about the divergent evolution of relative skilled wages in America and Europe that does not rely on local technology or policy shocks (see Davis (1998a, b)).

This chapter makes several analytic contributions. First, it develops a new presentation of the Findlay and Kierzkowski (1983) model that focuses on factor markets and links the results to the Dixit and Norman (1980) 'integrated equilibrium' framework. Second, we introduce within this setting a full general equilibrium with trade among two countries with divergent factor market institutions – one with rigid wages, the other with flexible wages. Finally, we develop a variety of comparative statics and consider the evolution of relative wages, unemployment, and the skill composition of the labour force.

We do not advance any single-cause account for the recent factor market developments. The results from the comparative statics suggests that one or more forces may in combination have contributed to the three wedges in experience between America and Europe we considered. We hope that the exercises we develop will inform the work of empirical researchers who investigate the relative importance of these factors in giving rise to these phenomena.

Notes

1 For example, Krugman (1997) writes 'In the last few years the impact of international trade on advanced-country wages has been hotly debated. Unusually, serious economists have not by and large argued about theory: with few exceptions they have agreed that a more or less classical Heckscher-Ohlin-Samuelson model is the best framework to use.'

2 It is well known that the UK experience has broadly been similar to that of the US. Hence in our stylised characterisation, the UK should be thought of as part of 'America' rather than 'Europe'.

3 Real wage rigidity in the context of the Findlay and Kierzkowski (1983) model has previously been considered in Flug and Galor (1986). However the case that they considered imposes severe restrictions that limit its applicability. There are two ways of thinking about these restrictions. One is to think of the policy as having raised the wage to such an extent that no goods price consistent with diversified production in this economy would ever support this wage in a flexible wage world. The alternative interpretation is that the jump in the wage is less dramatic, but Flug and Galor apply this to an economy that was completely specialised in production even before the minimum wage. A second limiting element of their approach is that most of their effort is spent considering the problem from the viewpoint of a small open economy. A drawback is that in almost all cases, this focuses on a world with complete specialisation in production. The one case in which production may be diversified is one in

which the pattern of production and the level of unemployment are indeterminate. In the one section of the paper in which they do consider a two-country large open economy, they again focus on the case with such a high minimum wage that this pushes the implementing country to full specialisation. Flug and Galor seem not to have perceived that the case of a more moderate, yet binding, minimum wage could leave both countries diversified in the neighbourhood of the initial equilibrium, yielding determinate trade and production patterns at all points in time. Nonetheless, several points of their analysis, notably the conditions under which the labour force composition is unaffected by imposition of a minimum wage, did prove helpful for our own work.

4 This choice follows Brecher (1974) and Davis (1998a). The modelling is not meant to be taken literally as a characterisation of European factor markets, where the institutions are both more subtle and varied. Rather it is a modelling shortcut to introduce rigidity and so induce unemployment. The exogeneity of the minimum wage ignores interesting problems of political economy, as well as the likely feedback from the real economy to the level at which the wage is set. This shortcut is justified by two facts. First, ignoring the political economy vastly simplifies the positive analysis. Second, whatever feedback mechanisms exist are evidently weak, given the high levels of unemployment. Thus ignoring these feedback effects is appropriate here.

In addition it might appear to be quite restrictive that we model the rigidity as a fixed minimum wage when we are alluding to factor market developments occurring over the course of decades. This is deceiving. It is a straightforward extension to allow the minimum wage to grow at the same rate as Hicks-neutral technical progress in both sectors, leaving the unemployment rate unaffected. Implicitly what is at stake is whether the level at which wages are rigid rises more or less slowly than that which would allow unemployment to remain unchanged. We consider the model with an evolving minimum wage only in Section 4, where we model the consequences of a productivity slowdown.

5 For various perspectives, see Wood (1994), Leamer (1995), and Krugman and Lawrence (1993).

References

Bertola, Giuseppe and Andrea Ichino (1995) 'Wage Inequality and Unemployment: United States vs. Europe', *NBER Macroeconomics Annual* (Cambridge, MA: NBER).

Brecher, Richard A. (1974) 'Minimum Wage Rates and the Pure Theory of International Trade', *Quarterly Journal of Economics*, vol. 88(1), pp. 98–116.

Davis, Donald R. (1998a) 'Does European Unemployment Prop Up American Wages? National Labour Markets and Global Trade', *American Economic Review*, vol. 88(3), pp. 478–94.

Davis, Donald R. (1998b) 'Technology, Unemployment, and Relative Wages in a Global Economy', *European Economic Review*, 42(9), pp. 1613–33.

Dixit, Avinash and Victor Norman (1980) *Theory of International Trade* (Cambridge: Cambridge University Press).

Dixit, Avinash and Joseph Stiglitz (1977) 'Monopolistic Competition and Optimum Product Diversity', *American Economic Review*, vol. 67(3), pp. 297–308.

Findlay, Ronald and Henryk Kierzkowski (1983) 'International Trade and Human Capital: A Simple General Equilibrium Model', *Journal of Political Economy*, vol. 91(6), pp. 957–78.

Flug, Karnit and Oded Galor (1986) 'Minimum Wage in a General Equilibrium Model of International Trade and Human Capital', *International Economic Review*, vol. 27(1), pp. 149–64.

Freeman, Richard B. and Lawrence F. Katz (1995) *Differences and Changes in Wage Structures* (Chicago: University of Chicago Press).

Helpman, Elhanan and Paul Krugman (1985) *Market Structure and Foreign Trade* (Cambridge, MA: MIT Press).

Katz, Lawrence F., Gary W. Loveman and David G. Blanchflower (1995) 'Changes in the Structure of Wages in Four OECD Countries', in Richard B. Freeman and Lawrence F. Katz, *Differences and Changes in Wage Structures* (Chicago: University of Chicago Press).

Katz, Lawrence F. and Kevin M. Murphy (1992) 'Changes in Relative Wages, 1963–1987: Supply and Demand Factors', *Quarterly Journal of Economics*, vol. 107(1), pp. 35–78.

Krugman, Paul (1995) 'Growing World Trade: Causes and Consequences', *Brookings Papers on Economic Activity*, vol. 1, pp. 327–77.

Krugman, Paul (1997) 'And Now for Something Completely Different: An Alternative Model of Trade, Education, and Inequality', mimeo, MIT.

Krugman, Paul and Robert Z. Lawrence (1993) 'Trade, Jobs, and Wages', NBER Working Paper no. 4478, September.

Leamer, Edward (1995) 'In Search of Stolper-Samuelson Effects Between Trade and US Wages', mimeo, Yale University and University of California at Los Angeles.

Wood, Adrian (1994) *North–South Trade, Employment and Inequality* (Oxford and New York: Oxford University Press).

3
Competition, Trade and Wages*

J. Peter Neary
University College, Dublin, Ireland, and CEPR

1 Introduction: The great debate

Perhaps the single most striking feature of rich-country labour markets in recent decades is what Nickell and Bell (1995) call 'the collapse in demand for the unskilled across the OECD'. In 'Anglo-Saxon' countries, this shows up as an increase in the premium paid to skilled relative to unskilled workers; in Continental Europe, it manifests itself as an increase in long-term unemployment among the unskilled. There seems to be fairly wide agreement that these differences reflect the response of different labour market institutions to common shocks. But there is no consensus on the nature of those shocks. Much popular discussion and some academic observers (such as Wood (1994) and Leamer (1998)) have blamed 'globalisation' in general, and increased imports from low-wage newly industrialised countries (NICs) in particular. By contrast, a majority of academic commentators have pointed instead to skill-biased technological progress as the explanation.

This 'trade versus technology' debate has prompted an extensive empirical literature.[1] As summarised and extended by Desjonqueres *et al.* (1999), three stylised facts in particular emerge from this literature. First, the rise in skill premia has been accompanied by increases in the ratio of skilled to unskilled employment in *all* sectors, not just those which use skilled labour intensively. Second, the skill premium has risen in less-developed and newly industrialising countries as well as in OECD countries. Third (though the evidence here is less clear-cut, especially for the United States), there has been no significant decline in the relative price of less-skill-intensive goods. All three of these stylised facts conflict with the view that the rise in skill premia is mainly due to

* Thanks for helpful discussions and suggestions to Carl Davidson, Alan Deardorff, Joep Konings, Paul Seabright, Joe Tharakan, Hylke Vandenbussche and Paul Walsh and to seminar participants at Ceras, Cérgy-Pontoise, Delta, Ecole Polytechnique and Erasmus (Rotterdam), at the Ecole de Printemps d'Aix-en-Provence, ERWIT 2000 in Copenhagen, the IEA Conference on *Globalisation and Labour Markets*, Nottingham, July 2000, and ETSG 2000 in Glasgow. This research is part of the Globalisation Programme of the Centre for Economic Performance at LSE, funded by the UK ESRC.

cheaper unskilled-labour-intensive imports. Indeed Desjonqueres *et al.* entitle their paper 'Another nail in the coffin' for the trade-based explanation.

My objective in this chapter is not to try and revive the trade explanation, not at least the standard version which emphasises the Stolper-Samuelson mechanism implied by the simple Heckscher-Ohlin-Samuelson (HOS) model. There is no reason to dispute the message of the empirical evidence to date, as summarised by Robbins (1996), 'HOS hits facts; facts win'. Instead, I want to explore theoretically two other themes suggested by this literature.

First is the issue of how well the alternative explanation, which relies on exogenous skill-biased technological progress, deals with the stylised facts. While it is obvious that this perspective can explain the increases in skill premia, I want to suggest that in general equilibrium it does not provide a coherent account of other aspects of labour market developments. This is despite the fact that the technology explanation is less specific, and hence has potentially greater explanatory power, than the trade one.

My second theme starts from the fact that, since Krugman (1995), almost all theoretical contributions to this debate have concentrated on competitive general equilibrium models. This constrains the discussion in significant ways. It means that 'increased foreign competition' can only take the form of reductions in the prices or increases in the quantities of imports. It precludes any discussion of the impact of trade or technology shocks on markups or profit rates. Finally, it is inconsistent with a small but suggestive number of empirical studies. Borjas and Ramey (1995), in a study using US data, found that the impact of foreign competition on the skill premium depended on the market structure of the industry penetrated and, in particular, that employment changes in a small group of trade-impacted concentrated industries could explain part of the aggregate rise in wage inequality. Similarly, Oliveira-Martins (1994) in a study using OECD data, found a positive impact of import penetration on wages in industries with low product differentiation and market segmentation. Finally, Sachs and Shatz (1994) found that industries which have declined in the OECD in the face of competition from NICs exhibited low skill intensities but paid higher wages, presumably reflecting the fact that they were also highly unionised. These empirical findings do not add up to a coherent picture of the interactions between imperfect competition, trade and wage inequality. But they suggest that it is worth trying to develop a framework which encompasses all these features.

This discussion sets the scene for the remainder of the chapter. In the next section, I review the Heckscher-Ohlin approach. With two factors that can be thought of as skilled and unskilled labour, and two sectors, each intensive in one of the factors, the model lends itself immediately to addressing the central issues in the debate. But, as I hope to show, not all its implications have been explored. Section 3 introduces a simple but new model of two-stage oligopolistic competition in the presence of a quota constraint and Section 4 draws out its implications for the trade versus technology debate. Section 5 presents some conclusions, and Appendices A and B give the detailed derivations underlying the results in Sections 2 and 3 respectively.

2   Trade versus technology in the Heckscher-Ohlin-Samuelson model

The basic outlines of the Heckscher-Ohlin story are well known. Yet a compact restatement seems desirable, both to put recent theoretical debates in perspective and to allow us to confront the trade and technology explanations with the stylised facts revealed by recent empirical work. This section draws on Jones (1965) to do just that.

Increased import competition

Begin then with the simplest setting of a competitive small open economy producing two goods, X_1 and X_2, using two factors, unskilled labour L and skilled labour S. Figure 3.1 illustrates the Stolper-Samuelson result. Each curve is a unit cost curve, showing the combinations of factor prices (w and r for unskilled and skilled labour respectively) that one sector can afford to pay and just break even. Given initial prices and technology, the locations of the curves are shown by the solid lines, so, if both goods are produced, equilibrium must be at point A. Finally, the slope of each sector's unit cost curve represents its employment ratio (skilled to unskilled), so sector 1 is relatively unskilled-labour intensive.

Now, assume an increase in import competition reflected in a fall in p, the relative price of the import-competing unskilled-labour-intensive good 1. That sector's unit cost curve shifts inwards as shown and, with the new equilibrium at B, the Stolper-Samuelson result follows immediately. The unskilled wage falls and the skilled wage rises. Algebraically, the result is given by a familiar equation (where a circumflex denotes a proportional change: $\hat{r} \equiv dr/r$):

$$\hat{r} - \hat{w} = -\frac{1}{\theta}\,\hat{p}. \tag{1}$$

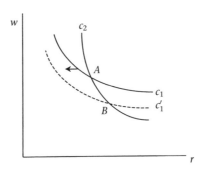

Figure 3.1   Effects of a fall in world prices

The left-hand side is the change in the skill premium (the relative wage of skilled workers). The denominator θ on the right-hand side indicates the relative factor intensities of the two sectors: it is positive since sector 1 is relatively unskilled-labour intensive.[2] Hence the standard result: a fall in the relative price of good 1 raises the skill premium. This might seem like a parsimonious explanation for the trends in relative wages in the OECD in recent decades. But note two corollaries. According to the model, the higher relative cost of skilled labour encourages a fall in the skilled–unskilled employment ratio in *both* sectors; and the fall in price of the import good X_1 should correspond to a *rise* in its relative price in the exporting country, mandating a *fall* in the skill premium there. Both these implications of the simple trade explanation are clearly contradicted by two of the stylised facts quoted in the introduction.

Does it matter that I have assumed a small open economy so far? Krugman (1995) has criticised this framework because the phenomenon to be explained is a generalised shift in labour demand towards skilled labour throughout the OECD. He argues that analysing this in a small open economy setting commits a fallacy of composition, and, as a first step towards a global analysis, he proposes examining both trade and technology shocks in a closed economy instead.[3] For a trade shock, the simplest way to do this is to assume a small relaxation in the tariff τ on imports from the rest of the world. Allowing for the endogenous adjustment of goods prices, the effect of such a relaxation on the skill premium is:

$$\hat{r} - \hat{w} = -\frac{\sigma_D}{\sigma_D + \sigma_S} \frac{1}{\theta} \hat{\tau} \tag{2}$$

where σ_D and σ_S are the elasticities of substitution in demand and supply respectively. (See Appendix A for details.) Equation (2) shows that a fall in the tariff has the same qualitative effect as a fall in relative prices from (1), but reduced by a fraction $\sigma_D/(\sigma_D + \sigma_S)$. The form of this fraction, the ratio of a demand elasticity to an excess demand elasticity, is familiar from elementary tax incidence theory, and its interpretation is the same. The greater the price responsiveness of aggregate supply relative to aggregate demand, the more the tariff reduction is shifted forward onto goods prices, and the less it affects the skill premium. (The result for the small open economy in (1) is of course the limiting case as σ_D tends towards infinity.) So the Stolper-Samuelson effect is dampened but not reversed by price changes. This suggests that much of the debate between Krugman (2000) and Leamer (2000) is off the point. Irrespective of whether goods prices are exogenous or endogenous, any explanation which relies exclusively on trade effects yields the counter-factual prediction that all sectors should shift to more unskilled-labour-intensive techniques.

Of course, Krugman is right to stress that a shock which hits all OECD countries (and so affects goods prices) must be of a sufficiently large magnitude if it is to explain the relatively large changes in the skill premium. In (2) I use the device of an equivalent tariff to model a surge in imports, but there are other ways of doing this. A natural alternative approach is to ask what change in domestic factor endowments would have the same effect on the skill premium as the increased import competition. In principle, this can be calculated by using the fact that an actual change in factor endowments would affect the skill premium as follows:

$$\hat{r} - \hat{w} = \frac{1}{\sigma}(\hat{L} - \hat{S}) \quad \text{where: } \sigma \equiv \lambda\theta(\sigma_D + \sigma_S). \tag{3}$$

Here σ is Jones's 'aggregate elasticity of substitution', which measures the effects on the skill premium of a change in factor endowments, taking into account the full adjustment of both supply and demand throughout the economy.[4] Combining (2) and (3) allows the 'factor content equivalent' of the increased imports to be calculated, and empirical estimates have found relatively small values for it. Yet another nail in the coffin of the trade explanation, apparently.

Technological progress

The trade explanation is easy to reject, in part, because it makes such precise predictions. Skill-biased technological progress is not as specific: as we will see, how it is distributed across sectors matters greatly. The issues can be explored by considering the effects of technological progress in the same two-sector Heckscher-Ohlin framework I have just used to address the trade explanation.

First, we need a simple way to parameterise technological progress. Following Jones (1965), let $\hat{b}_{ji}$ denote its effect on the unit input requirement of factor j in sector i at given factor prices. There are four $\hat{b}_{ji}$ terms and they can be combined in insightful ways. First, within each sector we can define the *extent* and the *bias* of technological progress as follows:

$$\pi_i \equiv \theta_{Li}\hat{b}_{Li} + \theta_{Si}\hat{b}_{Si}, \qquad \beta_i \equiv \hat{b}_{Li} - \hat{b}_{Si}, \qquad i = 1, 2. \tag{4}$$

Here π_i measures the reduction in unit cost in sector i at initial factor prices; while β_i measures the Hicksian bias of the technological progress: a positive value indicates that it is biased towards saving on unskilled labour – that it is *skill-biased*. Next, we can define two economy-wide indicators of the type of technological progress. Let π_j denote the sum of the b_{ji} terms for each factor j, weighted by their sectoral employment shares λ_{ji}:

$$\pi_j \equiv \lambda_{j1}\hat{b}_{j1} + \lambda_{j2}\hat{b}_{j2}, \qquad j = L, S. \tag{5}$$

Just as each π_i term indicates the extent to which the technological progress acts in the same way as an increase in the price of good i, so each π_j term indicates the extent to which it acts in the same way as an increase in the endowment of factor j. Then $\pi_L - \pi_S$ measures the aggregate *factor bias* of the technological progress, while $\pi_1 - \pi_2$ measures its *sector bias*.[5]

Armed with these definitions, consider first the effect of technological progress on the skilled–unskilled employment ratio in each sector:

$$\hat{S}_i - \hat{L}_i = -\sigma_i(\hat{r} - \hat{w}) + \beta_i. \tag{6}$$

Here σ_i is the elasticity of substitution between factors, and the bias term β_i indicates the effect of technological progress on the employment ratio at given factor prices. (Equation (6) applies whether goods prices are endogenous or not.) Now, recall two of the stylised facts already used to reject the simple trade explanation. The skill premium must rise throughout the economy: $\hat{r} > \hat{w}$; and the ratio of skilled to unskilled workers must rise in each sector: $\hat{S}_i > \hat{L}_i$. Equation (6) shows straight away that, if these stylised facts are to be explained by exogenous technological progress, then it must be skill-biased in *both* sectors. Moreover, the bias must be sufficiently great to offset the effect of the increased skill premium, which by itself tends to *lower* the skilled–unskilled ratio.

If technological progress cannot be Hicks-neutral and cannot be sector-specific, what is a natural way of specifying it? There seems no basis for assuming that substitution possibilities between skilled and unskilled workers are systematically lower in unskilled- than in skilled-labour-intensive sectors. Nor is there evidence that skill premia have risen by more in skilled-labour-intensive sectors. Hence equation (6) suggests that a natural benchmark to use is the case where the bias of technological progress is *uniform* across sectors. This implies that $\hat{b}_{ji}$ is the same in both sectors and so the bias term β_i is independent of sectors, and can be written simply as β. This implies the following relationship between the two aggregate bias terms:

$$\pi_1 - \pi_2 = \theta(\pi_L - \pi_S) = \theta\beta. \tag{7}$$

An immediate corollary is that uniform skill-biased technological progress benefits disproportionately the *unskilled*-labour-intensive sector. To see the implications of this, I turn now to the general equilibrium effects of technological progress.

Consider first the case of a small open economy. The effect of technological progress on relative factor prices when goods prices are parametric is exactly the same as the effect of a goods price change itself (compare equation (1)):

$$\hat{r} - \hat{w} = -\frac{1}{\theta}(\pi_1 - \pi_2). \tag{8}$$

In particular, all that matters is the sector bias of the technological change; its factor bias is irrelevant. This has the bizarre implication that if technological progress is uniform skill-biased in the form specified in (7), then it should *reduce* the skill premium: skill-biased technological progress encourages substitution away from unskilled workers, but this is outweighed by its favourable effect in disproportionately reducing costs in the unskilled-labour-intensive sector. Putting this differently, if skill-biased technological progress in a small open economy is to explain the rise in the skill premium, then it must be disproportionately concentrated in the skilled-labour-intensive sector, while at the same time sufficiently diffused throughout the economy to ensure from (6) that the skill ratio rises in both sectors.

These conclusions are modified when we switch to a large economy with goods prices determined endogenously. The effect of technological progress on the skill premium now has two components:[6]

$$\hat{r} - \hat{w} = -\frac{\sigma_D}{\sigma_D + \sigma_S}\frac{1}{\theta}(\pi_1 - \pi_2) + \frac{1}{\sigma}(\pi_L - \pi_S). \tag{9}$$

The first term is identical to the effect of a change in an import tariff as in (2); the second to that of a change in relative factor endowments, as in (3). If demand is relatively inelastic, the second term dominates, giving the required rise in the skill premium. This is especially true with uniform skill-biased technological progress, when (9) simplifies to:

$$\hat{r} - \hat{w} = \frac{1 - \lambda\theta\sigma_D}{\sigma}\beta. \tag{10}$$

Recalling that both λ and θ are less than one, the numerator is likely to be positive.

However, there is a final implication of technological progress in a large economy which is less plausible. Consider its effects on relative goods prices:

$$\hat{p} = -\frac{\sigma_S}{\sigma_S + \sigma_D}(\pi_1 - \pi_2) - \frac{\theta}{\sigma}(\pi_L - \pi_S). \tag{11}$$

As in the case of wages, technological progress has two effects, and the second one definitely tends to *lower* the relative price of the unskilled-labour-intensive good. This tendency is even more pronounced if technological progress is neutral skill-biased, when (11) becomes:

$$\hat{p} = -\frac{1 + \lambda\theta\sigma_S}{\sigma}\theta\beta. \tag{12}$$

Crucially, *both* sector and factor bias effects tend to *lower* the relative price of the unskilled-labour-intensive good. The same condition ($\lambda\theta\sigma_D < 1$) which was necessary to guarantee an increase in the skill premium in (10) now ensures that the relative price falls by *more* than θ times the proportionate bias of technological progress. This seems clearly at odds with the empirical evidence quoted in the introduction.

3   Increases in foreign competition

The previous section showed that simple competitive general equilibrium models do not justify a trade-based explanation for observed changes in labour markets; but neither are they easy to reconcile with an explanation which emphasises exogenous skill-biased technological progress. Moreover, as noted earlier, there are other reasons why it seems worthwhile to explore these issues in an imperfectly competitive framework. In this section, therefore, I introduce a very different model which does just that.

Consider first an individual industry, in which two firms, one home and one foreign, compete on the home market (which I assume is segmented from the rest of the world). The firms compete in two stages, first choosing their levels of investment, k and k^*, and then choosing their levels of output, x and y.[7] To highlight the workings of the model I assume extremely simple functional forms. Investment incurs quadratic costs of $\gamma k^2/2$ ($\gamma^* k^{*2}/2$ for the foreign firm) in the first stage, and reduces marginal production costs linearly in the second stage:

$$c = c_0 - \theta k, \qquad c^* = c_0^* - \theta k^*. \tag{13}$$

The home firm's profit function is therefore:

$$\pi(k, x, y) = -\gamma k^2/2 + (p - c)x, \tag{14}$$

where p, the price of the homogeneous good, is determined by a linear demand function:

$$p = a - b(x + y). \tag{15}$$

Begin with the case where competition from imports is unrestricted. The firms play a sub-game perfect Nash game in investment and outputs. In the second stage (with investment spending sunk) profit maximisation by each firm leads to first-order conditions for output (given by equation (B1) in Appendix B) which define the output reaction functions. These in turn can be solved for the stage-2 output levels as functions of the investment levels: $x(k, k^*)$ and $y(k, k^*)$.

In the first stage, each firm chooses its investment anticipating the effect this will have on competition in stage 2. For the home firm, this leads to the first-order condition:

$$\frac{d\pi}{dk} = \pi_k + \pi_y \frac{dy}{dk} = 0. \tag{16}$$

The first term on the right-hand side, π_k, represents the 'non-strategic' motive for investment: when this is zero, investment is at its socially efficient level. The second term represents the strategic motive. The home firm anticipates that a higher level of investment will lower its costs in the second stage, push the rival firm down its output reaction function, and so raise its profits. This gives it a strategic incentive to 'over-invest' relative to the efficient level. Exactly the same arguments apply to the foreign firm of course. Solving explicitly, the first-order conditions for investment are:

$$\gamma k = \mu\theta x \quad \text{and} \quad \gamma^* k^* = \mu\theta y, \tag{17}$$

where the parameter μ reflects the strategic effect. If firms did not behave strategically, μ would equal unity and investment would be at its efficient level. Strategic behaviour adds extra terms in dy/dk and dx/dk^* (both, from equation (B2) in Appendix B, equal to $-\theta/3b$) to the first-order conditions, raising the

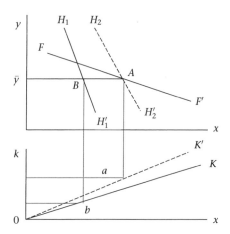

Figure 3.2 Effects of an import quota

value of μ to 4/3. Other things equal, strategic behaviour leads firms to over-invest by 33 per cent for a given level of output.

Figure 3.2, adapted from Neary and Leahy (2000), illustrates the special case where there is no foreign investment. The lower panel shows the home firm's first-order condition for investment from (17) with μ equal to either unity (along OK) or 4/3 (along OK'). The upper panel shows the output reaction functions (given explicitly by equation (B1) in Appendix B), with the appropriate values of k substituted to obtain the two home curves.[8] With unrestricted competition, equilibrium in the upper panel is at point A, where the foreign reaction function FF' intersects the strategic-investment home reaction function H_2H_2'; this corresponds to point a in the lower panel.

Now, assume that imports are restricted by a quota. To isolate its effects on the firms' strategic behaviour, assume initially that the quota is set at the free-trade level. Harris (1985) and Krishna (1989) considered the effects of a quota in a model with price (Bertrand) competition but no investment. They showed that, even when the quota is set at the free-trade level, it alters the equilibrium by changing the nature of strategic interaction between the firms. This effect has usually been assumed to apply only in Bertrand competition. However, it turns out that it also applies in Cournot competition, when firms first engage in investment.[9]

To show this, note that with foreign sales fixed by the quota, the strategic motive for investing (represented by the second term in the investment first-order condition (16)) disappears. Since the quota constraint prevents the foreign firm from responding to a cut in home sales by selling more, the home firm can reduce its investment from the free-trade level. Its only motive to invest is the non-strategic one, so the equilibrium is illustrated by point B in Figure 3.2. The foreign firm's quota-constrained reaction function is given by the kinked line $\bar{y}AF'$. Hence, with the foreign firm selling the free-trade level of imports, the home firm sells less. Since total sales are lower, the price must be higher and so the foreign firm earns higher profits. The home firm's investment locus shifts from OK' to OK in the lower panel, so its investment–sales combination is denoted by point b. Its sales are lower, but price is higher and it has saved on some inefficient investment. Its profits are therefore also likely to be higher.

Relaxing the assumption that the quota is set at the free-trade level of imports has straightforward effects. As the quota is tightened, the home firm moves down its efficient-investment reaction function $H_1H'_1$. Its sales and profits increase at the expense of the foreign firm. Relaxing the assumption that the foreign firm does not invest has no effect on the conclusions reached so far, but adds the extra prediction that the foreign firm has no incentive to invest strategically.[10] In this case, both firms invest efficiently.

So far, I have concentrated on the workings of the model. To show its relevance to the trade and wages debate, I need to reinterpret the policy change and to add a key assumption. The reinterpretation simply reverses the order in which the two equilibria are considered. Assume that imports are initially restricted by a quota and consider the effects of moving to free trade. The additional assumption concerns the factor intensities of the two components of costs. I assume that fixed costs (such as investments in marketing or R&D) require only skilled labour and that variable costs (i.e., production) require only unskilled labour.[11]

These two steps are simple in themselves, but their combined effect tells an interesting story about the effects of trade liberalisation. With the quota in place, both firms are in effect shielded from competition. In particular, their only concern in choosing their level of investment is to produce at minimum cost (trading off higher fixed costs of investment against lower production costs). Relaxing the quota changes the nature of the competition between the firms since the foreign firm can now potentially produce at a higher level (even if it does not choose to do so in equilibrium). To forestall this, the home firm now has an incentive to invest further, shifting its own reaction function outwards in order to force the foreign firm down its reaction function. The foreign firm faces a similar incentive and so it too invests beyond the cost-minimising level. Both firms behave more aggressively, which means that they increase their skill intensities. Hence, without any change in factor prices, trade liberalisation induces a skill-biased change in techniques.

Of course, factor prices may be expected to change. To establish how much, the model needs to be embedded in general equilibrium. This is no easy task in general, but it can be simplified by adopting a highly stylised approach which both reduces the relative scale of individual sectors and imposes an extreme symmetry across countries. Assume that the two countries are identical and that there is a continuum of industries, each identical to the one considered above. Each firm produces for the home or foreign market only, and takes factor prices as given in maximising its profits.[12] Aggregating across all domestic industrial sectors, equation (17) gives:

$$rS = \mu wL \tag{18}$$

where S and L represent aggregate demand for skilled and unskilled labour respectively, as in earlier sections, and the parameters γ and θ are replaced by factor prices r and w respectively.

Now, consider an across-the-board relaxation of import quotas. The strategic incentive to invest more aggressively raises μ; while the changes in factor demands depend on the output effects of the trade liberalisation. If quota levels are initially at the same levels as free-trade imports, then exporting firms raise their demand for skilled labour only, whereas import-competing firms raise their demand for both types of labour. If, more realistically, quota levels are initially below the free-trade import levels, exporting firms expand but import-competing firms reduce their demands for both factors. Finally, the induced changes in factor prices in general equilibrium depend on how factor markets respond. The simplest assumption is that both factors are supplied at less than infinite elasticity to the production sector of each economy:

$$\hat{S} - \hat{L} = \varepsilon(\hat{r} - \hat{w}) \tag{19}$$

where ε is the general-equilibrium elasticity of relative factor supply. Combining this with the total differential of (18) gives:

$$\hat{r} - \hat{w} = \frac{1}{1 + \varepsilon}\,\hat{\mu} \quad \text{and} \quad \hat{S} - \hat{L} = \frac{\varepsilon}{1 + \varepsilon}\,\hat{\mu}. \tag{20}$$

So, provided ε is positive, the relative return to skilled labour definitely rises, dampening but not reversing the initial rise in the ratio of skilled to unskilled employment demand in all sectors. Alternative assumptions about factor markets may modify these conclusions, but this remains the central case which may be expected to follow from relaxations of quotas in oligopolistic markets.

4   Extending and interpreting the model

The model presented in the last section provides a simple explanation of the effects of greater competition which is more consistent with the stylised facts than either of the competitive alternatives considered earlier. It would be going too far to suggest that the increase in OECD wage inequality can be attributed solely to relaxations of import quotas in oligopolistic markets. Nevertheless, in this section I want to argue that, despite many limitations, the model suggests a pattern of events, and a future research programme, which may illuminate a lot of what has happened in recent years.

The first point to emphasise is that the model's key result is robust to relaxing many of the assumptions made. For example, the assumption of homogeneous products is not restrictive. Suppose that, instead of (15), the demand function is $p = a - b(x + ey)$, where $e \leq 1$ is an inverse measure of product differentiation. It can then be checked that the strategic effect ($\mu - 1$), which equalled 1/3 with homogeneous goods, becomes $e^2/(4 - e^2)$, which is decreasing in e. So the qualitative prediction of strategic over-investment is robust to relaxing the assumption of homogeneous products, but the quantitative magnitude of 33 per cent is an upper bound within the class of linear demand functions.

Similarly, the extreme assumption that investment requires only skilled labour and production only unskilled labour can easily be relaxed. The essential feature is that their factor intensities differ in such a way that investment is more skill-intensive. This innocuous assumption is all that is needed to give the prediction that an intensification of competition raises the relative demand for skilled labour even if factor prices and import volume remain unchanged.

Finally, do the model's conclusions hinge on the assumption of Cournot rather than Bertrand competition? The workings of the model are unchanged, with the home firm investing strategically in free trade but not in the presence of a quota.[13] The first-order condition for home investment, equation (16), now becomes:

$$\frac{d\pi}{dk} = \pi_k + \pi_q \frac{dq}{dk} = 0 \tag{21}$$

where q is the foreign firm's price. Assuming goods are substitutes in demand, home profits are increasing in q: $\pi_q > 0$. The strategic effect therefore depends on how home investment affects the foreign firm's equilibrium price in the second stage game. With cost-reducing investment as in (13), the home price falls and, since prices are strategic complements, the foreign price too is pulled down. This gives the home firm a strategic *disincentive* to engage in investment, and so the effect highlighted in the last section is reversed. However, this is not the case if investment is *market-expanding*, tending to raise the price that consumers are willing to pay for home output. The foreign price then rises in unison, so a strategic incentive to over-invest relative to the efficient level is restored. This suggests that the effect of a quota relaxation in raising skill intensity is reasonably robust to alternative specifications of the nature of competition between firms and the technology of investment.[14]

Turning from robustness to interpretation, the effects highlighted by the model can be expected to follow any change which increases the degree of competition faced by home firms. In particular, there is nothing in the model which identifies foreign competition as coming from low-wage NICs: increased competition from countries at similar levels of economic development is even more consistent with the model. In this context it is worth mentioning the finding of Hine and Wright (1998) that trade has a disciplinary effect on UK manufacturing labour demand: but trade with other OECD countries has a stronger impact than trade with NICs.

Table 3.1   Alternative channels of effects on relative wages

Endogenous	Exogenous	
	Technology	Trade/Competition
Technology	(1)	(2)
Trade/Competition	(3)	(4)

A further consideration is that trade and technology are not necessarily competing explanations. Table 3.1 illustrates alternative channels whereby exogenous shocks can impinge on the wage structure. The diagonal cells, (1) and (4), indicate the direct channels, on which most commentators have focused: exogenous technology shocks in cell (1), exogenous trade shocks in cell (4). However, the off-diagonal cells are possibly more interesting. Cell (2) denotes trade-induced changes in techniques (observationally equivalent to changes in technology) such as those arising from quota relaxations as in Section 3 above.[15] Cell (3) denotes a different kind of change, whereby a change in technology can induce a change in trade patterns or in the extent of competition. For example, 'just-in-time' production techniques, falls in the costs of transporting intermediate goods, or improvements in communications may allow foreign firms to respond more flexibly and thus compete much more effectively. Their effects are thus very similar to policy-induced changes in the degree of competition as considered in Section 3. The model considered there seems more appropriate to all these shocks than the competitive models which dominate the literature to date.

5   Conclusion

Popular discussion and academic debate have focused on trade and technology as competing explanations for recent increases in the relative return to skills in OECD countries. In this chapter I have tried to broaden the discussion of these issues in two directions. First, I have suggested that the technology explanation should be subjected to the same scrutiny as the trade one. Second, I have argued that concentrating on models of perfect competition is inconsistent with some of the empirical evidence and misses some channels whereby increased import competition can impinge on factor markets.

I began by reviewing the stylised facts which emerge from a decade of empirical research on the fall in relative demand for unskilled labour in OECD countries. I noted that the Heckscher-Ohlin explanation, which blames increased competition from low-wage countries, is overwhelmingly rejected by the facts. I then turned to consider the technology explanation and, in particular, to question its consistency with the stylised facts in general equilibrium.

The key difficulty with this explanation is that, though skill-biased technological progress is bad news for unskilled workers, it is good news for sectors
which use them intensively. These sectors should have significantly lower costs,
which, in an economy that is competitive but not small, should translate into
significantly lower prices. These predictions seem inconsistent with the
empirical evidence. And they cannot be rejected by asserting that skill-biased
technological progress has only been important in skill-intensive sectors, since
this conflicts with a different stylised fact: skilled to unskilled employment
ratios have risen in *all* sectors despite economy-wide increases in skill premia.

I then introduced a model which highlights the effect of quantitative import
restrictions on technology choice by oligopolistic firms. I showed that the
model predicts that trade liberalisation encourages both exporting and import-
competing firms to invest more aggressively, raising the investment-intensity of
production in order to give themselves an advantage in competing against their
rivals. Assuming plausibly that investment requires relatively more skilled
labour, it follows that trade liberalisation raises the demand for skilled labour in
both exporting and importing countries, even at initial factor prices and even
if the initial import volume is unchanged. General equilibrium responses of
factor prices are likely to yield a rise in the skill premium which will dampen but
not reverse the increase in demand for skilled labour. Since this mechanism
operates in both countries, it is therefore consistent with all the stylised facts
summarised in Section 1.

Finally, I have argued that relaxations of quantitative import controls are not
the only type of shock to which the analysis is relevant. More generally, quota
relaxations can be viewed as a metaphor for any change which intensifies the
degree of competition in international markets. This includes changes which
should properly be attributed to technological progress itself, even though they
manifest themselves in more intense competition.

Fans of the *Hitchhiker's Guide to the Galaxy* may recall that the answer to
the question 'What is the secret of the universe?' was '42'. Most answers to the
question 'What is the percentage contribution of trade to the rise in OECD
wage inequality?' have been lower than that. But perhaps the second question is no better posed that the first. The analysis in this chapter implies that
empirically disentangling the effects of trade and technology is harder than
existing studies suggest; and that an imperfectly competitive framework may
be a more plausible one for understanding recent labour market developments.

Appendix A: Solving the Heckscher-Ohlin model

The change in the unit input coefficients in each sector may be written as:

$$\left.\begin{aligned} \hat{a}_{Li} &= -\theta_{Si}\sigma_i(\hat{w} - \hat{r}) - \hat{b}_{Li} \\ \hat{a}_{Si} &= \theta_{Li}\sigma_i(\hat{w} - \hat{r}) - \hat{b}_{Si} \end{aligned}\right\} i = 1, 2. \tag{A1}$$

Subtracting gives equation (6). Differentiating the price-equal-to-unit-cost equations in each sector gives:

$$\hat{p}_i + \hat{\tau}_i + \pi_i = \theta_{Li}\hat{w} + \theta_{Si}\hat{r} \qquad i = 1, 2. \tag{A2}$$

Subtracting (and setting $\hat{p}_1 - \hat{p}_2 = p$ and $\hat{\tau}_1 - \hat{\tau}_2 = \tau$) gives the Stolper-Samuelson relationship:

$$\hat{r} - \hat{w} = -\frac{1}{\theta}[\hat{p} + \hat{\tau} + (\pi_1 - \pi_2)]. \tag{A3}$$

When prices are endogenous, we must solve for them by equating aggregate supply and demand. In general this requires specifying the behaviour of the rest of the world (or, at least, its offer curve). Provided we assume that initial imports are zero, this can be avoided by simply positing a change in policy which imposes a wedge between home supply and demand (and hence home supply and demand prices). This is equivalent to modelling the change in trade policy as a reduction in the level of a *production subsidy* to the import-competing sector. (The income effects of this change will differ from a tariff, but this can be ignored since all income effects are zero in the neighbourhood of autarky.) Assuming homothetic tastes, the aggregate demand schedule may be written in differential form as:

$$\hat{X}_1 - \hat{X}_2 = -\sigma_D\hat{p}. \tag{A4}$$

To derive the aggregate supply schedule, consider first the total differentials of the two full employment conditions:

$$\lambda_{L1}\hat{X}_1 + \lambda_{L2}\hat{X}_2 = \pi_L + \delta_L(\hat{w} - \hat{r}) \tag{A5}$$

$$\lambda_{S1}\hat{X}_1 + \lambda_{S2}\hat{X}_2 = \pi_S - \delta_S(\hat{w} - \hat{r}). \tag{A6}$$

The terms δ_L and δ_S isolate the substitution effects in aggregate factor demand: they give the effects of a change in the factor-price ratio on the demand for unskilled and skilled labour respectively, holding outputs fixed. Subtracting gives the aggregate supply schedule in differential form:

$$\hat{X}_1 - \hat{X}_2 = \sigma_S[\hat{p} + \hat{\tau} + (\pi_1 - \pi_2)] + \frac{1}{\lambda}(\pi_L - \pi_S) \tag{A7}$$

where $\sigma_S \equiv (\delta_L + \delta_S)\lambda\theta$. Equate this to the change in aggregate demand from (A4) to obtain (11) in the text. Finally, substitute the solution for $\hat{p}$ into (A3) to obtain (2) and (9) in the text.

Appendix B: Computing the strategic effects in oligopoly

In free trade, the first-order conditions for output, which implicitly define the output reaction functions, are given by the following:

$$\begin{bmatrix} 2 & 1 \\ 1 & 2 \end{bmatrix}\begin{bmatrix} bx \\ by \end{bmatrix} = \begin{bmatrix} a - c \\ a - c^* \end{bmatrix}. \tag{B1}$$

These can be solved for the functions $x(k, k^*)$ and $y(k, k^*)$, since outputs are functions of the cost parameters, c and c^*, and hence of the investment levels k and k^*:

$$3b \begin{bmatrix} x \\ y \end{bmatrix} = \begin{bmatrix} (a - 2c_0 + c_0^*) + 2\theta k - \theta k^* \\ (a - 2c_0^* + c_0) + 2\theta k^* - \theta k \end{bmatrix}. \tag{B2}$$

The derivatives of these functions can now be used to calculate equation (17).

Notes

1   For representative overviews, see Francois and Nelson (1998), Haskel (1999), Johnson and Stafford (1999) and Slaughter (1998).
2   θ equals the determinant of the matrix of sectoral factor shares $\theta_{L1}\theta_{S2} - \theta_{L2}\theta_{S1}$, which simplifies to $\theta_{L1} - \theta_{L2}$. θ is less than one, which gives what Jones (1965) calls the 'magnification effect': the proportionate change in the skill premium exceeds the proportionate change in relative goods prices. So a modest change in goods prices could in principle explain a large change in the skill premium.
3   Of course, there is a dangerous, slippery slope here. Davis (1998a) criticises Krugman in turn for committing a different fallacy of composition, by allowing for endogenous price adjustment in a flex-wage 'America' and a rigid-wage 'Europe' without taking into account the constraints on mutual trade flows which are implied by these differences in labour market institutions. Davis's point is well taken in general, though the particular rigid-wage model he uses imposes an implausible degree of structure on the world economy.
4   λ equals the determinant of the matrix of factor-to-sector allocations $\lambda_{L1}\lambda_{S2} - \lambda_{L2}\lambda_{S1}$, which simplifies to $\lambda_{L1} - \lambda_{S1}$. Like θ, λ is less than one and is positive since sector 1 is relatively unskilled-labour intensive.
5   Jones (1965) calls these the 'differential factor effect' and the 'differential industry effect' respectively.
6   This equation contradicts Krugman's assertion (2000, p. 61) that 'When technological change occurs in a large economy, . . . [its] sectoral bias . . . has an effect which is ambiguous if it is there at all.' In Krugman's baseline case of fixed proportions technology, the weight $\sigma_D/(\sigma_D + \sigma_S)$ attached to the sectoral bias term reduces to unity (irrespective of whether preferences are Cobb-Douglas or not). However, Krugman is right to note that, with Hicks-neutral technological progress at a higher rate in sector 2, the skill premium does not rise if demands are inelastic. Hicks-neutral technological progress in both sectors implies: $\pi_L - \pi_S = \lambda(\pi_1 - \pi_2)$. Substituting into (9), $\hat{r} - \hat{w}$ reduces to $(\sigma_D - 1)\lambda(\pi_2 - \pi_1)/\sigma$. Hence the skill premium falls if σ_D is less than one. This result, which does *not* require fixed proportions in either sector, is stated explicitly in Jones (1965), p. 570.
7   Spencer and Brander (1983) is the classic presentation of this model in the trade literature. Neary and Leahy (2000) show how this approach can be extended to a wide range of intertemporal linkages. These papers, like most of the huge literature to which they contribute, concentrate on policy issues (in particular, the choice of optimal investment and export subsidies) and do not consider quotas.
8   The explicit expressions are $(2 - \mu\eta)bx = a - c_0 - by$, where $\eta \equiv \theta^2/b\gamma$ measures the relative effectiveness of investment for the home firm, and where μ equals 1 for the curve H_1H_1' and 4/3 for H_2H_2'.

9   After this was written, I found that Reitzes (1991) also considers these issues, though with a very different substantive focus.

10   Note that, unlike the one-stage game with Bertrand competition but no investment considered by Krishna (1989), assuming that the two firms continue to play simultaneously in the second stage need not pose problems for the existence of an equilibrium in pure strategies. Reitzes (1991) derives a necessary and sufficient condition for this, which I assume is satisfied.

11   Similar assumptions have been made in models of trade under monopolistic competition. Lawrence and Spiller (1983) distinguish between physical capital and labour (rather than skilled and unskilled labour) and assume that they are exclusively used in fixed and variable costs respectively. Flam and Helpman (1987) allow for differences in factor proportions between fixed costs (which they interpret as R&D costs incurred in product development) and variable costs. Many empirical studies of technology, trade and wages assume that the distinction between unskilled and skilled workers coincides with that between production and non-production workers.

12   The latter assumption is controversial, but can be justified when there is a continuum of oligopolistic industries. Gabszewicz and Vial (1972) were the first to point out that the properties of general equilibrium models with Cournot oligopolists are sensitive to the choice of numeraire. This has generated a large literature, which is generally pessimistic about the prospects of deriving a fully satisfactory model of oligopoly in general equilibrium. (See, for example, Dierker and Grodal (1999).) However, the approach I have adopted here seems intuitively plausible; assuming that firms take account of the effects of their actions on the full general equilibrium of the economy gives them an implausible degree of monopsony power. (See, for example, Melvin and Warne (1973).) Similar problems arise in models of monopolistic competition, and are routinely ignored in the many applications of the approach pioneered by Dixit and Stiglitz. See the discussion in d'Aspremont *et al.* (1996).

13   As noted in Note 10 above, an equilibrium in pure strategies does not exist if the firms set prices simultaneously in the presence of a quota. We must then assume that, in the second stage, either the home firm sets its prices as a Stackelberg leader (as in Harris (1985)), or that both firms continue to play simultaneously, in which case they adopt mixed strategies (as in Krishna (1989)). Provided goods are substitutes in demand, the qualitative outcome is the same.

14   With Cournot competition, market-expanding and cost-reducing investment generate the same strategic incentives. See Leahy and Neary (2000) for further details. All this can be expressed in terms of the taxonomy of business strategies of Fudenberg and Tirole (1984). (See also Neary and Leahy (2000).) In Cournot competition, investment of either kind makes firms 'tough' (in the sense that it reduces the rival's output and profits) so they have an incentive to behave like a 'top dog' and over-invest strategically. In Bertrand competition, cost-reducing investment lowers both firms' prices which reduces profits; each firm therefore has an incentive to behave like a 'puppy dog' and under-invest strategically. By contrast, market-expanding investment in Bertrand competition raises the prices which consumers are willing to pay for the products of *both* firms. Hence each firm behaves like a 'fat cat', over-investing relative to the non-strategic benchmark, thereby raising both its own and its rival's profits.

15   Trade-induced technological change has also been considered in models with outsourcing, as in Feenstra and Hanson (1996) and Jones (1997); with defensive innovation as in Thoenig and Verdier (2000); and with entry of new firms as in Vandenbussche and Konings (1998).

References

Borjas, G.J. and V.A. Ramey (1995) 'Foreign Competition, Market Power, and Wage Inequality', *Quarterly Journal of Economics*, vol. 110, pp. 1075–110.

d'Aspremont, C., R. Dos Santos Ferreira and L.-A. Gérard-Varet (1996) 'On the Dixit-Stiglitz Model of Monopolistic Competition', *American Economic Review*, vol. 86, pp. 623–9.

Davis, D.R. (1998a) 'Does European Unemployment Prop Up American Wages? National Labor Markets and Global Trade', *American Economic Review*, vol. 88, pp. 478–94.

Davis, D.R. (1998b) 'Technology, Unemployment and Relative Wages in a Global Economy', *European Economic Review*, vol. 42, pp. 1613–33.

Desjonqueres, T., S. Machin and J. van Reenan (1999) 'Another Nail in the Coffin? Or Can the Trade Based Explanation of Changing Skill Structures be Resurrected?' *Scandinavian Journal of Economics*, vol. 101, pp. 533–54.

Dierker, E. and B. Grodal (1999) 'The Price Normalization Problem in Imperfect Competition and the Objective of the Firm', *Economic Theory*, vol. 14, pp. 257–84.

Feenstra, R.C. and G.H. Hanson (1996) 'Globalization, Outsourcing, and Wage Inequality', *American Economic Review (Papers and Proceedings)*, vol. 86, pp. 240–5.

Flam, H. and E. Helpman (1987) 'Industrial Policy under Monopolistic Competition', *Journal of International Economics*, vol. 22, pp. 79–102.

Francois, J.F. and D. Nelson (1998) 'Trade, Technology, and Wages: General Equilibrium Mechanics', *Economic Journal*, vol. 108, pp. 1483–99.

Fudenberg, D. and J. Tirole (1984) 'The Fat-Cat Effect, the Puppy-Dog Ploy, and the Lean and Hungry Look', *American Economic Review (Papers and Proceedings)*, vol. 74, pp. 361–6.

Gabszewicz, J. and J.P. Vial (1972) 'Oligopoly à la Cournot in a General Equilibrium Analysis', *Journal of Economic Theory*, vol. 4, pp. 381–400.

Harris, R. (1985) 'Why Voluntary Export Restraints are "Voluntary" ', *Canadian Journal of Economics*, vol. 18, pp. 799–809.

Haskel, J.E. (1999) 'The Trade and Labour Approaches to Wage Inequality', mimeo., Queen Mary and Westfield College, London.

Hine, R.C. and P.W. Wright (1998) 'Trade with Low Wage Economies, Employment and Productivity in UK Manufacturing', *Economic Journal*, vol. 108, pp. 1500–10.

Johnson, G. and F. Stafford (1999) 'The Labor Market Implications of International Trade', in O. Ashenfelter and D. Card (eds), *Handbook of Labor Economics, Vol. 3B* (Amsterdam: North-Holland), pp. 2215–88.

Jones, R.W. (1965) 'The Structure of Simple General Equilibrium Models', *Journal of Political Economy*, vol. 73, pp. 557–72.

Jones, R.W. (1997) 'Trade, Technology, and Income Distribution', *Indian Economic Review*, vol. 32, pp. 129–40.

Krishna, K. (1989) 'Trade Restrictions as Facilitating Practices', *Journal of International Economics*, vol. 26, pp. 251–70.

Krugman, P. (1995) 'Growing World Trade: Causes and Consequences', *Brookings Papers on Economic Activity*, vol. 1, pp. 327–77.

Krugman, P. (2000) 'Technology, Trade and Factor Prices', *Journal of International Economics*, vol. 50, pp. 51–71.

Lawrence, C. and P.T. Spiller (1983) 'Product Diversity, Economies of Scale, and International Trade', *Quarterly Journal of Economics*, vol. 98, pp. 63–83.

Leahy, D. and J.P. Neary (2000) 'Robust Rules for Industrial Policy in Open Economies', presented to the Conference on Dynamics, Economic Growth and International Trade, University of Rome 'La Sapienza', June 2000.

Leamer, E.E. (1998) 'In Search of Stolper-Samuelson Linkages between International Trade and Lower Wages', in S. Collins (ed.), *Imports, Exports and the American Worker* (Washington, DC: Brookings Institution), pp. 141–202.

Leamer, E.E. (2000) 'What's the Use of Factor Contents?', *Journal of International Economics*, vol. 50, pp. 17–49.

Melvin, J.R. and R.D. Warne (1973) 'Monopoly and the Theory of International Trade', *Journal of International Economics*, vol. 3, pp. 117–34.

Neary, J.P. and D. Leahy (2000) 'Strategic Trade and Industrial Policy Towards Dynamic Oligopolies', *Economic Journal*, vol. 110, pp. 484–508.

Nickell, S. and B. Bell (1995) 'The Collapse in Demand for the Unskilled and Unemployment across the OECD', *Oxford Review of Economic Policy*, vol. 11, pp. 40–62.

Oliveira-Martins, J. (1994) 'Market Structure, Trade and Industry Wages', *OECD Economic Studies*, vol. 22, pp. 131–54.

Reitzes, J.D. (1991) 'The Impact of Quotas and Tariffs on Strategic R&D Behaviour', *International Economic Review*, vol. 32, pp. 985–1007.

Robbins, D. (1996) 'HOS Hits Facts; Facts Win: Evidence on Trade and Wages in the Developing World', mimeo, Harvard Institute for International Development.

Sachs, J.D. and Shatz, H.J. (1994) 'Trade and Jobs in US Manufacturing', Brookings Papers, pp. 1–69.

Slaughter, M.J. (1998) 'International Trade and Labour-Market Outcomes: Results, Questions, and Policy Options', *Economic Journal*, vol. 108, pp. 1452–62.

Spencer, B.J. and J.A. Brander (1983) 'International R&D Rivalry and Industrial Strategy', *Review of Economic Studies*, vol. 50, pp. 707–22.

Thoenig, M. and T. Verdier (2000) 'Trade-Induced Technical Bias and Wage Inequalities: A Theory of Defensive Innovation', mimeo, CREST and DELTA, Paris.

Vandenbussche, H. and J. Konings (1998) 'Globalization and the Effects of National Versus International Competition on the Labour Market: Theory and Evidence from Belgian Firm Level Data', *The World Economy*, vol. 21, pp. 1151–77.

Wood, A. (1994) *North–South Trade, Employment and Inequality: Changing Fortunes in a Skill-Driven World* (Oxford: Clarendon Press).

4

Fragmentation, Globalisation and Labour Markets*

Michael C. Burda
Humboldt University, Berlin, Germany, and CEPR

Barbara Dluhosch
University of the Federal Armed Forces, Hamburg, Germany

1 Introduction

Most contributions to the debate on the role of trade versus technology in explaining labour market developments see the two forces operating separately in independent spheres. In this chapter, we study the impact of trade on labour markets transmitted by its effect on choice of technology. Two observations in particular motivate our interest in this issue. First, not only final goods production but production itself is becoming increasingly global. Recent revisions of trade statistics, which give more detailed information on the nature of products traded, suggest that trade in intermediates has significantly outpaced trade in final goods. Second, a more detailed examination of labour statistics reveals that the increase in the skill premium was accompanied by substantial shifts in the structure of employment (OECD (1996, 1999, 2000)). In particular, employment in service activities rose in tandem with the exposure of locals to foreign competition. The increase in services employment was not limited to low-skilled, poorly paid jobs, but rather has exhibited a bimodal pattern with growth especially strong at the lower and the upper end of the wage scale. In addition, the employment of professional, management and sales-related personnel has increased substantially faster than in other high skilled groups.[1] These developments are indicative of fundamental changes in production methods and technology as the openness of economies increases. In addition, it suggests that the impact of trade on labour markets may be underrated in studies which neglect the indirect effect that increased openness has on labour markets via induced technical change.

The phenomenon of fragmentation is intimately related to globalisation. While globalisation remains the subject of endless academic and popular discussion, it is clear that the economic integration of the world's economies

* We thank Adrian Wood and Douglas Nelson for helpful comments. This research was supported by the Sonderforschungsbereich 373 of the Deutsche Forschungsgemeinschaft (DFG).

has risen markedly over the last few decades; the ratio of international trade to value added in the OECD rose from 24.6 per cent in 1960 to 42.7 per cent in 1996 (OECD (1998)).[2] Moreover, a number of fundamental developments are changing the ways that nations interact economically with each other. Mega-mergers and cross-border firm linkages have intensified trade in intermediate goods. An especially impressive development is the rise in outsourcing, allowing enterprises to extend activities across national boundaries and tailor production strategies to idiosyncratic attributes of local production sites. The word 'fragmentation' has been used to characterise these developments (e.g. Deardorff (1998); Jones and Kierzkowski (1990, 1999, 2001); Feenstra (1998); Kierzkowski (1998)).

This aspect of globalisation is the focus of our chapter. In particular, we ask the question: can the opening up of trade itself and the increasing fragmentation of world economic relations account for current labour market developments in OECD countries? In the model we propose, fragmentation is driven by Smithian division of labour and pure economies of scale, and results from cost competition among firms. To highlight these effects, we suppress any role for exogenous changes in technology.[3] Globalisation differs markedly from that derived in models of factor proportions or horizontal trade alone. North–South models of the HOS or Ricardian type are often difficult to reconcile with product and labour market developments in industrialised countries.[4] In our model, the removal of barriers to trade and factor mobility can induce an endogenous fragmentation of the value-added chain as the conscious choice of cost structure by monopolistically competitive firms. Trade-induced changes in production methods, rather than low wage competition, are responsible for an increase in the relative demand for skill. Furthermore, we focus our attention on fragmentation in a fully integrated economy, down-playing physical trade flows to emphasise the endogeneity of production and cost structures.

Because the model admits trade in differentiated final goods, it allows a useful distinction between horizontal and vertical globalisation. An expansion of the integrated trading region affects globalisation not only horizontally with respect to product variety, but also vertically as firms vary the specialisation of production stages. In the short run, it is likely that fragmentation will be accompanied by an increase in services employment as well as the skill premia, as observed in OECD countries. These implications can be reversed, however, as new firms enter the market.

The chapter is organised as follows. Section 2 offers a brief review of the literature on fragmentation and trade. Section 3 sets out our model of en-dogenous fragmentation in an integrated economy and illustrates the central role of labour markets in determining the cost of fragmentation, which we interpret as the price of business services. Section 4 reinterprets the model as a benchmark integrated economy and presents the central comparative statics results linking the size of the trading area to globalisation, as we understand it in this paper. Section 5 concludes.

2 Fragmentation and globalisation: A literature review

A large and growing body of research confirms that the intensification of trade is best characterised as vertical rather than horizontal. Krugman (1995) argues that export to GDP ratios in the range of 30 per cent can only be explained with reference to vertical specialisation-based trade. This applies in particular to countries with total trade exposure exceeding total economy value added. At the level of the OECD, Yeats (1998) estimates that the share of trade in parts and components within the SITC 7 category (i.e. machinery and transportation equipment) increased by 4 percentage points between 1978–95 and currently stands at more than 30 per cent. These numbers are considered representative for manufacturing in general. These estimates are consistent with those of Campa and Goldberg (1997), who examined input–output data of 20 industries at the two-digit SIC level from the UK, the US and Canada and found that in almost all industries the imported share of inputs (in total inputs) rose in the period 1975–95. Looking at the share of imported inputs in exports, Hummels, Rapoport and Yi (1998) found similar evidence.[5]

A number of contributions have featured the fragmentation of production processes as a concomitant feature of globalisation (see Francois (1990a, b), Jones and Kierzkowski (1990, 1999, 2001). Jones and Kierzkowski (1990) emphasise the role of producer services in the production process and in fragmentation without a formal model. In Jones and Kierzkowski (2001) specialisation in intermediates is driven by differences in factor intensities of stages of production and endowments if fragmentation occurs (see also Feenstra and Hanson (1996a, b)). In general, this work ignores the opportunity costs of resources employed in managing the fragmented value-added chain. Drawing on the examples of the photo-imaging and the pharmaceutical industries, Jones and Kierzkowski (1999) describe how fragmentation allows sharing of production blocks across various industries and how (due to indivisibilities and economies of scope) horizontal linkages among industries may be established as vertical specialisation deepens.

Francois (1990a) explicitly accounts for services and employs a family of production functions as proposed by Edwards and Starr (1987) and Francois and Nelson (1998) to display economies of scale as fragmentation increases, but features a single (homogeneous) labour market. Most importantly, Francois (1990a) stresses the endogeneity of the elasticity of substitution in demand along the lines of Lancaster (1979) so that via demand market size serves as a driving force for fragmentation (see also Dluhosch (2000)). In a related paper, Francois (1990b) assumes that services are produced with high-skilled labour only, while direct production uses unskilled labour but retains Lancaster preferences in demand, which he considers crucial for fragmentation (see Francois (1990b: p. 723, footnote 6)).

Another salient aspect of many models of globalisation is the use of Dixit and Stiglitz (1977) 'love-of-variety' preferences (Krugman (1980, 1981), Helpman (1981)). In principle, trade in these models is also driven by the demand side. Because consumers prefer a variety of goods, larger markets can sustain larger numbers of businesses; competition occurs via the number of firms, not via the scale of production.[6] Love of variety in intermediates may feature increases in productivity and scale in final goods production, but in the end this process is demand-driven as well. Some examples of this approach are Markusen (1989); Feenstra, Markusen and Zeile (1992); Feenstra and Markusen (1994); Krugman and Venables (1995); Ethier (1982); Romer (1987) and Matusz (1996).

While retaining a framework of imperfect competition, the model we present in the next section shifts the focus from demand to supply as an alternative engine of globalisation. We model fragmentation as an endogenous choice of cost-competitive firms in a general equilibrium setting with two factors of production. The scale of production of individual firms changes endogenously while the production process becomes more fragmented and global sourcing increases. Labour markets segmented by skill level turn out to be crucial for integration-driven fragmentation. Business services produced with skilled labour are necessary for managing global production and therefore determine the equilibrium extent of fragmentation. Explicit modelling of the supply side of fragmentation is a central contribution of our model.

3 Cost competition and technological choice under monopolistic competition in the closed economy

Household preferences and demand

The economy consists of a large number of identical households which can consume N differentiated, manufactured goods in quantities x_i as well as a homogeneous consumption service x_0, which also serves as the model's numeraire. Preferences over manufactured goods are described by the standard Dixit and Stiglitz (1977) symmetric CES function, which is nested in turn in Cobb-Douglas utility with expenditure shares of μ and $(1 - \mu)$ for manufactured goods and consumer services respectively. Given income Y, utility maximisation for the representative household gives rise to the familiar demand functions

$$x_i = \left(\sum_{j=1}^{N} p_j^{1-\eta} \right)^{-1} \mu Y p_i^{-\eta} \quad \text{for } i = 1, \dots, N \tag{1a}$$

$$x_0 = (1 - \mu)Y \tag{1b}$$

so that for N large, the elasticity of demand for manufactured goods is approximately η.

Manufactured goods and technology of cost reduction

Each of the manufactured goods described above is produced by a single firm under conditions of monopolistic competition. A central innovation in this paper is that the supplier of each manufactured good variety can influence its own cost structure by choosing the *length* or *roundaboutness* of production, and thereby the degree of specialisation of individual production stages. This aspect of the production technology is summarised by the positive real number z. Since we allow for non-integer values, it is best to think of z as an index of fragmentation or the degree of specialisation of stages in the value-added chain.[7] A small increase in fragmentation or specialisation dz (or an incremental lengthening of the production process) reduces direct production costs, but also generates overhead costs $p_z \mathrm{d}z$ (communication, management, organisational), so that p_z can be thought of as the cost of adding and managing an intermediate production stage.

To make the cost function consistent with a primal problem in two factors of production, we assume that direct production costs represent payments for the output of a perfectly competitive intermediate sector which employs skilled labour H_P and unskilled labour L_P using the constant returns production function $f(H_P, L_P)$ which is sold at price p_C.[8] We assume that fixed direct costs $\bar{F} > 0$ are invariant with respect to the number of production stages z, but that variable costs are subadditive, so that total direct production costs for a representative firm in producing x are given by $\bar{F} + v(z)x$, with $v' < 0$, $v'' > 0$. This is consistent with Adam Smith's (1776) idea that the size of the market determines the extent to which specialisation can increase productivity and reduce variable costs.[9] To facilitate analysis, we assume an isoelastic function $v(z) = \bar{v}/z^\gamma$.[10] Total production costs for firm i are then given by

$$\bar{F} + \frac{\bar{v}}{z^\gamma} x_i + p_z z_i. \tag{2}$$

Optimal firm behaviour and partial product market equilibrium

Since firms produce differentiated goods with identical technologies, describing (partial) product market equilibrium is straightforward. Profits π of the representative firm in manufacturing can be written as the difference between total revenues and total production costs:

$$\pi_i = p_i x_i - \left[\bar{F} + \frac{\bar{v}}{z^\gamma} x_i + p_z z_i \right]. \tag{3}$$

The ith firm maximises π_i in (3) by its choice of output level x_i and cost reduction z_i, taking p_z and its output demand curve (1a) as given. In what follows, we combine the first-order conditions (not shown) with the characterisation of partial product market equilibrium $p_i = p_j = p$, $x_i = x_j = x$ and $z_i = z_j = z$ for all firms i and j, which follows from the fact that manufactured goods enter utility symmetrically and are produced under identical cost conditions.

Short-run analysis: The case of no entry (n)

In a first variant of the model we explore the general equilibrium properties from a short-run perspective in which entry is restricted. With N fixed at $\bar{N}$, positive economic profits in the differentiated goods sector will be assumed. Optimal behaviour of firms in symmetric product market equilibrium yield the following expressions for the scale, the price and the extent of fragmentation in the differentiated goods sector:

$$x = \left(\frac{(\eta - 1)\mu Y}{\eta \bar{N}} \right)^{1+\gamma} \left(\frac{\gamma}{p_z} \right)^{\gamma} \Big/ \bar{v} \qquad (4n)$$

$$p = \left(\frac{\eta}{\eta - 1} \right)^{1+\gamma} \left(\frac{p_z \bar{N}}{\gamma \mu Y} \right)^{\gamma} \bar{v} \qquad (5n)$$

$$z = \frac{(\eta - 1)\gamma \mu Y}{\eta \bar{N} p_z}. \qquad (6n)$$

Partial equilibrium values of x, p and z thus depend on the relative price of fragmentation p_z and the scale of output Y. Equations (4n), (5n) and (6n) reveal the following partial equilibrium implications of our model of cost competition in the short run:

1. Production fragmentation z depends negatively on the costs of fragmentation, p_z, and positively on total value-added Y in the economy;
2. The price of manufactured output p (in terms of consumer services) depends positively on p_z and negatively on Y. While the markup remains constant, marginal costs are endogenous;
3. The scale of the firm x is no longer constant as in Dixit and Stiglitz (1977) and Krugman (1980, 1981), but depends on the incentives and ability of firms to reduce costs.

Long-run analysis: The case of free entry (f)

The assumption of no entry is unrealistic, especially in the medium to long run. The other extreme, free entry, implies that profits are driven to zero by endogenous variation of N which stands for both product variety and the number of firms.[11] Setting π in (3) equal to zero and substituting in (4) yields the following relationship between product variety N and income Y:

$$N = \frac{[1 - \gamma(\eta - 1)]\mu Y}{\eta \bar{F}}. \qquad (7)$$

To limit attention to economically meaningful equilibria, we will assume $\gamma < 1/(\eta - 1)$ throughout. Inserting (7) into the equilibrium conditions (4n),

(5n) and (6n) results in the following characterisation of symmetric product market equilibrium:

$$x = \left(\frac{\bar{F}(\eta - 1)}{[1 - \gamma(\eta - 1)]} \right)^{1+\gamma} \left(\frac{\gamma}{p_z} \right)^{\gamma} \Big/ \bar{v} \tag{4f}$$

$$p = \left(\frac{\eta}{\eta - 1} \right)^{1+\gamma} \left(\frac{[1 - \gamma(\eta - 1)]p_z}{\gamma \eta \bar{F}} \right)^{\gamma} \bar{v} \tag{5f}$$

$$z = \frac{(\eta - 1)\gamma \bar{F}}{[1 - \gamma(\eta - 1)]p_z}. \tag{6f}$$

On the basis of these equations we can again highlight the most important implications of our model from a perspective of partial symmetric product equilibrium:

1. The free-entry equilibrium of production fragmentation z now depends inversely on the cost p_z only; given p_z, both total demand Y (measured in terms of the numeraire) and the fraction spent on manufactures by consumers, μ, are irrelevant. This is because free entry allows limitless replication of production at a given cost structure, which is in turn determined by p_z;
2. The price of manufactured output p (in terms of consumer services) depends positively on p_z only. While marginal costs are endogenous, the markup remains constant though and, as γ approaches zero, converges to the familiar Lerner index of monopoly power (Lerner (1934));
3. As with the no-entry case, firm scale x is not constant, but now only depends negatively on the cost of fragmentation p_z. As γ approaches zero, x becomes constant (given the price of the fixed input), as in Krugman (1980, 1981);
4. An increase in market power (a decline in η) reduces both the output of firms and expenditures on cost reduction unambiguously.[12]

The supply of business and consumer services

Business services

Irrespective of whether they involve geographical reallocation of industries or the entry of new firms, the fragmentation of production requires additional resources in the form of coordination and communication. These resource requirements, which are increasing with the extent of fragmentation, are modelled explicitly as a demand for business services produced with skilled labour. It is here that the link between fragmentation and the labour market is established.[13] By suitable normalisation, the length of the production process of the representative firm z gives rise to an equal demand for business services, which can be interpreted as an intermediate input to manufacturing. Economy-wide demand for business services Z is then given by Nz. Business services are supplied in quantity Z at price p_z by competitive, profit maximising firms which use skilled labour H_S according to the constant returns production technology $Z = AH_S$. The derived demand for labour is thus infinitely elastic at Ap_Z, which in a competitive labour market will equal the equilibrium wage.

Consumer services

Consumer services are also supplied under conditions of perfect competition employing unskilled labour using the technology $x_0 = L_S$. Labour demand originating in this sector is thus infinitely elastic at 1, the value marginal product of unskilled labour in consumer services. We will assume throughout that $A > 1$; the assumption that consumer services are produced with low-skilled labour is consistent with below-average compensation in that sector (OECD (1999)).

Partial equilibrium in labour markets

Until now we have treated p_z as exogenous, in order to explore partial equilibrium aspects of the cost-reduction technology on products markets. Since Z is produced by profit-maximising firms using resources with value in alternative uses, its price should be determined in general equilibrium.[14] If p_z is endogenous, it will be influenced by conditions in labour markets, which in turn affects the extent of (vertical) globalisation (z) and the demand for labour, as we elaborate in the next section.

Labour is supplied inelastically by households in two forms, skilled $\bar{H}$ and unskilled $\bar{L}$ to perfectly competitive labour markets. Mobility between sectors is costless, so the demand curve for each type of labour in each sector is thus the 'supply price' to the other. The two relevant labour market equilibrium conditions are thus the equality of wage and value marginal product for both types of labour:

$$1 = p_C f_L(\bar{H} - H_S, \bar{L} - L_S) \tag{8}$$

$$Ap_Z = p_C f_H(\bar{H} - H_S, \bar{L} - L_S) \tag{9}$$

where p_C is the market price of the intermediate input, which is produced using f and which comprises the direct costs to the manufacturing sector.

Closing the model

No-entry case

The market price for business services equates demand for outsourcing services from $\bar{N}$ manufacturing firms (6n) with total supply (7):

$$\frac{(\eta - 1)\gamma\mu Y}{\eta p_z} = AH_S. \tag{10}$$

Finally, the model is closed using the market-clearing condition that the value of demand for the direct cost input in manufacturing equals supply:

$$\bar{N}[\bar{F} + \bar{v}z^{-\gamma}x] = p_C f(\bar{H} - H_S, \bar{L} - L_S). \tag{11}$$

We now have a system of nine equations (1b), (4n), (5n), (6n), (7), (8), (9), (10) and (11) in nine unknowns x_0, x, p, z, p_z, p_C, Y, L_S and H_S. The essential information can be distilled into a system of three equations in three unknowns p_z, H_S and L_S consisting of

$$p_z A = \frac{f_H}{f_L} \tag{12}$$

$$\frac{L_S}{(1 - \mu)} = \frac{\eta}{(\eta - 1)\gamma\mu} p_z A H_S \tag{13}$$

$$\overline{NF} + \frac{(\eta - 1)\mu}{\eta(1 - \mu)} L_S = \frac{f}{f_L}. \tag{14n}$$

Since $1/f_L = p_C$, the right-hand side of equation (14n) represents total direct costs in manufacturing (purchases of the intermediate input in terms of the numeraire), while the left side can be thought of as its decomposition into fixed $(\overline{NF})$ and variable $((\eta - 1)\mu/\eta(1 - \mu)L_S)$ components.

Free-entry case

Under free entry, the number of firms is given by (5f), making the equilibrium number of firms a linear function of income. Substituting (7) into (14n) yields a slightly different system of three equations in L_s, H_s and p_Z consisting of (12), (13) and

$$\frac{[\eta - \gamma(\eta - 1)]\mu}{\eta(1 - \mu)} = \frac{f}{L_s f_L}. \tag{14f}$$

4 International trade, fragmentation and globalisation

Interpreting the model in terms of trade and globalisation

While not modelled explicitly, the model contains two important implications for international trade. Like conventional intra-industry trade approaches, an enlargement of the trading area will have real effects on production patterns. Generally, two nations which open up to trade in differentiated output and produce as an integrated economy will demand more types of goods than in autarky. *Horizontal globalisation* means that the representative household can augment the variety of its consumption basket via purchases of 'foreign' goods. Trade in conventional models with differentiated goods has been used to explore the effects of opening up closed economies of similar development to trade (e.g. Brander (1981), Krugman (1980, 1981)). In addition, the removal of barriers to trade and mobility and higher volumes of operation induce firms to invest in more specialised production sites and economise on variable costs. *Vertical globalisation* refers to the process by which fragmentation of production is achieved, both within and across international boundaries. The distinction between deepening (vertical) and broadening (horizontal) globalisation is an important one.[15]

There are at least two ways to relate these two dimensions of globalisation to trade. One is to employ the Samuelsonian metaphor (Samuelson (1949)) and ignore national boundaries; it would be sufficient to study the effects of exogenous changes in factor endowments on the integrated economy.[16] Another approach is to model trade explicitly and ask whether the integrated economy can be replicated, as has been done in the intra-industry trade literature (see Helpman (1984)). If some goods are not traded, however (i.e. services), there is no guarantee that the integrated economy can be achieved. We take the former approach.

Our model predicts that an enlargement of the trading area – achieved for example by the removal of barriers to trade and mobility between countries – will have two effects. First, a horizontal effect reflected in the number of firms in manufacturing (N) of the traditional intra-industry sort. Second, however, an enlarged market for a given trading region, *ceteris paribus*, will increase incentives for individual firms to economise on variable costs by outsourcing or fragmenting the production process (z). In this sense, an enlarged market associated with trade can drive an endogenous evolution of technology, which in turn affects the international division of labour.[17] There is, however, no reason to believe *a priori* that increased trade will necessarily lead to more fragmentation. Next we explore formally the conditions under which a larger trading area in the integrated economy will increase the degree of fragmentation of the representative firm, z, and how this affects labour markets in general equilibrium.

Comparative static analysis of the impact of trading area size on fragmentation and labour markets

A variable of central importance to the model economy is the price of business services – the market price of fragmentation. From equations (4)–(6), it determines the degree of vertical versus horizontal globalisation in this model via its influence over the degree of fragmentation at the individual firm level (z), the relative price of manufactured goods (p) and the optimal scale of the firm (x). In general equilibrium, p_z will depend on the technology of business services production as well as the opportunity cost of skilled labour in the manufacturing sector, and thus will also depend on productivity of *unskilled* labour in alternative uses. It will also depend on the availability of factors; intuitively an increase in the supply of skilled labour is more prone to depress the price of skilled business services than an increase in the supply of unskilled labour, because the latter would increase total demand without contributing to its supply. A formal comparative static analysis can help reveal under which conditions trade increases vertical globalisation.

The enlargement of the trading area is modelled as an exogenous increase in factors of production: $\hat{H} > 0$, $\hat{L} - \omega\hat{H}$ with $\omega \geq 0$. When $\omega = 1$, factor endowments are increased equiproportionally. In the analysis which follows, conditions on ω are identified for which cost competition leads to vertical globalisation of production – an increase in the number of production sites for the representative firm ($dz > 0$), as opposed to an increase in the number of products ($dN > 0$). Since labour market implications of an increase in the integrated economy may differ we again differentiate between the polar cases of no entry and free entry associated with the short and the long run respectively. For the *aggregate* economy, an increase in fragmentation in the long run can be achieved either via an increase in that activity at the firm level, or by an increase in the number of firms.

Short-run analysis: Comparative statics without entry

We make use of the following familiar notation from Jones (1965): percentage change in a variable is denoted by a circumflex (e.g. $\hat{x}$ for dx/x), λ_{ij} is the share of input i employed by sector j. Log-differentiating (12), (13) and (14n) results in a system of three equations in $\hat{p}_z$, $\hat{H}_S$ and $\hat{L}_S$:

$$
\begin{bmatrix}
-\dfrac{(1-\lambda_{LP})}{\lambda_{LP}} & \dfrac{(1-\lambda_{HP})}{\lambda_{HP}} & -\sigma \\[2ex]
1 & -1 & -1 \\[2ex]
S\sigma + \dfrac{(1-\lambda_{LP})}{\lambda_{LP}}[\theta_{HP} + (1-\theta_{HP})\sigma] & -(1-\sigma)\theta_{HP}\dfrac{(1-\lambda_{HP})}{\lambda_{HP}} & 0
\end{bmatrix}
\begin{bmatrix}
\hat{L}_S \\[2ex]
\hat{H}_S \\[2ex]
\hat{p}_z
\end{bmatrix}
$$

$$
=
\begin{bmatrix}
-\left(\dfrac{\omega\lambda_{HP} - \lambda_{LP}}{\lambda_{LP}\lambda_{HP}}\right) \\[2ex]
0 \\[2ex]
\dfrac{\lambda_{LP}\theta_{HP}(\sigma - 1) + [(1 - \theta_{HP})\sigma + \theta_{HP}]\omega\lambda_{HP}}{\lambda_{LP}\lambda_{HP}}
\end{bmatrix}
\hat{\bar{H}} \quad (15)
$$

where $S = \{[(\eta - 1)\mu L_S/\eta(1 - \mu)]/[(\eta - 1)\mu L_S/\eta(1 - \mu)] + \overline{NF}\}$ is the fraction of direct costs in manufacturing represented by variable costs in equilibrium.

The differential system (15) expresses the (logarithmic) evolution of three central variables – skilled employment in business services, unskilled employment in consumer services and the price of business services in terms of the numeraire – as a function of a small change in the size of the market, when entry of new firms is excluded. Because we have treated the more general case elsewhere (Burda and Dluhosch (2000)), in what follows we present results only for the Cobb-Douglas specification of f, which obtains as $\sigma \to 1$. The Cobb-Douglas case has the advantage of simplicity without some of the ambiguity which characterises the model with more general production technologies.

Employment in services

From a labour market perspective, the response of employment in the two service sectors to an expansion of the size of the trading area is of central interest. In the case of unit substitution elasticity in f, these are:

$$\hat{L}_S = \frac{S\lambda_{LP} + (1-S)\omega\lambda_{HP} + (1-\lambda_{LP})}{\lambda_{LP}\lambda_{HP}\Delta_N}\hat{H} > 0 \tag{16}$$

$$\hat{H}_S = -\frac{1-\lambda_{LP}(1-S)+\omega\lambda_{HP}(1-S)}{\lambda_{LP}\lambda_{HP}\Delta_N}\hat{H} > 0 \tag{17}$$

where $\Delta_N = -(1-\lambda_{LP}+S\lambda_{LP})/\lambda_{HP}\lambda_{LP}$, which is unambiguously negative. Under these conditions, a 'bimodal growth' pattern in high- and low-skill services results from *any* expansion of the market size (for all values of ω).[18]

To summarise, the model yields a short-term response to an increase in market size which is in line with current developments in OECD countries which show a bimodal (high- and low-skill) increase in services employment. A requirement for this result is a sufficiently large elasticity of substitution between skilled and unskilled labour in the manufacturing sector, where the critical value is less than unity.

Market price of business services and fragmentation

As noted above, sufficient statistics for the degree of fragmentation and the associated labour market effects are the degree of firm-level fragmentation (z) and the price of fragmentation ($\hat{p}_z$). Inspection of (6n) reveals that the necessary and sufficient condition for firm-level fragmentation is $\hat{Y} > \hat{p}_z$ or, since $L_S = (1-\mu)Y$, $\hat{L}_S > \hat{p}_z$. Equivalently, since z is simply aggregate fragmentation divided by the number of firms $AH_S/\bar{N}$, condition (17) is also necessary and sufficient for firm-level fragmentation to rise. Thus, in the short run it is possible to observe that fragmentation at the level of the firm is increasing, even while the price of fragmentation is rising. The Cobb-Douglas case is unambiguous in the short run however, with H_S, Z and z all increasing.

Labour market effects: Relative wages

The effect of trade on wages is a central issue in the debate on inequality.[19] It is well known that exogenous labour-saving technical progress is a primary candidate for explaining the current labour market malaise in many OECD countries. In our model, a similar effect can be attributed to the endogenous reaction of producers to an expansion of the trading area. In particular, the assumption of constant returns in the two competing uses for labour guarantees that the relative value of the output of the business services sector is the sole determinant of the relative wage structure. We thus exclude not only exogenous technical change as a source of changing wage inequality, but also any endogenous variation of the marginal physical products in the service sectors resulting from changing employment levels. Variation of the price of business services is thus the sole determinant of the wage structure. The comparative statics result for $\hat{p}_z$ is

$$\hat{p}_z = -\frac{(\omega\lambda_{HP}-\lambda_{LP})S-(1-\lambda_{LP})+\omega(1-\lambda_{HP})}{\lambda_{LP}\lambda_{HP}\Delta_N}\hat{H}. \tag{18}$$

To sign (18) unambiguously, it is convenient to express parameter restrictions in terms of ω. With $\Delta_N < 0$, the price of fragmentation rises in short-run equilibrium without entry if and only if

$$\omega > \frac{1 - \lambda_{LP}(1 - S)}{1 - \lambda_{HP}(1 - S)}. \tag{19}$$

This would require $\lambda_{LP} > \lambda_{HP}$, or that manufacturing is relatively less skill-intensive than both 'services' taken together.

It is important to note that if (19) holds, an increase in the trading area leads not only to an increase in fragmentation and its market price, but also raises the skilled wage ($p_Z A$), increases income inequality and induces an apparent skill bias in manufacturing, if the business service sector is included. This result stands in contrast to the usual Heckscher-Ohlin logic, since a relative increase in the world supply of skilled labour ($\omega < 1$) could in principle lead to an *increase* in its relative wage and an increase in relative manufacturing employment, even though manufacturing uses skilled labour less intensively than business services. Given that much of world trade is 'North–North', the model thus suggests that integration of skill-abundant regions could in principle also cause rising inequality, at least in the short run.

Long-run analysis: Comparative statics with free entry

In the case of free entry and zero profits, log-differentiating (12), (13) and (14f) yields the following system in $\hat{p}_z$, $\hat{H}_S$ and $\hat{L}_S$:

$$\begin{bmatrix} -\dfrac{(1 - \lambda_{LP})}{\lambda_{LP}} & \dfrac{(1 - \lambda_{HP})}{\lambda_{HP}} & -\sigma \\ 1 & -1 & -1 \\ \sigma + \dfrac{(1 - \lambda_{LP})}{\lambda_{LP}}[\theta_{HP} + (1 - \theta_{HP})\sigma] & -(1 - \sigma)\theta_{HP}\dfrac{(1 - \lambda_{HP})}{\lambda_{HP}} & 0 \end{bmatrix} \begin{bmatrix} \hat{L}_S \\ \hat{H}_S \\ \hat{p}_z \end{bmatrix}$$

$$= \begin{bmatrix} -\left(\dfrac{\omega\lambda_{HP} - \lambda_{LP}}{\lambda_{LP}\lambda_{HP}}\right) \\ 0 \\ \dfrac{\lambda_{LP}\theta_{HP}(\sigma - 1) + [(1 - \theta_{HP})\sigma + \theta_{HP}]\omega\lambda_{HP}}{\lambda_{LP}\lambda_{HP}} \end{bmatrix} \hat{H}. \tag{20}$$

Note that the determinant of the matrix in (20), Δ_F, is now given by

$$\Delta_F = -\frac{\sigma}{\lambda_{HP}\lambda_{LP}}\{(1 - \lambda_{LP})(1 - \lambda_{HP}) + \sigma\theta_{HP}(1 - \lambda_{HP})\lambda_{LP} +$$

$$(1 - \theta_{HP})(1 - \lambda_{HP})\lambda_{LP} + \lambda_{HP}(1 - \lambda_{LP})[\theta_{HP} + \sigma(1 - \theta_{HP})] + \lambda_{HP}\lambda_{LP}\sigma\} \tag{21}$$

and is unambiguously negative; in the Cobb-Douglas case with free entry, we have $\Delta_F = -1/\lambda_{HP}\lambda_{LP}$. Again, we consider below the solution of the model in the Cobb-Douglas case ($\sigma = 1$).

Employment in services

When entry is unrestricted, the change in employment of services workers $\hat{L}_S$ and $\hat{H}_S$ is given by:

$$\hat{L}_S = \omega\hat{\hat{H}} \tag{22}$$

$$\hat{H}_S = \hat{\hat{H}}. \tag{23}$$

Clearly, the economy scales up in the employment of both types of labour, increasing by the same percentage in which endowments are assumed to increase. In the long run with free entry, there is no evidence of bias, as sectoral employment increases homothetically.[20]

The market price of business services, fragmentation and relative wages

Equation (6f) implies that equilibrium fragmentation under free entry is a function of the market price for business services p_z only. For this reason, the long-run behaviour of the relative price of business services p_Z – the price of coordinating fragmented production processes – is of central interest. If p_Z declines in the long run, then the representative firm will have a larger scale of production and be more globalised. In the Cobb-Douglas case, the solution of (20) for p_Z is given by

$$\hat{p}_z = (\omega - 1)\hat{\hat{H}}. \tag{24}$$

Thus, in the long run a necessary and sufficient condition for an increase in firm-level fragmentation is $\omega < 1$. If instead $\omega > 1$, then the long run is characterised by an increase in the price of and a decrease in the level of fragmentation. By (23), the evolution of total employment in and output of business services depends only on the scale of the expansion of the skilled endowment, and ω determines whether long-run globalisation is horizontal (in product variety) or vertical (in the extent of production fragmentation).

Since the variables in the differentiated goods sector depend only on $\hat{p}_z$, it follows directly from (16) that fragmentation in the long run may be fundamentally different from the short run. In particular, firm-level fragmentation will rise with free entry if and only if growth in the endowment of low-skilled workers is exceeded by that of high-skilled workers. In the short run, in contrast, fragmentation may occur with an increase in wage inequality. From (17) and (24) one could easily imagine a situation in which a uniform expansion of the trading area initially induces an increase in business services employment and fragmentation as well as wage inequality, all of which are reversed as new firms enter the market. In fact, overshooting of business services employment will occur if

$$\hat{H}_S = -\frac{1 - \lambda_{LP}(1 - S) + \omega\lambda_{HP}(1 - S)}{\lambda_{LP}\lambda_{HP}\Delta_N}\hat{\hat{H}} > \hat{H}$$

or if $\omega > \lambda_{LP}/\lambda_{HP}$.

5 Conclusions

The objectives of this chapter were twofold: first, to model partial and general equilibrium implications of cost competition and fragmentation in a model of monopolistic competition, and second, to ascertain to what extent trade alone can explain recent global trends in fragmentation and apparent skill bias in domestic labour markets. We describe a general equilibrium model in which trade and fragmentation are driven not by exogenous differences in factor endowments or technology, but by the sheer size of the market. Increased openness induces firms to cut costs; under certain conditions, removal of barriers to trade and mobility can lead to a decline in costs of organising and managing the value-added chain and thereby to more fragmented production structures. The result is a finer vertical division of labour and outsourcing similar to that observed in the process of globalisation. Although trade drives technology in this model, the potential for explaining observed fragmentation in the OECD as a function of increased trade seems greater in the short run, when the number of firms is held constant. In the long run when free entry has driven profits to zero, firm-level fragmentation can be reversed.

This chapter is a study of the behaviour of the integrated economy as a metaphor for trade in the world economy. We maintain that this is an informative approximation, even if trade flows are not explicitly studied. By stressing cost competition, our model offers a trade account of labour market developments which differs from the traditional factor-proportions explanations. In our framework, globalisation implies a shift in relative labour demand which can reverse the usual effects implied by the Rybczynski Theorem, at least in the short run. In the variable-entry case, it is necessary that the relative price of managing more complex production declines endogenously. With a fixed number of firms, necessary and sufficient conditions are decidedly weaker. Overall, the possibility that some component of technological change in the process of globalisation might be induced can explain why trade and technology are empirically difficult to disentangle in their contribution to the immiseration of low-skilled labour in industrialised countries.

Notes

1   In the period March 1995 to March 2000, 54.3 per cent of net US employment growth occurred in managerial and professional occupational categories; 29.9 per cent came in the category 'executive, administrative, and managerial'. During the same period, the groups 'precision production, craft, and repair' and 'operators, fabricators, and laborers' accounted for only 10.5 per cent and 0.6 per cent of new net job growth, respectively.

2   Some observers have noted however that the world is no more integrated today than it was at the turn of the last century; one frequently reads of 'globalisation cycles' in economic history. See Bairoch (1989), Williamson (1998), Baldwin and Martin (1999).

3   For a discussion of globalisation related to intermediates production and out-sourcing driven by factor proportions and Ricardian differences, see Sanyal and Jones (1982), Sanyal (1983), Feenstra and Hanson (1996a, b), and Deardorff (1998); outsourcing related to factor intensities of multinationals is discussed by Slaughter (2000). In a related paper, Burda and Dluhosch (2000) investigate to what extent fragmentation of production obtains for more general constant returns production functions.

4   An overwhelming majority of studies from the perspective of both trade volumes (Sachs and Shatz (1996), Cooper (1994), but see also Wood (1994)) and prices have found little evidence of globalisation along HOS-lines (Lücke (1998)). Furthermore, while these models predict substitution from skilled towards unskilled labour, the unskilled–skilled ratio has in fact fallen in virtually all industries (Berman, Bound and Machin (1998)).

5   The same pattern of increases in outsourcing and intra-industry trade in components is also displayed by area and industry studies (Ng and Yeats (1999), Jones and Kierz-kowski (1999)).

6   Krugman (1981) avoids this issue by assuming differentiated products segmented on the demand-side along industry groups.

7   Since our model applies largely to industry or economy-wide phenomena and not to the firm, ignoring the integer problem will not be an important issue here.

8   We assume that f has the usual properties; that is, $f_H, f_L > 0$; $f_{HH}, f_{LL} < 0$; $f_{LH} > 0$; and $f_{HH}f_{LL} - (f_{LH})^2 = 0$. One way of thinking about this is to regard the input as being supplied by a perfectly competitive manpower industry to the manufacturing sector in the form of a composite of the two labour types at minimum cost conditions, given factor prices.

9   Fixed costs might also be affected by choice of z, but since we are interested in the effect of relative cost differences we focus on variable costs.

10   This implies that marginal costs at $z = 0$ are infinite. Below we also impose explicit bounds on γ so that fragmentation is not 'too effective' in cost reduction.

11   Again, we ignore integer issues here.

12   To see this note that

$$dz/d\eta = \frac{\gamma\bar{F}[1 - \gamma(\eta - 1)] + (\eta - 1)\gamma^2\bar{F}}{[1 - \gamma(\eta - 1)]^2 p_z} = \frac{\gamma\bar{F}}{[1 - \gamma(\eta - 1)]^2 p_z} > 0.$$

13   Some of these channels are stressed by Harris (1995). Becker and Murphy (1992) point out that the division of labour is more often determined by costs of coordinating the various activities rather than size of the market. Our formulation is consistent with the fact that average compensation in business services is higher than in the overall economy (OECD (1999)).

14   In the original work by Kennedy (1964), Samuelson (1965) and von Weizsäcker (unpublished) on factor bias in technological change, these resource requirements were not explicitly modelled.

15   Our model thus extends Krugman (1980), who ruled out scale effects in a constant elasticity setting (p. 200). In our model, firms can change scale across different zero-profit equilibria as they 'economise' on variable costs.

16   This is in line with the widely held view that intensifying trade has resulted from declining trade barriers (see Wood (1994)).

17   This possibility has been discussed informally in the context of outsourcing by Feenstra (1998).

18   In the general case of nonunitary elasticity of substitution, Burda and Dluhosch (2000) show that a necessary and sufficient condition on σ for $\hat{L}_S > 0$ is

$$\sigma > 1 - \frac{\omega}{\lambda_{LP}\theta_{HP} + \omega\lambda_{HP}(1 - \theta_{HP})},$$

and the corresponding necessary and sufficient condition for positive $\hat{H}_S > 0$ is

$$\sigma > 1 - \frac{S\lambda_{LP} + (1 - S)\omega\lambda_{HP} + (1 - \lambda_{LP})}{[\lambda_{LP}\theta_{HP} + (1 - \theta_{HP})\omega\lambda_{HP}]}.$$

Since the fractions appearing on the right-hand side of the two expressions are unambiguously positive, one plausible sufficient condition for both forms of service employment to increase is $\sigma \geq 1$.

19   See, for example, the 1997 Symposium in the *Journal of Economic Perspectives* and the references therein.

20   With a more general constant return production function, Burda and Dluhosch (2000) show that the interval of σ for which bimodal growth in services obtains under free entry is given by

$$\left[\max\left(1 - \frac{\min(\omega, 1)}{\lambda_{LP}\theta_{HP} + (1 - \theta_{HP})\omega\lambda_{HP}}, 0\right), \infty\right].$$

References

Bairoch, P. (1989) 'European Trade Policy, 1815–1914' in P. Mathias and S. Pollard (eds), *The Cambridge Economic History of Europe VIII* (Cambridge: Cambridge University Press), pp. 1–160.

Baldwin, R.E and P. Martin (1999) 'Two Waves of Globalisation: Superficial Similarities, Fundamental Differences', in H. Siebert (ed.) *Globalisation and Labor* (Tübingen: Mohr Siebeck), pp. 3–58.

Becker, G.S. and K.M. Murphy (1992) 'The Division of Labor, Coordination Costs, and Knowledge', *Quarterly Journal of Economics*, vol. 107(4), pp. 1137–60.

Berman, E., J. Bound and S. Machin (1998) 'Implications of Skill-Biased Technological Change', *Quarterly Journal of Economics*, vol. 113(4), pp. 1245–79.

Brander, J.A. (1981) 'Intra-Industry Trade in Identical Commodities', *Journal of International Economics*, vol. 11(1), pp. 1–14.

Burda, M.C. and B. Dluhosch (2000) 'Cost Competition, Fragmentation, and Globalisation', presented at the Delphi 2000 conference 'Globalisation: Trade, Financial and Political Economy Aspects', Delphi.

Campa, J. and L.S. Goldberg (1997) 'The Evolving External Orientation of Manufacturing: A Profile of Four Countries', *Federal Reserve Bank of New York Economic Policy Review*, vol. 3(2), pp. 53–81.

Cooper, R. (1994) 'Foreign Trade, Wages, and Unemployment', in H. Giersch (ed.) *Fighting Europe's Unemployment in the 1990s* (Berlin: Springer), pp. 93–111.

Cortes, O. and S. Jean (1997) 'International Trade Spurs Productivity', presented at the 1997 EEA Annual Meeting, Toulouse.

Deardorff, A.V. (1998) 'Fragmentation in Simple Trade Models', presented at the Annual ASSA Meeting, Chicago.

Dixit, A. and J.E. Stiglitz (1977) 'Monopolistic Competition and Optimum Product Diversity', *American Economic Review*, vol. 67(3), pp. 297–308.

Dluhosch, B. (2000) *Industrial Location and Economic Integration* (Cheltenham and North-ampton, MA: Edward Elgar).

Edwards, B.K. and R.M. Starr (1987) 'A Note on Indivisibilities, Specialization and Econ-omies of Scale', *American Economic Review*, vol. 77(1), pp. 192–4.

Ethier, W.J. (1982) 'National and International Returns to Scale in the Modern Theory of International Trade', *American Economic Review*, vol. 72(3), pp. 389–405.

Feenstra, R.C (1998) 'Integration of Trade and Disintegration of Production in the Global Economy', *Journal of Economic Perspectives*, vol. 12(4), pp. 31–50.

Feenstra, R.C. and G.H. Hanson (1996a) 'Globalisation, Outsourcing, and Wage Inequal-ity', *American Economic Review (Papers and Proceedings)*, vol. 86(2), pp. 240–5.

Feenstra, R.C. and G.H. Hanson (1996b) 'Foreign Investment, Outsourcing, and Rela-tive Wages', in R.C. Feenstra, G.M. Grossman and D.A. Irwin (eds), *The Political Economy of Trade Policy: Papers in Honor of Jagdish Bhagwati* (Cambridge MA: MIT Press), pp. 89–127.

Feenstra, R.C. and J.R. Markusen (1994) 'Accounting for Growth with New Inputs', *International Economic Review*, vol. 35(2), pp. 429–47.

Feenstra, R.C., J.R. Markusen and W. Zeile (1992) 'Accounting for Growth with New Inputs: Theory and Evidence', *American Economic Review (Papers and Proceedings)*, vol. 82(2), pp. 415–21.

Francois, J. (1990a) 'Producer Services, Scale, and the Division of Labour', *Oxford Economic Papers*, vol. 42(4), pp. 715–29.

Francois, J. (1990b) 'Trade in Producer Services and Returns Due to Specialization under Monopolistic Competition', *Canadian Journal of Economics*, vol. 23(1), pp. 109–24.

Francois, J. and D. Nelson (1998) 'A Geometry of Specialization', *CEPR Working Paper* no. 1,813.

Harris, R.G. (1995) 'Trade and Communication Costs', *Canadian Journal of Economics*, vol. 28, Special Issue, pp. S46–S75.

Helpman, E. (1981) 'International Trade in the Presence of Product Differentiation, Economies of Scale and Imperfect Competition: A Chamberlin-Heckscher-Ohlin Approach', *Journal of International Economics*, vol. 11(3), pp. 305–40.

Helpman, E. (1984) 'Increasing Returns, Imperfect Markets, and Trade Theory', in R. Jones, P. Kenen, G. Grossman and K. Rogoff (eds), *Handbook of International Economics Volume I* (Amsterdam: North Holland), pp. 325–65.

Hummels, D., D. Rapoport and K.-M. Yi (1998) 'Vertical Specialization and the Chang-ing Nature of World Trade', *Federal Reserve Bank of New York Policy Review*, vol. 4(2), pp. 79–99.

Jones, R. (1965) 'The Structure of Simple General Equilibrium Models', *Journal of Political Economy*, vol. 73(6), pp. 557–72.

Jones, R. and H. Kierzkowski (1990) 'The Role of Services in Production and International Trade: A Theoretical Framework', in R.W. Jones and A.O. Krueger (eds), *The Political Economy of International Trade* (Oxford: Basil Blackwell).

Jones, R. and H. Kierzkowski (1999) 'Horizontal Aspects of Vertical Fragmentation', mimeo, University of Rochester and Graduate Institute of International Studies, Uni-versity of Geneva.

Jones, R. and H. Kierzkowski (2001) 'Globalisation and the Consequences of Inter-national Fragmentation', in R. Dornbusch, G. Calvo and M. Obstfeld (eds), *Money, Capital Mobility and Trade. Festschrift in Honor of Robert A. Mundell* (Cambridge, MA: MIT Press), pp. 365–84.

Kennedy, C. (1964) 'Induced Bias in Innovation and the Theory of Distribution', *Economic Journal*, vol. 74, pp. 541–7.

Kierzkowski, H. (1998) 'Trade Restructuring and Globalisation: New Challenges for the Transition Economies', report prepared for the WTO, March.

Krugman, P.R. (1980) 'Scale Economies, Product Differentiation, and the Pattern of Trade', *American Economic Review*, vol. 70(5), pp. 950–9.

Krugman, P.R. (1981) 'Intraindustry Specialization and the Gains from Trade', *Journal of Political Economy*, vol. 89(5), pp. 959–73.

Krugman, P.R. (1995) 'Growing World Trade: Causes and Consequences', *Brookings Papers on Economic Activity 1: Macroeconomics*, pp. 327–62.

Krugman, P.R. and A.J. Venables (1995) 'Globalisation and the Inequality of Nations', *Quarterly Journal of Economics*, vol. 110(4), pp. 857–80.

Lancaster, K. (1979) *Variety, Equity, and Efficiency* (Oxford: Basil Blackwell).

Lerner, A. (1934) 'The Concept of Monopoly and the Measurement of Monopoly Power', *Review of Economic Studies*, vol. 1(3), pp. 157–75.

Lücke, M. (1998) 'Searching for the Cause of Declining Low-Skilled Wages and Employment: Sectoral Value Added Prices in 11 OECD Countries Since 1970', mimeo, Kiel Institute of World Economics.

Markusen, J.R. (1989) 'Trade in Producer Services and in Other Specialized Intermediate Inputs', *American Economic Review*, vol. 79(1), pp. 85–95.

Matusz, S.J. (1996) 'International Trade, the Division of Labor, and Unemployment', *International Economic Review*, vol. 37(1), pp. 71–84.

Ng, F. and A. Yeats (1999) 'Production Sharing in East Asia: Who Does What for Whom and Why?' *World Bank Policy Research Working Paper* no. 2197.

OECD (1996) *Services: Statistics on Value Added and Employment* (Paris: OECD).

OECD (1998) *National Accounts* vol. I, *1960–96* (Paris: OECD).

OECD (1999) *National Accounts* vol. II (Paris: OECD).

OECD (2000) *Labour Force Statistics 1978/98* (Paris: OECD).

Romer, P.M. (1987) 'Growth Based on Increasing Returns Due to Specialization', *American Economic Review*, vol. 77(1), pp. 56–62.

Sachs, J. and H.J. Shatz (1996) 'U.S. Trade with Developing Countries and Wage Inequality', *American Economic Review (Papers and Proceedings)*, vol. 86(2), pp. 234–9.

Sanyal, K.K. (1983) 'Vertical Specialization in a Ricardian Model with a Continuum of Stages of Production', *Economica*, vol. 50, pp. 71–8.

Sanyal, K.K. and R.W. Jones (1982) 'The Theory of Trade in Middle Products', *American Economic Review*, vol. 72(1), pp. 16–31.

Samuelson, P.A. (1949) 'International Factor Price Equalization Once Again', *Economic Journal*, vol. 59, pp. 181–97.

Samuelson, P.A. (1965) 'A Theory of Induced Innovation along Kennedy-Weizsäcker Lines', *Review of Economics and Statistics*, vol. 47(4), pp. 343–56.

Slaughter, M.J. (2000) 'Production Transfer within Multinational Enterprises and American Wages', *Journal of International Economics*, vol. 50(2), pp. 449–72.

Smith, A. (1776) *An Inquiry of the Nature and Causes of the Wealth of Nations* (Oxford: Clarendon Press edn).

Wood, A. (1994) *North–South Trade, Employment and Inequality* (Oxford: Oxford University Press).

Yeats, A.J. (1998) 'Just How Big is Global Production Sharing?' *World Bank Policy Research Working Paper* no. 1,871.

Williamson, J. (1998) 'Globalisation, Labor Markets and Policy Backlash in the Past', *Journal of Economic Perspectives*, vol. 12(4), pp. 51–72.

5
Globalisation, Employment and Income: Analysing the Adjustment Process*

Carl Davidson and Steven J. Matusz
Michigan State University, USA

1 Introduction

Textbook models of international trade always posit well-functioning, friction-less factor markets. Policy-induced changes in relative output prices lead to the instantaneous reallocation of resources. While trade may result in some winners and losers (*à la* Stolper-Samuelson), factors are never unemployed and (ignoring terms-of-trade effects) the efficiency gains from trade liberalisation always result in aggregate net benefits.

Rather than focusing on the well understood benefits of liberalisation, some policy makers and editorialists tend to focus on the potentially costly aspects of resource reallocation. Most workers who lose their jobs due to liberalisation will find new employment opportunities, but there is typically a period of active search before such opportunities are found. Indeed, some workers may find that they have to re-tool before qualifying for employment in growing sectors. At the other end of the spectrum, some workers with little training and little innate ability may find themselves facing employment prospects so bleak that they choose to exit the labour force. Depending on the magnitude of the various effects, it is conceptually possible for the losses that occur during transition to outweigh the steady-state benefits of trade reform.

The purpose of this chapter is to construct and analyse a general equilibrium trade model that explicitly accounts for the dynamic aspects of labour market adjustment. Unlike earlier work in this area, we show how empirically observable parameters of the labour market determine the rate at which labour is released from the contracting sector and is absorbed into the expanding sector and therefore influence the magnitude and extent of the losses associated with trade reform.[1] As a by-product of the analysis, we are also able to show how the same parameters exert their own independent influence on the pattern and volume of trade.

* We gratefully acknowledge useful comments and suggestions provided to us by Rodney Falvey and other participants at the Conference on Globalisation and Labour Markets held at the University of Nottingham, 7–8 July 2000. We are fully responsible for the shortcomings that remain.

After developing the model in the next section, we parameterise it in Section 3 and use it to trace out the movement of the unemployment rate subsequent to the removal of a 5 per cent import tariff. We find that the unemployment rate overshoots its new steady-state level as expected. We turn to the welfare analysis in Section 4 where we show that subsequent to liberalisation, the value of net output (measured at world prices) falls below what it would have been had the tariff not been removed and remains below that benchmark level for an extended length of time. However, the value of output ultimately rises above the level that would have been obtained had the tariff not been removed. In our numeric exercise, the present discounted value of output under free trade is higher than it is with the tariff in place. In Section 5, we show how our model can be used to shed some light on the Bhagwati-Dehejia thesis that increased globalisation has led to increased job turnover, and therefore has affected the distribution of income (Bhagwati (1998)). Finally, we provide some suggestions for future research in Section 6.

2 The model

Labour market dynamics

To keep the model simple and to focus on labour market dynamics, we assume that labour is the only input in the production process. To allow us to examine the issues of interest, we introduce training costs and search frictions into the labour market. In particular, we assume that a worker must first undertake a period of training in order to obtain a job in either sector. Once training is complete, the worker must conduct a time-consuming search for employment.[2]

We formulate the model in a continuous-time framework and assume that transitions from one employment or training status to another follow a Poisson process. Eight parameters completely specify all transitions in this economy (four parameters for each of two sectors).[3] Unemployed workers searching for employment in sector i find jobs at rate $e_i > 0$. Employed workers in sector i lose their jobs at rate $b_i > 0$. Finally, workers training for employment in sector i exit the training process at rate $\tau_i > 0$. The Poisson process allows the nice interpretation that, for example, the expected duration of a spell of unemployment in sector i is $1/e_i$.[4]

We want the model to be able to capture the notion that some skills are general while others are job-specific. General skills are those that transfer across jobs while job-specific skills do not. We therefore assume that in each sector there is a probability $\phi_i \in [0, 1]$ that a sector-i worker who loses his job can forego retraining and can immediately begin searching for a new job in the same sector.

The dynamics that occur within a given sector are illustrated in Figure 5.1 and are made explicit in (1)–(3). Define L_i^E, L_i^S, L_i^T as the measure of workers employed, searching for employment, or training for employment in the ith sector. Let a dot above a variable indicate the derivative of that variable with respect

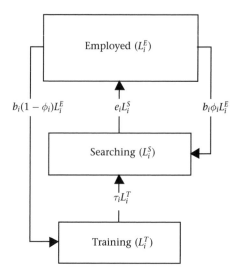

Figure 5.1

to time. Then the measure of workers in each category evolves as follows:

$$\dot{L}_i^E = e_i L_i^S - b_i L_i^E \tag{1}$$

$$\dot{L}_i^S = \phi_i b_i L_i^E + \tau_i L_i^T - e_i L_i^S \tag{2}$$

$$\dot{L}_i^T = (1 - \phi_i) b_i L_i^E - \tau_i L_i^T. \tag{3}$$

The change in employment over time equals the measure of workers who successfully complete the search process ($e_i L_i^S$) less the measure of separations ($b_i L_i^E$). The pool of searchers expands when workers lose their jobs but retain their skills ($\phi_i b_i L_i^E$) and when workers complete training ($\tau_i L_i^T$). On the other hand, the pool contracts when searchers successfully find employment ($e_i L_i^S$). Finally, the measure of workers in training expands when workers lose their jobs and require retraining prior to search ($(1 - \phi_i) b_i L_i^E$) and shrinks when workers complete training ($\tau_i L_i^T$).

Let L_i represent the total measure of workers attached to sector i. By definition, $L_i = L_i^T + L_i^S + L_i^E$. In writing (1)–(3), we have implicitly assumed that L_i is held constant. For example, all workers who are training in sector i were once employed in that sector. There are no inflows from the other sector. In fact, intersectoral flows play a critical role in the adjustment process and we explicitly consider such flows below when we discuss the impact of trade liberalisation. Until then, we have two adding-up constraints, expressed as (4) and (5):

$$\dot{L}_i^E + \dot{L}_i^S + \dot{L}_i^T = \dot{L}_i = 0 \tag{4}$$

$$L_1 + L_2 \leq L \tag{5}$$

where L is the total measure of labour available in the economy. The inequality in (5) allows for the possibility that some workers may choose to opt out of the labour force.[5]

Given L_i, it is straightforward to solve (1)–(3) for the steady-state values of L_i^E, L_i^S and L_i^T. Doing so, we obtain (6)–(8).

$$L_i^E = \left(\frac{e_i \tau_i}{(1 - \phi_i)e_i b_i + (e_i + b_i)\tau_i} \right) L_i \tag{6}$$

$$L_i^S = \left(\frac{b_i \tau_i}{(1 - \phi_i)e_i b_i + (e_i + b_i)\tau_i} \right) L_i \tag{7}$$

$$L_i^T = \left(\frac{(1 - \phi_i)e_i b_i}{(1 - \phi_i)e_i b_i + (e_i + b_i)\tau_i} \right) L_i \tag{8}$$

The allocation of labour across sectors

In the previous section, we took the allocation of labour (L_1 and L_2) across sectors as given. We show in this section how these values are determined endogenously by the behaviour of income-maximising workers.[6] In our model, workers cannot choose to become employed. Rather, they choose a sector in which to train. Each worker makes this decision based on the discounted lifetime income that he could expect to earn if he were to train in a particular sector. Once this decision is made, the worker undertakes training until its (exogenously determined) completion, at which time he becomes a searcher, and then ultimately an employee. The purpose of this section is to formalise this decision process.

As stated in the introduction, we would like our model to account for worker heterogeneity in terms of innate abilities. To this end, we define the ability level of a type-j worker as a_j and assume that this parameter is uniformly distributed over the interval $[0, 1]$. We then assume that higher-ability workers are more productive than lower-ability workers.[7] In particular, we assume that a worker with ability a_j can produce $q_i a_j$ units of output when employed in sector i. In what follows, we assume that labour is the only input, so that

$$w_i(a_j) = p_i q_i a_j. \tag{9}$$

where p_i is the price of the ith good and $w_i(a_j)$ is the wage earned by a type-j worker employed in sector i.

We now have all of the assumptions necessary to determine the discounted expected lifetime income of a type-j worker contingent upon his current labour market status. Let $V_i^E(a_j)$ represent the discounted expected lifetime income of a type-j worker who is currently employed in sector i, let $V_i^S(a_j)$ represent the discounted expected lifetime income of a worker who is searching for a job in sector i, and let $V_i^T(a_j)$ represent the discounted expected lifetime income of a type-j worker who is currently training for a job in sector i. Given the discount rate r and the wage rate w_i, the asset-value equation for a worker who is employed in the ith sector can be written as

$$rV_i^E(a_j) = w_i(a_j) + b_i[\phi_i V_i^S(a_j) + (1 - \phi_i)V_i^T(a_j) - V_i^E(a_j)]. \tag{10}$$

To interpret (10), think of the discounted expected income generated by employment as an asset. Then $rV_i^E(a_j)$ is the flow income that is generated by the asset. This is equal to the instantaneous wage adjusted by the capital loss that would be realised if employment were terminated. The capital loss is represented by the expression in brackets. In the event of job loss, there is a probability (ϕ_i) that the worker will not have to retrain before searching for a new job. In that event, the worker has an asset with a value of $V_i^S(a_j)$. Otherwise, the worker does have to retrain and therefore has an asset worth $V_i^T(a_j)$. The capital loss is multiplied by b_i, the rate at which losses are realised.[8]

For simplicity, we assume that workers who are currently searching for employment earn no income and incur no explicit costs. As such, the asset-value equation for a searching worker can be expressed as:

$$rV_i^S(a_j) = e_i[V_i^E(a_j) - V_i^S(a_j)]. \tag{11}$$

Since searchers earn no income, the flow value of the asset just equals the capital gain (the expression in square brackets) multiplied by the rate at which the gain is realised.

Finally, we assume that those engaged in training earn no income, but must pay an instantaneous cost equal to $p_i c_i$, where c_i is measured in units of sector-i output. Workers exit training and begin searching at a flow rate of τ_i. Given these assumptions, the asset-value equation for a worker who is currently training becomes:

$$rV_i^T(a_j) = -p_i c_i + \tau_i[V_i^S(a_j) - V_i^T(a_j)]. \tag{12}$$

Given a worker's level of ability, equations (10)–(12) can be solved for the six endogenous variables ($V_i^E(a_j)$, $V_i^T(a_j)$ and $V_i^S(a_j)$) in terms of the exogenous parameters of the model. Defining $D_i \equiv (r + \tau_i)(r + e_i + b_i) + (1 - \phi_i)e_i b_i$ to lighten the notation, we then have:

$$rV_i^E(a_j) = \left\{\frac{(r + \tau_i)(r + e_i)}{D_i}\right\} w_i(a_j) - \left\{\frac{(1 - \phi_i)(r + e_i)b_i}{D_i}\right\} p_i c_i \tag{13}$$

$$rV_i^S(a_j) = \left\{\frac{(r + \tau_i)e_i}{D_i}\right\} w_i(a_j) - \left\{\frac{(1 - \phi_i)e_i b_i}{D_i}\right\} p_i c_i \tag{14}$$

$$rV_i^T(a_j) = \left\{\frac{e_i \tau_i}{D_i}\right\} w_i(a_j) - \left\{\frac{r(r + e_i + b_i) + (1 - \phi_i)e_i b_i}{D_i}\right\} p_i c_i. \tag{15}$$

Equations (13)–(15) have fairly clean interpretations. First, suppose that the discount rate is zero and that all skills are job-specific, so that $\phi_i = 0$. Then the lifetime income for a worker is independent of the worker's current status.

This follows from the fact that the Poisson process implies that the expected durations of employment, search, and training are equal to $1/b_i$, $1/e_i$, and $1/\tau_i$ respectively. Therefore the ratio of time spent on the job relative to total time (employed, searching, or training) is $e_i\tau_i/D_i$. Likewise, the ratio of time spent training relative to total time is e_ib_i/D_i.

Putting the pieces together implies that the flow rate of income is a weighted average of the income earned when employed and the costs incurred while training, where the weights equal the share of time spent in each activity.[9] The existence of a strictly positive discount rate implies that more weight is placed on the current activity at the expense of the weight placed on the future activity. For example, an employed person places more weight on the current wage than on the future costs of training, while a person who is training places more weight on training costs than on the wage. Finally, greater transferability of skills (higher values for ϕ_i) implies a smaller share of a worker's lifetime spent in training.[10]

From (12)–(15), it is clear that, regardless of current status, discounted expected lifetime income is *increasing* in the wage rate, the share of skills that are transferable, the rate at which training is completed, and the rate at which searching workers become employed. Regardless of current status, discounted expected lifetime income is *decreasing* in the job separation rate and in the cost of training. An increase in the discount rate places more weight on the current activity. Therefore, an increase in the discount rate increases the discounted expected lifetime income of a worker who is currently employed, but reduces the discounted expected lifetime income of a worker who is currently training or searching.

Now begin by considering an untrained worker of ability a_j who is trying to determine whether to train for a job in sector i or whether to opt out of the labour force. A worker will choose to train for a job in sector i if and only if the following two conditions are satisfied:

$$V_i^T(a_j) \geq V_k^T(a_j) \quad i \neq k \tag{16}$$

$$V_i^T(a_j) \geq 0. \tag{17}$$

At this point, it is useful to provide an interpretation of our two sectors so that we may sensibly place more structure on the model.

We can think of sector 1 as the 'low-tech' sector where jobs are plentiful. In the limiting case, studied below, e_1 tends to infinity and jobs are instantaneously found. Furthermore, we can envision the skills necessary to perform any particular task in this sector as being very much specific to the job. For example, a store clerk may need to learn the layout of the store in which he is employed, the procedures involved in opening the store in the morning, the functioning of a particular type of cash register, and so on. These sorts of skills do not transfer across jobs. We capture this notion by setting $\phi_1 = 0$. By contrast, we can think of sector 2 as the 'high-tech' sector where more training is necessary for employment and where jobs are not instantaneously available upon completion of the training. Formally, this means $c_2 > c_1$, $\tau_2 < \tau_1$ and e_2 is strictly finite. In addition, the sector-2 jobs that are available require relatively more general, and therefore transferable, knowledge. For example, the most important part of a lawyer's training is learning the law. Therefore we assume that $0 < \phi_2 < 1$.

Given our interpretation of the two sectors, it seems reasonable to set up the model so that higher-ability workers sort into the high-tech sector and lower-ability workers sort into the low-tech sector. This will be the case only if expected lifetime training costs are higher in sector 2 than in sector 1 and if expected lifetime income increases more rapidly with ability in sector 2 than it does in sector 1.[11] These restrictions are implicit in the way that we have drawn the $V_i^T(a_j)$ curves in Figure 5.2, that is, a representative worker's discounted expected lifetime income if he obtains training in sector i. It is easily seen from inspection of (14) that these curves are linear and increasing in a_j.

Using (9) to substitute for the wage, letting e_1 tend to infinity and setting $\phi_1 = 0$, we can solve (15) for the level of ability at which the discounted expected lifetime income of training in sector 1 equals zero. Denoting this level of ability by a_L, we have

$$a_L = \frac{r + b_1}{\tau_1} \frac{1}{q_1}. \tag{18}$$

A worker with ability $a_j < a_L$ would earn negative lifetime income if he were to enter the labour force. That is, the income he could expect to earn while actually employed cannot compensate for the costs incurred while training. There exist no appealing job opportunities in this economy for these low-ability workers.

The ability level denoted by a_H in Figure 5.2 is the solution to $V_1^T(a_j) = V_2^T(a_j)$. This is the critical level of ability below which workers

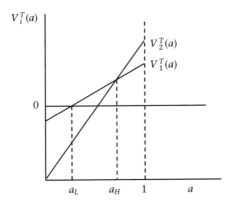

Figure 5.2

choose to train in sector 1 (or opt out of the labour force for sufficiently low ability). Workers with $a_j > a_H$ choose to train in sector 2.

Recall that we have assumed a uniform distribution of ability. Therefore, the proportion of the labour force sorting into the low-tech sector is $(a_H - a_L)$ and the proportion sorting into the high-tech sector is $(1 - a_H)$. Defining L_0 to be the measure of workers who opt out of the labour force, we then have

$$L_0 = a_L L \tag{19a}$$

$$L_1 = (a_H - a_L)L \tag{19b}$$

$$L_2 = (1 - a_H)L. \tag{19c}$$

Equilibrium

Substituting (9) into (15), it is easy to see that $V_i^T(a_j)$ is proportional to p_i. This implies that the ability level at which $V_i^T(a_j) = 0$ is independent of price. In the context of Figure 5.2, a higher value of p_i merely rotates the $V_i^T(a_j)$ curve counter clockwise about its intercept with respect to the ability axis.

Consider the steady-state supply side of the economy. Take good 1 to be the numeraire and define $p \equiv p_2$. For a sufficiently low value of p, the discounted expected lifetime income of training in sector 2 just equals that for training in sector 1 for the person with the highest ability level (i.e. for the person for whom $a_j = 1$). In terms of Figure 5.2, this means that $a_H = 1$. Given the assumed parameters of the model, this means that in the steady state no one would choose to train in sector 2 and therefore there would ultimately be no employment or production in that sector. As p increases, a_H falls and the proportion of the labour force training in sector 2 expands while the proportion training in sector 1 falls. This leads to more output of good 2 and less of good 1 in the steady state. As p tends to infinity, the $V_2^T(a_j)$ curve becomes vertical. There are some workers who just do not have sufficiently high ability to profitably train in sector 2. To an extent, this is an artefact of our assumption that training costs in sector i are paid in units of that sector's output. Increases in p_i raise both the wage and the cost of training simultaneously.[12]

Combining the logic in the previous paragraph with an assumption that all workers have identical homothetic preferences, we can sketch the relative demand (RD) and steady-state relative supply curves (RS) for this economy (see Figure 5.3). The intersection of the two curves determines the steady-state value of autarkic prices.

Observe that demand shifts change both outputs *and* prices despite the fact that we have assumed a Ricardian production technology. This follows from the fact that workers have heterogeneous abilities, of which some are better suited to the low-tech sector and some of which are better suited to the high-tech sector.

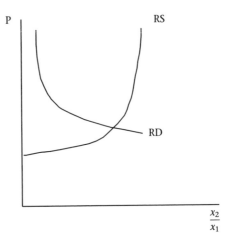

Figure 5.3

Note also that there is a role for absolute advantage (in terms of the production technology) in determining the pattern of trade. To see this, imagine two countries identical in every respect except that one country is proportionately more productive in both sectors compared with the other country. At any given price, w_2/w_1 will be the same in both countries (holding worker ability constant). However, in the high-productivity country w_i is relatively large compared with training costs in both sectors. As such, some workers who would opt out of the labour force in the low-productivity country choose to train in sector 1 in the high-productivity country. Furthermore, some workers with moderate ability who would train in sector 1 in the low-productivity country will choose to train in sector 2 in the high-productivity country. Output in both sectors expands, but the expansion is not necessarily proportional. Which sector experiences the greater expansion depends on the complex interaction of all of the remaining parameters in the model.

The final point to make is that labour market characteristics exert their own independent influence on autarky prices and therefore the pattern of comparative advantage.[13] Suppose, for example, that there is an increase in the rate at which workers in sector 1 complete training. This change leads to an upward shift of the $V_1^T(a_j)$ curve, drawing low-ability workers into sector 1 who had originally opted out of the labour force and drawing moderate-ability workers into sector 1 who had originally chosen to train in sector 2. In the new steady state, the output of good 1 will have increased, while the output of good 2 will have fallen.

As an alternative, suppose that b_2 increases; that is, the job separation rate for workers in sector 2 increases. This reduces the discounted income from working in sector 2, making such employment less attractive. The marginal moderate-ability workers who had been training in this sector immediately switch to train in sector 1. Over time, as workers become separated from their sector-2 jobs, they too switch. In the end, the output of good 2 falls because fewer workers choose sector 2, and because (for any worker who stays in sector 2) a smaller fraction of time is actually spent employed. On the other hand, the output of good 1 increases. Both effects work to increase the price of good 2 relative to good 1.

An increase in e_2 would have exactly the opposite effect. By increasing discounted expected lifetime income, more workers are drawn to sector 2 at the expense of sector 1. Furthermore, each worker attached to sector 2 spends a larger fraction of his life employed. Similar results hold for an increase in ϕ_2.

In summary, we have constructed a model that allows us to study the impact of trade on the distribution of labour between high-tech and low-tech jobs and, by implication, the steady-state levels of output, unemployment and training. The model also allows us to show how labour market parameters can exert an independent influence on the pattern of comparative advantage. Furthermore, the parameters of our model are generally observable. However, changes in the economic environment that lead to a new steady state take time to play themselves out. For proper policy analysis, it is important to know the behaviour of the economy along the adjustment path. For example, removal of an import tariff might very well yield long-run benefits, but the short-term adjustment costs could potentially dominate. This is the issue that we address in the next section.

3   Gradual adjustment following trade reform

The time path of employment following tariff removal

Suppose that the country under consideration is a small importer of the low-tech good (i.e. an importer of x_1). Further suppose that the country begins from a steady-state equilibrium and is considering the removal of an import tariff (T_1). With the tariff in place, $p_1 = 1 + T_1$. After removal of the tariff, $p_1 = 1$. As shown in Figure 5.4, the $V_1^T(a_j)$ curve rotates clockwise while the $V_2^T(a_j)$ curve remains unchanged.[14] The net result is that a_H falls, meaning that more workers will choose to train in sector 2 and fewer will choose to train in sector 1. But the shift between sectors occurs gradually. Recall that for simplicity we have assumed that the rate at which workers become employed in sector 1 is infinite so that there is no period of search. At the instant of trade liberalisation, all workers with ability $a_j \in [a'_H, a_H]$ who were training in sector 1 will switch to training in sector 2. However, assuming that the tariff was initially small enough, workers in that ability range who are employed in sector 1 at the moment of liberalisation will choose to remain so until they are exogenously separated. That is, as long as $V_1^E(a_j) > V_2^T(a_j)$, no one will voluntarily quit their job. However, once separated, these workers will begin training in sector 2. Therefore, the measure of trainers in sector 2 will jump up

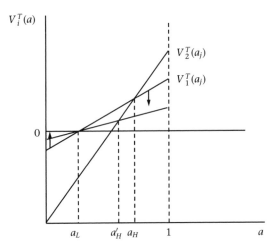

Figure 5.4

at the instant of liberalisation, then gradually continue to expand until the new steady-state equilibrium is attained.

The path taken by the measure of sector-2 searchers is less clear and depends on the relative magnitudes of the parameters in that sector. Suppose, for instance, that training is relatively quick, but searchers take a long time to find employment. Then the initial bulge in trainers will transmit itself to the pool of searchers, which will climb rapidly, overshoot its steady-state level, and then return to the steady-state level. On the other hand, if training is lengthy compared with the time required by searchers to find a job, the bulge of trainers will be released only gradually into the search pool and the measure of searchers will increase monotonically toward the new steady-state level.[15] In any event, the steady-state level of unemployment is bound to expand, since the measure of unemployed workers is a fraction of the measure of people tied to sector 2, which is larger in the new steady state (there is no unemployment in sector 1).[16]

We want to stress that we are able to provide an analytic closed-form solution for the entire adjustment path. This is a unique feature of our model. A more typical approach might require linearisation of the adjustment path near the new steady state. We do not need to make such an approximation. The closed-form solution to the complete system of differential equations is contained in Appendix A. Unfortunately, the solution is rather opaque and does not provide much insight on its own. We therefore close this section by providing results from a numerical exercise in order to gain some sense regarding the likely speed of adjustment.[17]

A numeric example

We do not claim that this particular parameterisation mimics an actual economy. In particular, it would be too much to ask of this simple two-sector model to accurately reflect *all* characteristics of a particular economy (e.g. the unemployment rate, the average duration of employment, the average duration of unemployment, the share of workers in the high-tech sector, and so on), but the numbers we have chosen strike us as lying in the range one might expect to see in many industrial countries.

In this exercise, we assume that we are dealing with a small country that begins with a 5 per cent tariff on imports of x_1. At time zero, the tariff is fully removed. We assume that tariff revenues had been redistributed in a lump-sum fashion, so their loss does not affect anyone's decision regarding the sector in which to train. Without loss of generality, we assume that units are normalised so that the world price of good 2 equals the world price of good 1. We summarise the values chosen for the remaining parameters that are used in this exercise in Table 5.1.

In our numeric example, we interpret one period as one year. Therefore, setting $b_1 = 1$ implies that the expected tenure for a low-skill job is one year. By contrast, the expected tenure for a high-skill job is ten years. This latter figure is roughly in line with the average job destruction rate in US manufacturing as reported by Davis, Haltiwanger and Schuh (1996). A value of 2 for e_2 means that the average duration of a spell of unemployment is six months. This is probably too long for the US, with actual unemployment spells being closer to three months. However, doubling e_2 (and therefore halving the expected duration of unemployment) would lead to excessively low values of unemployment in this simple version of the model.

The values for τ_1 and τ_2 imply training periods of one week and three months for low-skill and high-skill jobs, respectively. Combining this with the values of q_1, q_2, c_1 and c_2 implies training costs of approximately one week of wages for a worker of average productivity in sector 1 (for low-skill jobs), and approximately ten months' worth of wages for a worker of average productivity in sector 2. To calculate these figures, just note that the total amount of training cost for a worker training in sector i equals c_i/τ_i. A worker of average ability in sector 1 produces $[(a_L + a_H)/2]q_1$ during the course of a year. A worker of average ability in sector 2 produces $[(1 + a_H)/2]q_2$ in one year. Given the parameterisation provided in Table 5.1, $a_L \approx 0$ and $a_H \approx 0.192$. Therefore, a worker of average ability in sector 2 produces approximately 0.834 units of output in a year, whereas a worker of average ability in sector 1 produces approximately 0.096 units of output. That is, the average high-skilled worker produces between eight and nine times more output per year as the average low-skilled worker.

Table 5.1 Parameter values

q_1	q_2	b_1	b_2	e_2	τ_1	τ_2	c_1	c_2	ϕ_2	r
1	7	1	0.1	2	12	.5	1	4	0.5	0.03

The outcome of this exercise is illustrated in Figures 5.5–5.7. Figure 5.5 shows that the measure of unemployed workers shoots up immediately following liberalisation.[18] Given this parameterisation, overshooting does occur, with the measure of the unemployment pool declining after just one period and nearing the new steady state within about five periods.

Figure 5.6 shows that the labour force dips immediately following liberalisation, returning fairly quickly to the steady-state level. The dip is caused by workers exiting sector-1 employment to begin training in sector 2 and by workers who had been training in sector 1 (where the duration of training was short) starting to train in sector 2 (where training takes longer). Compared with the time required to return the measure of searchers to the steady state, a slightly shorter period is required for the labour force to return to the steady state. This follows because, in our parameterisation, training is a less time-intensive process than searching.

Figure 5.7 combines the information contained in Figures 5.5 and 5.6 to illustrate the movement of the unemployment rate over time. Again, the unemployment rate overshoots the steady-state level, but begins coming down after one period and closely approximates the new steady-state level after roughly four periods.

In examining Figures 5.5–5.7, two features stand out. First, the length of the adjustment period is neither trivial, nor does it appear to be excessive. Second, the magnitude of the short-run effect is noticeable. The unemployment rate climbs nearly three-quarters of a percentage point during the first year after

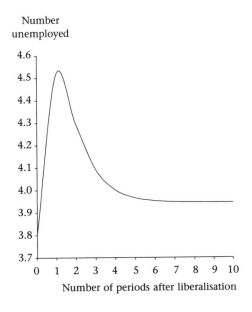

Figure 5.5

Labour force
participation rate

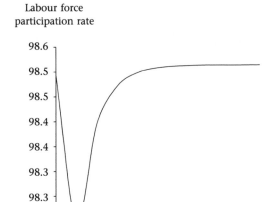

Number of periods after liberalisation

Figure 5.6

Per cent
unemployed

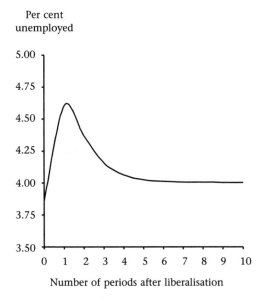

Number of periods after liberalisation

Figure 5.7

liberalisation before returning to a level less than one-fifth of a percentage point higher than in the initial steady state.

4   The welfare impact of trade reform

Even though labour is the only input in our model, workers are heterogeneous and therefore trade reform will benefit some workers while harming others.

First consider those workers with ability levels below a_L. In our model, such workers receive no income and therefore they are unaffected by reform. In a more elaborate version of the model, we might assume that such workers receive public assistance. We would then have to ask how that assistance is funded and how the funding changes with the removal of the tariff. These individuals benefit if the nominal amount of the assistance remains unchanged since the real value would increase in terms of x_1 while remaining the same in terms of x_2.

Clearly all workers who remain in sector 1 are harmed by the reform. When employed, their wage is unchanged in terms of x_1 but falls in terms of x_2. Similarly, those workers who are initially in sector 2 clearly benefit, with their wage increasing in terms of x_1 while remaining constant in terms of x_2.[19]

Now consider workers who switch sectors. On the one hand, sector 2 is more attractive after trade reform, so some workers are drawn into that sector. On the other hand, sector 1 is less attractive after reform, so some workers are pushed out of sector 1 into sector 2. We can envision these effects in two stages. First, hold constant the function $V_1^T(a_j)$ while shifting $V_2^T(a_j)$ upward by the amount corresponding to trade reform. Any workers moving under these circumstances are better off. Now, shift $V_1^T(a_j)$ down, commensurate with trade reform. The remaining movers are worse off than they would have been had the tariff not been removed, but the reduction in welfare is softened by the ability to switch sectors.

Perhaps a more interesting question regards the impact on overall welfare. A complete analysis of this question would require us to postulate some utility function so that we might talk about both the consumption and production aspects of reform. However, we can obtain some interesting results by focusing exclusively on the production side of the economy.

Define $Y(t)$ as the value of output (net of training costs) produced at time t and measured using world prices.

Even though the new steady state is plagued by higher unemployment, we show in Appendix B that the free-trade steady-state equilibrium is efficient. As such, steady-state 'welfare' with free trade is higher than steady-state 'welfare' with the tariff. In this context, 'welfare' is measured by the value of output net of training costs measured at world prices. However, welfare along the adjustment path is certainly lower than it is at the new steady state, and possibly lower than it was in the initial steady state. Could it be that the losses during the adjustment path outweigh the long-run gains from liberalisation? The answer to this is no, since we have shown in Appendix B that the free-trade equilibrium is dynamically efficient (which means that a small movement away from the free-trade equilibrium lowers welfare, taking into account the adjustment path). But, it is conceivable that the short-run losses during the adjustment process might eat away almost all of the long-run gains. This is an empirical question, but the model provides clear guidance regarding the proper data necessary to evaluate the experiment.

Formally, define $R_i^E(t)$ as the measure of workers who *remain* employed in sector i subsequent to liberalisation. Define $S_{12}^{E_1}(t)$ as the measure of workers who *eventually switch* from sector 1 to sector 2, but who are employed in sector 1 at time t. A similar expression, $S_{12}^{E_2}(t)$, represents the measure of workers who were employed in sector 1 prior to liberalisation, but are employed in sector 2 at time t. We then have the following:

$$Y(t) = \left\{ R_1^E \left(\frac{a_L + a_H'}{2} \right) q_1 + S_{12}^{E_1}(t) \left(\frac{a_H' + a_H}{2} \right) q_1 - L_1^T(t)c_1 \right\}$$

$$+ p^* \left\{ R_2^E \left(\frac{1 + a_H}{2} \right) q_2 + S_{12}^{E_2}(t) \left(\frac{a_H' + a_H}{2} \right) q_2 - L_2^T(t)c_2 \right\}. \qquad (20)$$

To derive (20), note that the average ability for workers who remain in sector 1 is $(a_L + a_H')/2$, implying that average output per worker employed in that sector is $[(a_L + a_H')/2]q_1$. The other terms are obtained similarly.

We show $Y(t)$ as the solid line in Figure 5.8 for $t = 0, \ldots, 10$. The dashed horizontal line represents the value of steady-state output prior to liberalisation. Conforming with the intuition discussed above, the value of output falls below its pre-liberalisation level for the first several years after liberalisation. In this example, based on the parameters of Table 5.1, output does not

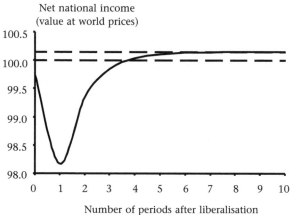

Net national income
(value at world prices)

Figure 5.8

climb above the pre-liberalisation level until sometime during the fourth year after the reform.

Reform is beneficial only if net losses during the early years of reform are compensated by the future gains. Formally, let W_{FT} represent the present discounted value of welfare under free trade, and let W_{SS} represent the present discounted value of welfare consistent with the tariff-distorted steady state. Then removal of the tariff is beneficial if and only if $\hat{W} = (W_{FT} - W_{SS})/W_{SS} > 0$, where

$$W_{SS} = \int_0^\infty e^{-rt} Y_{SS}\, dt \tag{21a}$$

$$W_{FT} = \int_0^\infty e^{-rt} Y_{FT}(t)\, dt. \tag{21b}$$

Based on the parameters in Table 5.1, $\hat{W} = 0.0002$. That is, there is a welfare gain, but the gain is less than 0.02 per cent of pre-liberalisation income. The measured welfare gain would be larger if we simply compare steady states. In this example, steady-state income with free trade is approximately 0.14 per cent higher than steady-state income in the distorted economy.[20] While adjustment costs do not reverse the benefits of tariff reform, they are substantial.[21] Thus, although Appendix B tells us that this economy will benefit from liberalisation, our numerical exercise tells us that the gains will be almost trivial.

5   The Bhagwati-Dehejia thesis

Our main concern in this chapter so far has been to develop a tractable model suited to predicting adjustment costs based on observable parameters. We can also use our model, however, to shed some light on the raging debate regarding the impact of globalisation on the distribution of income.

As is well documented, income distributions within OECD countries have worsened, with the rich getting richer and the poor getting poorer. At the same time, imports from developing countries have exploded. The natural inclination among many economists is to apply the Stolper-Samuelson theorem to argue that increased globalisation caused deterioration of the income distribution. The problem is that (depending upon one's interpretation) the data do not seem to support this hypothesis.[22]

Bhagwati and Dehejia (1994) have suggested the possibility that globalisation might impact relative income even without Stolper-Samuelson effects. They hypothesise that increased globalisation means increasing competition, with razor-thin profit margins. Firms that are competitive today might be out of business tomorrow. They refer to this phenomenon as 'kaleidoscopic comparative advantage' and argue that one implication is that job turnover rates might have increased due to this effect. In turn, the higher rates of job turnover might reduce incentives for workers to acquire human capital, flattening out the growth profile of earnings. They argue that this could result in an increase in the income differential between skilled and unskilled workers if skilled workers have greater transferability of workplace skills than do unskilled workers (as we model).[23] While our model is not tailored to address this thesis head on, we clearly have the machinery to explore some possibilities.

Suppose that globalisation implies an increase in b_1 and b_2, all else equal.[24] Consider first what happens when b_1 increases. Sector 1 becomes less attractive. Some low-ability workers are pushed into economic inactivity. Some higher-ability workers are pushed into sector 2. Workers who remain in sector 1 spend a higher fraction of their lifetime in training and a smaller fraction actually employed. Whether the total amount of training goes up or down depends on the interaction of a smaller sector size with more time spent in training by those who continue to work in the sector.

Similar effects are seen in sector 2. An increase in b_2 will make sector 2 less attractive. Some lower-ability workers will be pushed into sector 1. Those workers who remain in sector 2 will spend a smaller fraction of their lifetime working, and a larger fraction searching and in training. Whether sector 2 shrinks or expands depends upon the magnitude by which b_2 increases compared with the increase in b_1. Even here, there is no simple comparison because all of the other parameters have a role to play.

We can use our model to derive three results, all of which are consistent with the Bhagwati-Dehejia thesis. First, if both turnover rates increase proportionately, it is likely that workers will shift out of sector 2 and into sector 1, and there will be a reduction in the aggregate amount of training. Second, higher turnover rates imply lower lifetime incomes for all agents, but the impact is proportionately less for agents with higher ability. Therefore we can infer that such an increase in turnover rates will improve the welfare of the highest-ability workers with respect to the welfare of the lowest-ability workers. Finally, the degree to which income falls as a result of higher turnover is inversely related to the ease with which skills transfer between jobs.

To illustrate these results, we differentiate (15) with respect to b_1, holding all other variables constant. Doing so, we find

$$\hat{V}_2^T(a_j) = -\left\{ \left(1 + \frac{p_2 c_2}{rV_2^T(a_j)}\right) \left(\frac{rb_2 + (1-\phi_2)e_2 b_2}{D_2}\right) - \frac{\tau_2 b_2}{D_2} \right\} \hat{b}_2 \qquad (22a)$$

$$\hat{V}_1^T(a_j) = -\left\{ \left(1 + \frac{p_1 c_1}{rV_1^T(a_j)}\right) \left(\frac{b_1}{D_1}\right) \right\} \hat{b}_1. \qquad (22b)$$

At the initial steady state, $rV_1^T(a_H) = rV_2^T(a_H)$. By assumption, training costs are low in sector 1, so $p_1 c_1 < p_2 c_2$. The fractions b_1/D_1 and $(rb_2 + (1-\phi_2)e_2 b_2)/D_2$ are not directly comparable. Given the parameters in Table 5.1, b_1/D_1 has the slightly larger value. However, in our example, $\hat{V}_2^T(a_H)/\hat{b}_2 < \hat{V}_1^T(a_H)/\hat{b}_1 < 0$. A proportionate increase in b_1 and b_2 reduces the expected lifetime income from training in sector 2 by more than the reduction in sector 1 for the person with ability a_H. Workers therefore shift gradually from sector 2 to sector 1, illustrating our first result.

Inspection of (22a) and (22b) reveals that the proportionate impact on expected lifetime income of an increase in b_i diminishes as ability increases, therefore confirming our second result. Higher turnover rates in both sectors hurt everyone, but mostly impact those with the lowest abilities (i.e. workers in the bottom tail of the income distribution).

Finally, differentiating the right-hand side of (22a) with respect to ϕ_2 shows that the coefficient on $\hat{b}_2$ becomes smaller in absolute value as skills become more transferable across jobs (i.e. as ϕ_2 increases), therefore reducing the elasticity of $V_2^T(a_j)$ with respect to b_2. This confirms our third result.[25]

6   Conclusion

The vast majority of public debate about trade policy centres on its impact on the jobless and the poor and the short-run adjustment costs generated by changes in the pattern of trade. With only a few notable exceptions, the vast majority of the academic literature on trade policy ignores such issues. In this chapter, we have offered a simple model of trade that incorporates some of the more important features that the public seems concerned about. In our opinion, the two most important features are unemployment and a class of workers who are shut out of the labour market because they do not have the ability to acquire the skills required for the jobs that are available. We have shown that not only is it possible to build a simple model with such features, but that it is also possible to solve analytically for the adjustment path that connects steady states.[26] This allows us to weigh the short-run costs of adjustment against any long-run gains that may arise from changes in trade policy. Moreover, the key parameters of our model (labour market turnover rates) are all observable, making it a natural framework for future policy analysis.

Our main goal in this chapter was to demonstrate the usefulness of the model in dealing with some basic issues. For example, we began by examining the impact of globalisation on unemployment and economic welfare. We show that, in our model, the short-run costs of adjustment cannot outweigh the long-run gains from globalisation. However, our numeric exercise suggests that adjustment costs are substantial in the short run (the value of output net of training costs falls by more than 1.5 per cent one year after liberalisation), and that they may be large enough to eat away almost all the long-run efficiency gains.

We also examined the impact of globalisation on the distribution of income. When we assume that protection is removed from the low-skill sector, we obtain results of a Stolper-Samuelson type, even though labour is the only input in our model. In this case, those workers who continue to be attached to the low-skill sector are worse off while those who were initially attached to the high-skill sector benefit. Liberalisation causes some workers to switch from the low-skill to the high-skill sector. Of those who shift between sectors, those with higher abilities benefit from the liberalisation, while those with lower abilities are harmed.

Our model also provides support for the Bhagwati-Dehejia thesis that if globalisation leads to higher job turnover it may lead to a more unequal distribution of income. In particular, we show that an increase in job turnover has a smaller (negative) impact on workers of higher ability compared with lower ability and greater transferability of skills across jobs reduces the sensitivity of lifetime income to changes in job turnover.

In the future, we intend to use our model to address some issues that have received very little attention in the trade literature. Since our model explicitly allows for unemployment and heterogeneity in skills across workers and jobs (which generates a non-trivial income distribution), we can carry out careful policy analysis of a wide variety of labour market policies aimed at helping the jobless and the poor who are adversely affected by changes in the pattern of trade. For example, we could incorporate training subsidies, unemployment compensation, trade adjustment assistance, government-sponsored training or job search services and wage subsidies with virtually no change to the underlying structure of the model. We could then choose a target (say, a certain level of income for low-ability workers) and find the policy that achieves the target with the smallest social cost. Moreover, by varying the turnover rates to mimic the structure of the labour markets in different regions of the world, we can investigate how the optimal policy depends on the flexibility of the labour market. After all, there is little reason to believe that policies that may be effective in the United States, where the durations of employment and unemployment are low relative to Europe and Japan, will be equally effective in other parts of the world where turnover rates are vastly different.

Appendix A

We sketch the derivation of closed-form solutions for the adjustment path in this appendix. In addition to the notation introduced in the text, define $S_{12}^{T_2}(t)$ as the measure of workers who switch from sector 1 to sector 2 and are training at time t. Similarly define $S_{12}^{S_2}(t)$ as the measure of workers who switch from sector 1 to sector 2 and are searching at time t. The system of differential equations then can be written as in (A1)–(A4):

$$\dot{S}_{12}^{E_1} = -b_2 S_{12}^{E_1} \tag{A1}$$

$$\dot{S}_{12}^{E_2} = e_2 S_{12}^{S_2} - b_2 S_{12}^{E_2} \tag{A2}$$

$$\dot{S}_{12}^{S_2} = b_2 \phi_2 S_{12}^{E_2} + \tau_2 S_{12}^{T_2} - e_2 S_{12}^{S_2} \tag{A3}$$

$$(a_H - a_H')L = S_{12}^{E_1} + S_{12}^{E_2} + S_{12}^{S_2} + S_{12}^{T_2} \tag{A4}$$

where, for notational convenience, we have suppressed the time argument.

Equation (A4) is a simple differential equation, the solution of which is

$$S_{12}^{E_1}(t) = \frac{\tau_1}{\tau_1 + b_1}(a_H - a_H')L\,e^{-b_1 t}. \tag{A5}$$

In solving (A1), we make use of the initial condition that $S_{12}^{E_2}(0) = [\tau_1/(\tau_1 + b_1)](a_H - a_H')L$.

To solve (A2)–(A4), first substitute (A5) into (A4) and then solve for $S_{12}^{T_2}$ in terms of $S_{12}^{E_2}$ and $S_{12}^{S_2}$. Substitute the result into (A3). Then (A2) and (A3) form a system of two differential equations which can be written in matrix form:

$$\begin{bmatrix} \dot{S}_{12}^{E_2} \\ \dot{S}_{12}^{S_2} \end{bmatrix} = \begin{bmatrix} -b_2 & e_2 \\ b_2\phi_2 - \tau_2 & -(e_2 + \tau_2) \end{bmatrix} \begin{bmatrix} S_{12}^{E_2} \\ S_{12}^{S_2} \end{bmatrix} + \begin{bmatrix} 0 \\ h(t) \end{bmatrix} \tag{A6}$$

where $h(t) = \tau_2(a_H - a_H')L\{1 - [\tau_1/(\tau_1 + b_1)]\,e^{-b_1 t}\}$. The method for solving a system of this form is provided by Boyce and DiPrima (1977, pp. 329–31). Using the initial conditions that $S_{12}^{E_2}(0) = S_{12}^{S_2}(0) = 0$, the solutions are

$$S_{12}^{E_2}(t) = \frac{e_2\tau_2(a_H - a_H')L}{\lambda_1\lambda_2} + \frac{e_2\tau_1\tau_2(a_H - a_H')L}{(\tau_1 + b_1)(\lambda_2 - \lambda_1)}\left[\frac{e^{\lambda_1 t}}{\lambda_1 + b_1} - \frac{e^{\lambda_2 t}}{\lambda_2 + b_1}\right]$$

$$- \frac{e_2\tau_2(a_H - a_H')L}{\lambda_2 - \lambda_1}\left[\frac{e^{\lambda_1 t}}{\lambda_1} - \frac{e^{\lambda_2 t}}{\lambda_2}\right]$$

$$- \frac{e_2\tau_1\tau_2(a_H - a_H')L}{(\tau_1 + b_1)(\lambda_1 + b_1)(\lambda_2 + b_1)}\,e^{-b_1 t} \tag{A7}$$

$$S_{12}^{S_2}(t) = \frac{\tau_2 b_2(a_H - a_H')L}{\lambda_2\lambda_1} + \frac{\tau_1\tau_2(a_H - a_H')L}{(\tau_1 + b_1)(\lambda_2 - \lambda_1)}$$

$$\times \left[\frac{b_2 + \lambda_1}{b_1 + \lambda_1}e^{\lambda_1 t} - \frac{b_2 + \lambda_2}{b_1 + \lambda_2}e^{\lambda_2 t}\right]$$

$$- \frac{\tau_2(a_H - a_H')L}{(\lambda_2 - \lambda_1)}\left[\frac{b_2 + \lambda_1}{\lambda_1}e^{\lambda_1 t} - \frac{b_2 + \lambda_2}{\lambda_2}e^{\lambda_2 t}\right]$$

$$- \frac{\tau_1\tau_2(b_2 - b_1)(a_H - a_H')L}{(\tau_1 + b_1)(\lambda_1 + b_1)(\lambda_2 + b_1)}\,e^{-b_1 t} \tag{A8}$$

where λ_1 and λ_2 are the eigenvalues of the coefficient matrix in (A6) and are equal to:

$$\lambda_1 = \frac{-(b_2 + e_2 + \tau_2) - \sqrt{(b_2 + e_2 + \tau_2)^2 - 4b_2 e_2(1 - \phi_2)}}{2} \tag{A9a}$$

$$\lambda_2 = \frac{-(b_2 + e_2 + \tau_2) + \sqrt{(b_2 + e_2 + \tau_2)^2 - 4b_2 e_2(1 - \phi_2)}}{2}. \tag{A9b}$$

Appendix B

Our goal is to show that the equilibrium in our model is efficient. To do so, we must calculate the dynamic marginal product of labour in each sector and show that these values are equal in the market equilibrium.

The dynamic marginal product of labour in a sector measures the increase in net output that occurs if the steady state is disturbed by adding an additional worker to that sector taking into account the adjustment path to the new steady state. To calculate the dynamic marginal products we follow the method developed in Diamond (1980).

We begin by defining $\chi_i(\theta)$ as the present discounted value of output net of training costs produced in sector i when a (small) measure θ of new workers is added to that sector. These workers are assumed to have ability level a_H. Equilibrium is efficient if $\chi_1'(\theta) = \chi_2'(\theta)$.

Start with sector 1. We have[27]

$$\chi_1(\theta) \equiv \int_0^\infty e^{-rt}\{a_H q_1 \theta I(t) - \theta c_1[1 - I(t)]\}\, dt \tag{B1}$$

where $\dot{\theta}_1^E = \tau_1\theta - (\tau_1 + b_1)\theta_1^E$ and $I(t)$ is an indicator function that takes on the value of 1 when the worker is employed and equals zero at all other times. To find $\chi_1'(\theta)$ we start by using the fundamental equation of dynamic programming which states that

$$r\chi_1(\theta) = a_H q_1 \theta I(t) - \theta c_1[1 - I(t)] + \frac{\partial \chi_1}{\partial \theta_1^E}\,\dot{\theta}_1^E. \tag{B2}$$

Substituting for $\dot{\theta}_1^E$ from above allows us to write this as

$$r\chi_1(\theta) = a_H q_1 \theta I(t) - \theta c_1[1 - I(t)] + \frac{\partial \chi_1}{\partial \theta_1^E}\{\tau_1\theta - (\tau_1 + b_1)\theta_1^E\}. \tag{B3}$$

Differentiating with respect to θ yields

$$r\chi_1'(\theta) = a_H q_1 I(t) - c_1\{1 - I(t)\} + \tau_1 \frac{\partial \chi_1}{\partial \theta_1^E} \tag{B4}$$

but, at the initial moment, none of the new workers are employed. That is, $I(0) = 0$, so that we have

$$r\chi_1'(\theta) = -c_1 + \tau_1 \frac{\partial \chi_1}{\partial \theta_1^E}. \tag{B5}$$

To complete our derivation, we must now calculate $\partial \chi_1/\partial \theta_1^E$. To do so, we solve (B3) for $\partial \chi_1/\partial \theta_1^E$. We obtain

$$\frac{\partial \chi_1}{\partial \theta_1^E} = \frac{r\chi_1 - a_H q_1 \theta I(t) + \theta c_1[1 - I(t)]}{\tau_1\theta - (\tau_1 + b_1)\theta_1^E}. \tag{B6}$$

In the initial steady state, the right-hand side of this equation equals 0/0. Applying L'Hopital's Rule, we have (note that we are differentiating with respect to θ_1^E, which is the same as $\theta I(t)$)

$$\frac{\partial \chi_1}{\partial \theta_1^E} = \frac{r \frac{\partial \chi_1}{\partial \theta_1^E} - a_H q_1 - c_1}{-(\tau_1 + b_1)} \tag{B7}$$

or

$$\frac{\partial \chi_1}{\partial \theta_1^E} = \frac{a_H q_1 + c_1}{r + \tau_1 + b_1}. \tag{B8}$$

We can now substitute this value into (A2) to obtain the dynamic marginal product of labour in sector 1:

$$r\chi_1'(\theta) = \frac{\tau_1 a_H q_1 - (r + b_1)c_1}{r + \tau_1 + b_1} \tag{B9}$$

Note that this dynamic marginal product equals $rV_1^E(a_H)$.

Turn next to sector 2. We have

$$\chi_2(\theta) \equiv \int_0^\infty e^{-rt} \{ a_H p_2 q_2 \theta I(t) - c_2 p_2 \theta [1 - I(t) - H(t)] \} \, dt \tag{B10}$$

where, $\dot{\theta}_2^E = e\theta_2^S - b_2 \theta_2^E$, $\dot{\theta}_2^S = \tau_2 \theta + (b_2 \phi - \tau_2)\theta_2^E - (\tau_2 + e)\theta_2^S$, $I(t)$ is an indicator function that equals 1 when the worker is employed and zero otherwise and $H(t)$ is an indicator function which equals 1 when the worker is searching and zero otherwise.

As above, we start by applying the fundamental equation of dynamic programming which implies that

$$r\chi_2(\theta) = a_H p_2 q_2 \theta I(t) - c_2 p_2 \theta [1 - I(t) - H(t)] + \frac{\partial \chi_2}{\partial \theta_2^E} \dot{\theta}_2^E + \frac{\partial \chi_2}{\partial \theta_2^S} \dot{\theta}_2^S. \tag{B11}$$

If we now use the equations of motion to substitute for $\dot{\theta}_2^E$ and $\dot{\theta}_2^S$ and then differentiate with respect θ to we obtain

$$r\chi_2'(\theta) = a_H p_2 q_2 I(t) - c_2 p_2 [1 - I(t) - H(t)] + \frac{\partial \chi_2}{\partial \theta_2^S} \tau_2. \tag{B12}$$

But, in the initial steady state (at $t = 0$), we know that $I(0) = H(0) = 0$; so that

$$r\chi_2'(\theta) = -c_2 p_2 + \tau_2 \frac{\partial \chi_2}{\partial \theta_2^S}. \tag{B13}$$

The final step requires us to solve for $\partial \chi_2 / \partial \theta_2^S$ and then substitute that value into (B13). Again following Diamond (1980), we differentiate the fundamental equation of dynamic programming with respect to θ_2^E and θ_2^S. We obtain

$$\begin{bmatrix} \dfrac{\partial \chi_2}{\partial \theta_2^E} \\[2ex] \dfrac{\partial \chi_2}{\partial \theta_2^S} \end{bmatrix} = [(a_H p_2 q_2 + c_2 p_2) \quad c_2 p_2] \begin{bmatrix} r + b_2 & -(b_2 \phi - \tau_2) \\ -e_2 & (r + \tau_2 + e_2) \end{bmatrix}^{-1}. \tag{B14}$$

Solving this system of equations for $\partial \chi_2 / \partial \theta_2^S$ yields

$$\frac{\partial \chi_2}{\partial \theta_2^S} = \frac{p_2\{a_H q_2 e_2 + c_2(e_2 + r + b_2)\}}{(r + b_2)(r + \tau_2 + e_2) + e_2 \tau_2 - e \phi b_2}. \tag{B15}$$

Substituting (B15) into (B13) and collecting terms results in

$$r \chi_2'(\theta) = \frac{p_2\{a_H q_2 e_2 - [(r + b_2)(r + e_2) - e_2 \phi b_2]c_2\}}{(r + b_2)(r + \tau_2 + e_2) + e_2 \tau_2 - e_2 \phi b_2}. \tag{B16}$$

Note that (B16) is also equal to $r V_2^T(a_H)$. Thus, since the dynamic marginal products both equal the expected lifetime income for a worker training in that sector, and, since workers are allocated so that the expected lifetime income from training is the same in both sectors, the dynamic marginal products are equal in equilibrium. As a result, equilibrium is efficient.

Notes

1 For example, see Lapan (1976), Magee (1972), Baldwin, Mutti and Richardson (1980), and Neary (1982). Winters and Takacs (1991) examine the likely impact on employment in the British footwear industry should trade restrictions be lifted. Their study, based upon the natural rate of voluntary separations observed in that industry, is similar in spirit to ours. However, they miss some important general equilibrium effects by focusing on a single industry.

2 We introduce worker heterogeneity in the next section where we assume that workers differ in their basic ability and therefore productivity differs across the population.

3 Generalisation to any number of sectors is a fairly trivial task. None of our qualitative results depend on the number of sectors.

4 In this chapter, we treat the labour market turnover rates as exogenous. In reality, these rates can be affected by a variety of factors. Workers can affect their re-employment probability by varying search intensity, the rate at which jobs dissolve may be affected by trade policy, and the length of the training period may depend on worker effort and/or the amount of resources devoted to training by firms. Including these features in order to make the model more realistic would cause us to sacrifice tractability. In particular, adding these features would make it impossible to obtain a closed-form solution for the adjustment path. Future research will be required in order to determine how sensitive our results are to these assumptions.

5 In calculating the economy's unemployment rate, we exclude from the definition of the labour force those who are training. When in the text we refer to someone who is not in the labour force, we mean to refer to someone who is neither training, nor searching, nor employed.

6 Assuming risk-neutrality, there is no difference between the decisions made by income-maximising workers and those made by utility-maximising workers in our model. To lighten the already cumbersome notation, we therefore formulate the decision-making process based on income maximisation. However, we will have to deflate income by an appropriate price index when we consider welfare effects resulting from a change in prices.

7 We could also allow training costs to vary by ability without changing any of the substantive results that follow.

8   Shapiro and Stiglitz (1984) provide the generic technique for deriving the asset-value equations in their footnote 8. Consider a small interval of time $[0, t]$. During this period of time, the expected lifetime utility of a worker employed in sector i is

$$V_i^E(a_j) = w_i t + e^{-rt}[b_i t \phi_i V_i^S(a_j) + b_i t(1 - \phi_i)V_i^T(a_j) + (1 - b_i t)V_i^E(a_j)].$$

Substitute $1 - rt$ for e^{-rt}, solve for $V_i^E(a_j)$ as a function of $V_i^S(a_j)$ and $V_i^T(a_j)$ and take the limit of the resulting expression as $t \to 0$ to obtain (10). All remaining asset-value equations are derived in similar fashion.

9   The share of time spent searching (during which no income is earned) is $\tau_i b_i / D_i$.

10   For example, when $\phi_i = 1$, no worker ever returns to training once training is completed. All elements of (13) and (14) associated with training costs vanish.

11   These conditions are necessary, but not sufficient. It might be possible, for example, that all workers would choose to train in sector 1 if training costs are extremely high in sector 2.

12   As we will see below, the same logic implies that changes in trade policy that result only in changing prices cannot squeeze workers out of the labour market.

13   See Davidson, Martin and Matusz (1999) where we make the same point in the context of a very different model.

14   If we defined $V_i^T(a_j)$ as the value of discounted real income for a worker who is currently training, then the $V_i^T(a_j)$ curve would shift up, because the wage for workers in sector 2 would increase in terms of x_1 while remaining constant in terms of x_2. It does not matter if we use real or nominal income when we discuss resource allocation. However, discussion of welfare effects should obviously be based on changes in real income if prices change.

15   However, the labour force (which excludes those training) will take a longer time to return to its steady-state level. Therefore, it is still possible for the unemployment rate to first rise above its steady-state level.

16   It is conceivable that some parameter configurations could result in a lower unemployment rate. This follows since the number of trainers (who would not be counted as part of the labour force) is a fraction of the number of workers tied to sector 1 plus a (different) fraction of the number of workers tied to sector 2. Clearly, the number of trainers could be lower in the new steady state, meaning that the labour force would be higher. We don't think that this case is likely, however, since we view sector 2 as entailing more training than sector 1.

17   We used Mathcad 2000 Professional to calculate all of the numeric results. Our calculation routine is available on request.

18   In this exercise, we normalise the number of potential workers to equal 100. Therefore a number such as 4.0 can be interpreted to mean that 4.0 per cent of all potential workers (including those not in the labour force) are looking for jobs.

19   For both sets of workers, the value of training costs moves in the same direction as the value of wages, but it is easy to demonstrate that the wage effect dominates the welfare consideration.

20   This value is surprisingly similar to Krugman's view that the efficiency gain due to removal of the main trade barriers in the US would be roughly 0.25 per cent of income. See Krugman (1990, p. 104).

21   Our results contrasts sharply with the findings of Magee (1972) and Baldwin, Mutti and Richardson (1980) where discounted adjustment due to liberalisation are estimated to be well under 5 per cent of the discounted efficiency gains. Of course, both of these earlier studies treated the depth and length of the adjustment process in a rather ad hoc manner.

22 See, for example, Lawrence and Slaughter (1993). There is significant debate regarding the proper way to examine the data, with some economists arguing that the only way for globalisation to affect relative incomes is via price changes, and others arguing for the relevance of the quantity of labour embodied in the trade bundle. It is way beyond the scope of our paper to examine this debate.

23 See Bhagwati and Dehejia (1994) or Bhagwati (1998) for a more detailed exposition.

24 More generally, increased turnover might also imply a higher job acquisition rate in sector 2.

25 The analysis in this section focuses on the impact of increased turnover on the expected lifetime income of those in training. However, it is clear from (10)–(12) that incomes for employed workers and searchers are positively related to the income of trainers.

26 There can be no doubt that our model is overly simplistic. It includes only a single factor of production and all of the labour market turnover rates are exogenous. In the future, we hope to find ways to relax these assumptions without sacrificing the tractability of the model.

27 The equation of motion for $\dot{\theta}_1^E$ is obtained in the following manner. Since search is not required to find employment in sector 1, we have $\dot{\theta}_1^E = \tau_1 \theta_1^T - b_1 \theta_1^E$. Now, we know that the total measure of trainers (out of the θ) in sector 1 is equal to the difference between θ and the measure of employed workers in that sector. Substituting for θ_1^T yields the desired result.

References

Baldwin, R.E., J.H. Mutti and J.D. Richardson (1980) 'Welfare Effects on the United States of a Significant Multilateral Tariff Reduction', *Journal of International Economics*, vol. 10(3), pp. 405–23.

Bhagwati, J. (1998) 'Trade and Wages: A Malign Relationship?' in S. Collins (ed.), *Imports, Exports, and the American Worker* (Washington DC: Brookings Institution Press).

Bhagwati, J. and V. Dehejia (1994) 'Freer Trade and Wages of the Unskilled – Is Marx Striking Again?' in J. Bhagwati and M. Kosters (eds), *Trade and Wages: Leveling Wages Down?* (Washington DC: AEI Press).

Boyce, W. and R. DiPrima (1977) *Elementary Differential Equations and Boundary Value Problems* (New York: John Wiley & Sons).

Davidson, C., L. Martin and S. Matusz (1999) 'Trade and Search-Generated Unemployment', *Journal of International Economics*, vol. 48(2), pp. 271–99.

Davis, S., J. Haltiwanger and S. Schuh (1996) *Job Creation and Destruction* (Cambridge MA: MIT Press).

Diamond, P. (1980) 'An Alternative to Steady State Comparisons', *Economics Letters*, vol. 1(1), pp. 7–9.

Krugman, P. (1990) *The Age of Diminished Expectations – U.S. Economic Policy in the 1990s* (Cambridge MA: MIT Press).

Lapan, H. (1976) 'International Trade, Factor Market Distortions, and the Optimal Dynamic Subsidy', *American Economic Review*, vol. 66(3), pp. 335–46.

Lawrence, R. and M. Slaughter (1993) 'International Trade and American Wages in the 1980s: Giant Sucking Sound or Small Hiccup?', *Brookings Papers on Economic Activity: Microeconomics 2*, pp. 161–226.

Magee, S.P. (1972) 'The Welfare Effects of Restrictions on U.S. Trade', *Brookings Papers on Economic Activity 3*, pp. 645–701.

Neary, J.P. (1982) 'Intersectoral Capital Mobility, Wage Stickiness, and the Case for Adjustment Assistance', in J. Bhagwati (ed.) *Import Competition and Response* (Chicago: University of Chicago Press), pp. 39–67.

Shapiro, C. and J. Stiglitz (1984) 'Equilibrium Unemployment as a Worker Discipline Device', *American Economic Review*, vol. 74(3), pp. 433–44.

Winters, L.A. and W.E. Takacs (1991) 'Labour Adjustment Costs and British Footwear Protection', *Oxford Economic Papers*, vol. 43(3), pp. 479–501.

6

Sectoral Transformation and Labour Market Flows*

David Greenaway, Richard Upward and Peter Wright
Leverhulme Centre for Research on Globalisation and Economic Policy, University of Nottingham, UK

1 Introduction

In this chapter we examine the dynamics of adjustment in the labour market, and in particular the movement of workers between industries. It is often assumed that the speed with which the labour market must adjust has increased due to globalisation and/or technological change. If this is the case, then these forces may be responsible for greater instability in the workplace, the displacement of growing numbers of (especially unskilled) workers from declining sectors, longer periods of unemployment and wage losses.

We address two main issues. First, we ask whether there is any evidence that the speed of labour reallocation has actually increased. We examine the flows of workers between industries in the UK over the post-war period, and show how these flows can be related to the dramatic changes in the sectoral composition of the UK economy. Second, we examine the impact of worker reallocation on individuals' labour market outcomes. We draw on a range of empirical evidence to analyse whether workers who move between industries face longer periods of unemployment and greater wage losses than workers who remain in the same industry.

From a theoretical viewpoint, measuring the relative costs of intra- and inter-industry adjustment is important because it provides a direct test of the *smooth adjustment hypothesis*. This states that adjustment costs will be lower (and hence adjustment smoother) when the economy is faced with increases in intra-industry trade as opposed to inter-industry trade.[1] From a policy perspective, measuring adjustment costs is important because it relates directly to the impact of increased globalisation or technological change on different groups of workers. The most widely discussed development in many OECD labour markets is the growing wage inequality between skilled and unskilled

* We are grateful for the comments of two anonymous referees and the participants at the IEA conference in Nottingham, July 2000. Any remaining errors are our own. Financial assistance from the Leverhulme Trust under Programme Grant F114/BF and from the ESRC under award number L138251007 are gratefully acknowledged.

workers, and it is important to know whether the mobility of different groups of labour is a factor contributing to increased inequality.

Section 2 examines the pattern of sectoral transformation in the United Kingdom over the last 50 years, and the flows of workers that have resulted. We draw a distinction between the *gross* flows of workers, which are directly related to measures of tenure and turnover, with the *net* flows of workers, which determine the extent of sectoral transformation. We then compare measures of sectoral mobility with more frequently used measures of labour adjustment, such as job tenure and regional mobility. Section 3 provides a simple framework for modelling the observed movements of labour between sectors which is consistent with the observed flows of workers. In Section 4 we examine the consequences of sectoral transformation for individual labour market outcomes, in terms of wages and unemployment. In Section 5 we conclude by examining the policy implications of our findings on the extent and costs of sectoral adjustment.

2   Sectoral transformation and labour market flows

What do we mean by sectoral transformation, and what does this imply for worker flows? In the simplest case we might associate sectoral transformation with the long-run decline of one aggregate sector and the expansion of another. This occurs if there are changes in profitable opportunities between sectors, which manifest themselves in differential rates of job creation and destruction. This causes workers to leave the declining sector for the expanding sector. However, they may not be able to move between sectors costlessly. They may experience a period of unemployment, they may have to spend a period retraining, or they may leave the labour market altogether. Workers may also face changes in the wage they receive after they have moved to a new sector.

Two conclusions emerge from this simple framework. First, for a given rate of job creation and destruction in each sector, an increase in the difficulty of moving sector increases the unemployment attributable to sectoral transformation. Second, for a given cost of moving sector, an increase in the rate of sectoral transformation increases the inflow and hence the level of unemployment.

Sectoral transformation in the UK, 1950–2000

How does this stylised picture of sectoral transformation compare to the actual experience of the UK economy? The pattern of employment in the UK has changed markedly since the Second World War. The top half of Table 6.1 sets out labour reallocation across seven broad sectors between 1950 and 2000. The proportion employed in distribution and services has more than doubled, and now accounts for 70 per cent of the workforce. Manufacturing, by contrast, now provides only 16 per cent of employment compared to nearly 40 per cent in 1950. The bottom half of the table shows how manufacturing employment declined faster in the 1970s and 1980s than in other decades, and that the

Table 6.1 Changing employment shares in the UK, 1950–2000

(a) % of employees in employment	1950	1960	1970	1980	1990[a]	2000[ab]
Agriculture, forestry and fishing	5.60	4.10	1.74	1.57	1.37	1.27
Mining, supply of elec., gas and water	5.16	4.73	3.68	3.19	1.74	0.86
Manufacturing	38.02	37.66	38.69	30.28	20.52	16.52
Transport, storage and communication	8.00	6.97	6.94	6.52	6.07	6.09
Construction	6.66	6.51	5.88	5.37	5.36	4.73
Wholesale and retail distribution	12.74	13.88	12.08	14.61	15.79	17.04
Services	23.82	26.16	30.98	38.47	49.15	53.50
(b) Change in % over decade		1950s	1960s	1970s	1980s	1990s
Agriculture, forestry and fishing		−1.50	−2.35	−0.18	−0.20	−0.10
Mining, supply of elec., gas and water		−0.44	−1.04	−0.50	−1.44	−0.88
Manufacturing		−0.36	1.03	−8.41	−9.76	−4.00
Transport, storage and communication		−1.03	−0.03	−0.42	−0.45	0.02
Construction		−0.15	−0.62	−0.51	−0.01	−0.64
Wholesale and retail distribution		1.14	−1.80	2.53	1.18	1.25
Services		2.34	4.82	7.48	10.68	4.35

Notes:
[a] Figures for 1990 and 2000 refer to UK; earlier years refer to GB.
[b] December 1999.
Sources: Ministry of Labour Gazette, Department of Employment Gazette, Employment Gazette and *Labour Market Trends* (various years).

speed of decline has halved in the last decade. Similarly, the increase in the size of the service sector accelerated in every decade up to the 1990s.

The rate of restructuring through time can be summarised via a *turbulence index* which provides a measure of the rate of change of industry employment shares:

$$\frac{1}{2} \sum_i \left| \Delta \left(\frac{N_i}{N} \right) \right| \tag{1}$$

where N_i is employment in industry i. There are two important caveats in the calculation of such indices. First, since they measure absolute changes in employment shares, an expansion of a sector followed by an immediate contraction of the same size will be picked up as two periods of turbulence. Thus the index may pick up relative expansion and contraction of sectors over the business cycle. This can be ameliorated by extending the time period over which the difference is taken. Second, the level of industrial aggregation matters. At higher levels of aggregation movements of employment within a sector will not affect the index. At lower levels these will be picked up as movements between more disaggregated sectors.

Figure 6.1 plots three different turbulence indices for the UK, all of which indicate that the 1970s and 1980s saw greater sectoral employment realloca-tion than any decade since the war. In the 1990s, the rate of restructuring

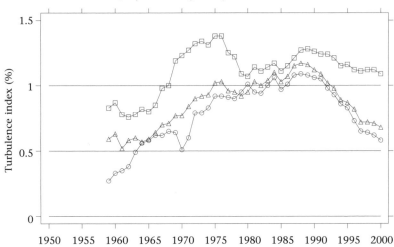

Figure 6.1   Turbulence indices for the United Kingdom

decelerated rapidly and returned to levels similar to those that prevailed in the 1960s.[2] We compare a turbulence index based on seven sectors with one based on 24, and we compare an annual (moving average) index with one based on ten-year changes.

The divergence of the seven- and 24-sector indices is a result of the fact that in the 1950s and 1960s employment shares changed *within* manufacturing sectors, which the 24-sector index is picking up but the seven-sector index misses. In the 1970s and 1980s on the other hand, embracing the period of most acute de-industrialisation, most adjustment is directly from manufacturing to services, which both indices pick up.

A comparison of a decade-based index with a ten-year moving average of the annual index also indicates the relative importance of short- and long-run factors. From 1950 to 1980 these indices diverge periodically since temporary shocks are an important cause of sectoral employment change. From 1980 to 2000 the indices move more closely together since, over this period, employment is consistently moving from manufacturing to services and reverse flows are rare.

Gross and net worker flows

Our stylised description of sectoral transformation suggested that workers flow from the declining to the expanding sector, albeit with some possible intervening period of unemployment or non-participation. This suggests that

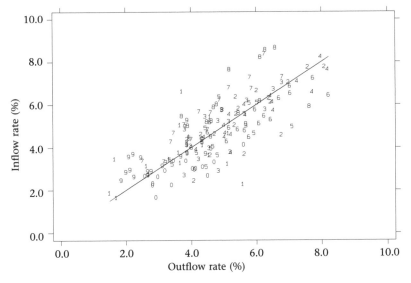

Figure 6.2   Inflow and outflow rates by 1-digit SIC 1975–95

declining sectors have high outflow rates, and expanding sectors high inflow rates. Is this what we observe?

Figure 6.2 shows job-to-job inflow and outflow rates between ten sectors of economic activity in the UK for each year from 1975 to 1995.[3] The 45-degree line equates inflow and outflow rates. Two features stand out. First, inflows and outflows are of similar size. Second, they are *positively* correlated.[4] Although a considerable number who leave declining sectors enter expanding sectors each year, an almost equal number of people move in the opposite direction. The fact that inflows and outflows are of a similar size suggests that gross flows, the total movement of labour between sectors, are far greater than net flows, the movement of labour which contributes to changing employment shares.

To calculate gross and net flows we construct a matrix **G** which contains the number of individuals in each sector in each year t, conditional on their sector at $t - 1$. Total gross flows are the sum of the off-diagonal elements of **G**, and proportionate gross flows are simply the probability of switching industry between t and $t + 1$. Total net flows are the sum of the elements of $|\mathbf{G} - \mathbf{G}'|$, divided by two to avoid double counting.[5] Gross and net flows will increase as the number of sectors increases, and the extent to which this happens indicates the extent to which flows occur within more finely disaggregated sectors. We therefore compute gross flows between two aggregate sectors, ten 1-digit sectors, and between firms.[6] Net flows are calculated between two aggregate sectors and ten 1-digit sectors only.[7] We also distinguish between gross and net flows which occur directly between jobs, and those which occur between

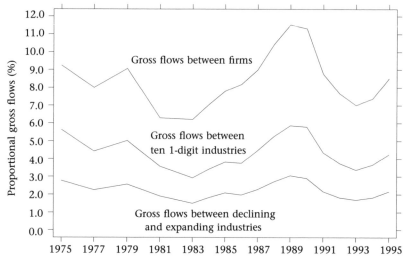

Figure 6.3   Gross flows between sectors, 1975–95

employment and non-employment. This gives a measure of the extent to which adjustment occurs via an intervening state.

Figure 6.3 shows that gross flows are procyclical, which suggests sector-to-sector flows are dominated by voluntary moves, with individuals moving when times are good rather than bad.[8] Whilst between 7 per cent and 11 per cent of individuals change firms each year, only 2–3 per cent switch from the declining to the expanding sector or *vice versa*. There is therefore considerable intra-sectoral movement of labour, which is consistent with the observation on US firm-level data that much job creation and destruction occurs within narrowly defined industries (Davis and Haltiwanger (1992)).

Comparing Figures 6.3 and 6.4, gross flows are approximately ten times greater than net flows. Some 2–3 per cent of the workforce switches from the declining to the expanding sector in any twelve-month period, while the net flow between the same two sectors is between 0.1 per cent and 0.5 per cent. However, the changes in sectoral employment during this period, shown in Table 6.1, would require net flows of greater than 1 per cent per year. It is clear, therefore, that direct job-to-job sectoral flows cannot account for this adjustment. Rather, it is the differential movement of workers into and out of non-employment which has facilitated the change in sectoral employment.

Figure 6.5 plots gross and net flows between employment and non-employment.[9] Note that net flows are much larger than net flows between sectors, and nearly half as big as gross flows. This is because flows from employment to non-employment are counter-cyclical, while flows in the reverse direction to employment are procyclical. There is therefore less of a tendency for them to cancel each other out.

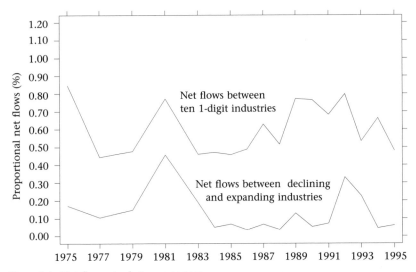

Figure 6.4   Net flow rates between sectors

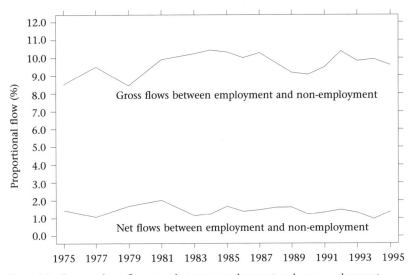

Figure 6.5   Gross and net flow rates between employment and non-employment

What do these patterns of gross and net flows imply for measures of sectoral transformation? An increase in sectoral transformation implies an increase in the differential rates of job creation and destruction in the expanding and declining sectors. This causes an increase in net worker flows. However, *gross* worker flows might actually decrease in response to increased rates of job creation and destruction. A given rate of job creation and destruction may be accommodated by widely varying gross flow rates, because the balanced flows may increase or decrease with no impact on adjustment. Because workers may move between pre-existing jobs and in equal and opposite directions there is no necessary relationship between gross flows and sectoral transformation.

Gross flow rates are informative, however, as a measure of the 'flexibility' of the labour market in terms of the ease with which employers can adjust labour demand and employees can adjust labour supply. Blanchflower and Freeman (1994), for example, use estimates of transition rates between employment, un-employment and out of the labour force as a measure of the increased flexibility of the UK labour market over the 1980s. Despite the widespread belief that labour adjustment costs have fallen in the UK over this period, there is very little evidence of this in our transition rates. The gross flows of workers between jobs appear procyclical with little trend. This is supported by the consensus view that job turnover has not declined significantly over the last 20 years.

Other measures of adjustment

Job tenure

An alternative way to look at changing patterns of employment is via job stability. If job reallocation has increased in response to the greater require-ments of restructuring, we might expect to find that average job tenure has declined. However, as we have seen, increasing turbulence has ambiguous impacts on gross flows and therefore on tenure. Furthermore, increased job instability may be caused by increased reallocation within rather than between sectors. Finally, increased movement may be voluntary. The fact that gross flow rates (Figure 6.3) are procyclical suggests that job-to-job sectoral moves are dominated by quits rather than layoffs.

Even if decreasing tenure were indicative of greater reallocation of workers across sectors, recent evidence for the UK from Gregg and Wadsworth (1995) and Burgess and Rees (1996) suggests that, contrary to popular perception, there is little evidence that the *average* length of jobs declined dramatically over the 1970s and 1980s. It does appear, however, that jobs for older workers and less-skilled men have become less stable, which suggests that it is peripheral workers who have found it increasingly difficult to move and it is not a general phenomenon. We return to this issue in Section 4.

Regional adjustment

In the UK, much of the focus has been on regional rather than sectoral mobil-ity,[10] and the impact of the housing market on regional mobility has attracted particular attention. Hughes and McCormick (1981) point to rigidities in the public rented sector, and Oswald (1996) to the expansion of home ownership at the expense of the private rented sector as the key impediment to mobility. However, the links between regional and sectoral mobility have not been made explicit. If housing market rigidities do cause workers to be less mobile between regions, does this have an effect on mobility between sectors? If sectors are geographically evenly spread, one would expect the relationship to be rather unimportant, since individuals will be able to switch sectors without moving region. If, as seems more plausible, sectors are unevenly distributed regionally, the relationship will be stronger.

Table 6.2 reports estimates of the average probability of moving between and within sectors and regions, split by employment status at $t-1$. These probabilities are another way of expressing gross flow rates between sectors and regions. The second column in panel (a) shows that the probability of moving to the expanding from the declining sector is just 0.02 for individuals who remain at the same address between $t-1$ and t. This probability increases to 0.05 for those who move addresses within region, while individuals who move region are by far the most likely to switch from the declining to the expanding sector, with a probability of 0.15. A similar pattern can be seen in the first column of panel (b): the probability of moving sectors between two consecutive years is highest for those who have also moved address or region. Panel (c) shows there is also a much higher probability of *leaving* non-employment for those who move region. The probability of remaining in non-employment is only 0.59 for those who move region, compared to 0.77 for those who move address within region and 0.83 for those who remain at the same address.

Thus, Table 6.2 shows that individuals who are geographically mobile are more mobile between jobs and more mobile between non-employment and

Table 6.2 Average gross flow rates by geographical mobility, 1975–95

	New firm, Declining sector	New firm, Expanding sector	Not Employed
(a) Employed at $t-1$ in declining sector			
Same address	0.05	0.02	0.06
Same region (new address)	0.09	0.05	0.10
New region	0.23	0.15	0.18
Total	0.06	0.03	0.06
(b) Employed at $t-1$ in expanding sector			
Same address	0.02	0.06	0.06
Same region (new address)	0.04	0.13	0.11
New region	0.06	0.32	0.20
Total	0.02	0.07	0.06
(c) Not employed at $t-1$			
Same address	0.06	0.11	0.83
Same region (new address)	0.07	0.16	0.77
New region	0.12	0.30	0.59
Total	0.06	0.01	0.82

Source: Authors' calculations from LFS.

employment. However, there are some important caveats to this. The third column shows that individuals who are geographically mobile are more likely to *enter* as well as *exit* non-employment. The probability of entering non-employment from the declining sector is 0.18 for an individual who also moves region, compared to 0.06 for an individual who remains at the same address. It should also be noted that the proportion of the sample who move region is extremely small: while about 10 per cent of the sample move address each year, the proportion who move region is less that 1 per cent. Thus, while there is clearly a relationship between flexibility in terms of regional mobility, sectoral mobility and non-employment, it is not necessarily important in terms of its overall contribution to the sectoral transformation of the economy.

Summary

The rate of sectoral transformation accelerated through the 1970s and 1980s and became increasingly dominated by movements of employment from manufacturing to services. However, flows of workers are not dominated by simple movements from declining to expanding sectors. Intra-sectoral movements are common and many individuals move from expanding to declining sectors. Thus gross flows dominate net flows. Whilst there have been large shifts in employment between sectors, only a small proportion of the adjustment is made up of individuals moving directly from one sector to another, with flows into and out of non-employment playing a large part in the adjustment process. Finally, other measures of labour market adjustment, such as job tenure and regional mobility are not necessarily useful in determining whether the adjustment of sectoral employment has become more rapid.

3   Why do individuals move sector?

We need to recognise that the majority of worker flows are not directly from the declining to the expanding sector: intra-sectoral flows are common, as are flows in the 'wrong' direction, from the expanding to the declining sector. Essentially, these facts can be explained by allowing for heterogeneous firms which create and destroy jobs within sectors, and heterogeneous workers who are searching for their best match.

Intra-sectoral worker flows are consistent with models of job creation and destruction such as those formulated by Mortensen and Pissarides (1994), in which firms within as well as between sectors experience idiosyncratic shocks. This leads to simultaneous job creation and destruction even within narrowly defined industries, as evidenced by Davis and Haltiwanger (1992). Matching models such as Jovanovic (1979) suggest that worker movements can be explained in a framework where firms and workers are searching for their most suitable job match. In models of this kind, the wage of worker i, w_{ist}, is given by:

$$w_{ist} = m \cdot p_{st} f'_{st}(x, z_{st}) = m w_{st}. \tag{2}$$

Wages depend on: the marginal product of labour in sector s at time t (measured in efficiency units, x); the output price in sector s at time $t(p_{st})$; sector-specific factors (z_{st}); and the quality of the match between the worker and employer (m). It is assumed that the quality of the match is not known prior to hiring. Following its realisation, poorly suited individuals receive a low wage and well-suited individuals a high wage. Low-paid poorly-matched workers will seek more profitable alternatives. Thus an individual may choose to move to a declining sector if their anticipated match quality is high, since this may more than outweigh a lower wage per efficiency unit. Hence we will observe gross flows both into and out of the declining sector, even in equilibrium. The total number of gross flows depends on the cost of moving sector and the spread of matching returns, because the lower the cost the greater the incentive to seek the highest possible match, and the greater the spread the greater the likelihood of an individual receiving a poor match. Net flows between sectors occur as long as there is a difference in expected net returns, perhaps because of differences in the wages paid per efficiency unit or, if unemployment is present, in the expected probability of job offers.

Within this framework, what is the effect of a shock which alters profitable opportunities differentially across sectors? Suppose there is a decline in output price (p_{st}) or an unfavourable movement in z_{st} for the declining sector. This causes a decrease in the wage the firm is willing to pay per efficiency unit, which has several consequences. First, a number of workers who were previously satisfied with their match in the declining sector will seek jobs in the expanding sector. Likewise those who would have moved in the opposite direction now find this unattractive. Second, if there is some institutional limit on how far the wage can fall, firms lay off workers. Hence there will be an increase in net flows from the declining to the expanding sectors and possibly also into non-employment.

These models imply that authors such as Lilien (1982) may be misinterpreting the impact of demand shifts on worker flows, since many observed job changes may be occurring for matching reasons, rather than because the sector in which an individual is employed has been subject to a shock. This difficulty also bedevils empirical work which focuses on individual 'displaced workers' (e.g. Kletzer (1996)), where identifying those whose job moves are enforced by sectoral shocks is similarly problematic.

4   The consequences of adjustment

We have shown that industrial turbulence was highest in the UK during the 1970s and the 1980s, and that a large proportion of the required net flows of workers occurred between employment and non-employment. In other words, changes in employment between sectors was facilitated by the movement of workers in and out of employment. Does this matter – what are the costs associated with this movement?

Sectoral adjustment and wages

Aggregate effects

If a shift in labour demand across sectors causes a shortage of labour in the expanding sectors, we would expect a shift in the structure of wages across sectors, until equilibrium is restored. However, Nickell (1996) argues that the movement of employment from production to service sectors was not accompanied by dramatic changes in the average real wage set in each sector. The most obvious shift in wages in most industrialised countries has been the increasing gap between skilled and unskilled workers, rather than between service sector and manufacturing workers.

However, the model presented in Section 3 suggests that the average wage within a sector is a poor indicator of demand in that sector. Although favourable shocks lead to expanding sectors paying higher wages per efficiency unit than declining sectors, this will encourage net movement to the expanding sector since the number of individuals who anticipate higher wages from such a move will increase. The average wage of movers will therefore be higher than the wage they received previously. However, those with good-quality matches in their existing job will be least likely to move. Therefore the average quality of match in the declining sector will increase. Jovanovic and Moffitt (1990) show that 'a contracting sector … will therefore have higher wages than an expanding sector. The scenario above more or less describes US experience over the past 15 years or so: the manufacturing sector has shrunk while services have expanded, but manufacturing wages have tended to exceed those in the service sector.'

Individual effects

A large body of evidence suggests that workers accumulate human capital which may be specific to a particular firm or job match. This is one reason why workers who are involuntarily displaced from their jobs suffer wage losses, which will tend to be higher for more senior workers.[11] It also seems likely that some element of human capital may be specific to an industry, rather than to a particular firm. Clearly this has implications for workers forced to move as a result of sectoral transformation, since workers will lose returns to their current industry. As well as being of importance to the individual, the extent to which skills are industry specific is of interest in determining the cost of aggregate adjustment, since this will determine the ease with which workers move from one industry to another. Indeed, the view that these costs may be substantial underpins the smooth adjustment hypothesis.

For the US, Neal (1995) finds that workers can transfer skills acquired in one firm to another in the same sector, while workers who change industry suffer wage losses, suggesting that industry-level skills are important. For the UK, Haynes, Upward and Wright (2002) show that crude returns to industry tenure appear to be large. However once the correlations between the measures of tenure and unobserved match-specific components of the wage are controlled for, returns to industry tenure are much smaller than returns to occupational tenure which implies that workers moving between industries suffer no greater wage losses than workers moving within industries, provided they remain in the same occupation. Further, they also find that returns to job tenure are much smaller than returns to firm tenure, which is the usual measure in the literature. This is unsurprising, since a job may be associated with a particular nominal wage, and so longer tenure may lead to a declining real wage if individuals get 'stuck' in a job. In a recent study of returns to tenure, Altonji and Williams (1997) suggest the best estimate for returns to ten years' firm tenure is about 0.11. The results of Haynes *et al.* suggest that it is not firm tenure itself which causes this increase, but occupational, and to a lesser extent, industry tenure.

Sectoral adjustment and unemployment

Aggregate effects

As we have seen, an important consequence of sectoral transformation is that a substantial proportion of those displaced are unable to move directly from contracting to expanding sectors. Hence sectoral transformation and reallocation may be an important source of aggregate unemployment. Indeed aggregate unemployment may increase if the rate of change of sectoral transformation has risen or if individuals have become less mobile between sectors for a given level of adjustment. For the US, Lilien (1982) finds that inter-sectoral shocks were positively correlated with US unemployment. However, Abraham and Katz (1986) point out that, if manufacturing employment is more cyclical than services, then the dispersion of employment growth rates may increase anyway during slumps, even without any permanent reallocation of labour.[12] Hence, a positive correlation between the variance of employment growth and unemployment is not necessarily evidence for the impact of restructuring. More recent studies (e.g. Brainard and Cutler (1993)) have sought to remedy this and have generally been supportive of the 'sectoral shift hypothesis' that inter-sectoral shocks are an important source of fluctuations in the unemployment rate.

Individual effects

Unemployment spells also represent an important cost of sectoral transformation to individuals. An examination of the movement of workers into and out of unemployment can also shed light on the proposition that labour market adjustments to intra-industry trade are less costly in terms of dislocation than adjustments to inter-industry trade. Previous literature here is rare,[13] though Murphy and Topel (1987) and Fallick (1993) provide evidence that individuals who change industry tend to have longer unemployment durations than those who return to the same industry. They suggest that the greater wage losses of movers mean that individuals are prepared to stay unemployed for longer to return to their original sector and avoid losing returns to sector-specific skills. The greater the sector-specificity of skills the greater the persistence of induced unemployment. This has been tested on Canadian data by Thomas (1996), who finds that the link between increased aggregate unemployment and increased immobility of labour is relatively weak.

Haynes, Upward and Wright (2000) compare unemployment durations of those who find work in the sector in which they were originally employed, and those who find work in a new sector. They also examine what personal circumstances affect the probability of individual movement and the duration of unemployment spells. Table 6.3 shows that individuals in the US experience a higher incidence of unemployment than in the UK. Further, a larger proportion of spells in the US end in a return to the same sector: 46.5 per cent compared to 20.4 per cent. A correspondingly higher proportion of UK spells therefore end in a movement to a new sector.[14]

One notable difference in the US data is that 13.6 per cent of spells are coded as 'temporarily laid off' and it would be expected that such individuals are more likely to return to their previous employer, and therefore remain in the same sector. This phenomenon is rare in the UK, and indeed is not recognised as an explicit category in the data.

Table 6.4 shows the probability of moving to particular states from employment. The average duration of spells in the US is shorter with, for both countries, the duration being shortest for those spells ending in a return to the same industry.[15]

It is important to note that the use of raw data is potentially misleading, however, since an individual who is unemployed for a long time, but finds a job in a new sector, could have taken even longer to find a job in the same sector. That is, one outcome 'censors' the other. To allow for this Haynes *et al.* adopt a competing risk model to allow for the possibility of multiple exit states from unemployment. They find that the longer mean duration observed in the UK is not the result of a less sharply declining unemployment hazard (which means the unemployed find it increasingly hard to find a job), so much as a lower overall hazard in the UK (which means that they are always less likely

Table 6.3   Characteristics of unemployment in the UK and the US

	UK	US
Annual incidence of unemployment (spells/year)	0.264	0.348
Exit into job, of which	0.567	0.703
(a) Exit into same industry	0.204	0.465
(b) Exit into new industry	0.363	0.238
Temporarily laid off	–	0.136

Source: Haynes, Upward and Wright (2000).

Table 6.4 Flows from unemployment and mean durations in the UK and US

Status at $t-1$		Status at $t+1$			
		Employed same industry	Employed new industry	Unemployed/ Out of labour force	Censored[b]
United Kingdom	Employed	0.20 (7.01)[a]	0.36 (8.34)	0.17 (11.30)	0.26 (28.21)
United States	Employed	0.46 (4.04)	0.24 (4.07)	0.15 (7.43)	0.15 (14.92)

Notes:
[a] Numbers in brackets indicate mean duration in months.
[b] Following status not known because of right censoring (occurs after end of sample period).
Source: Haynes, Upward and Wright (2000).

to exit unemployment). They also find that, in both countries, the hazard to staying in the same sector declines faster than the hazard to finding a job in a new sector. This suggests that, in both countries, individuals are more likely to switch sector the longer they are unemployed. A plausible explanation for this is that individuals initially attempt to find jobs that complement their general and specific skills but move sector as this prospect diminishes. This is particularly the case for workers who would be expected to have higher levels of sector-specific skills (older workers, for example), which is consistent with the hypothesis that finding a job in the original sector is less costly than finding a job in a new sector, at least for shorter unemployment durations. Indeed, even if it were the case that rewards in the new sector were higher, their results suggest that other costs of moving are sufficiently large to encourage search in the original sector.[16]

A further interesting result is that workers in both countries who enter unemployment from manufacturing are more likely to change sectors. If, as is thought to be the case, the manufacturing sector has experienced long-term decline, this provides some evidence of a relationship between sectoral transformation and factor mobility, as might be expected.

Whilst these results seem to be supportive of the smooth adjustment hypothesis the real world is more complicated than this characterisation suggests. It should be noted that in the UK, the conditional probability of staying in the same sector is generally lower than that of moving. This may be for a number of reasons: the rate of turbulence in the US may be lower, and workers that are displaced can return to the same industries; the costs of moving sector in the US may be higher, discouraging movement; institutional arrangements in the US may facilitate the return of a worker to the same sector – for example via temporary layoffs.

The effects of sectoral mobility on skilled and unskilled workers

A central theme in the literature on the relationship between globalisation and labour markets has been the effects of increased trade on the distribution of income between high- and low-skill workers. The analysis of sectoral mobility provides an alternative, but neglected, view of the effects of international trade (or technological change) on the distribution of income and employment between skilled and unskilled workers. As stressed by Haskel and Slaughter (1999), in an economy with many sectors the movement of factors of production (e.g. labour) between sectors provides an alternative mechanism for absorbing changes in the relative demand and supply of those factors. However, it is not obvious what differences in sectoral mobility one might observe between skilled and unskilled workers. The latter might find it more difficult to move to new opportunities in expanding sectors, in which case they would tend to have lower mobility rates than skilled workers. Alternatively, if unskilled workers are more likely to be *forced* to move they may have higher mobility rates, and in particular higher transition rates into unemployment.

Figures 6.6 and 6.7 break down the patterns of gross flow rates by four simple occupational categories: skilled non-manual, skilled manual, unskilled non-manual and unskilled manual.[17] It is clear that less-skilled workers have higher gross flow rates both between jobs and between jobs and non-employment. What is particularly noticeable is the large differential in flow rates between employment and non-employment. Figure 6.7 shows that in economic down-turns layoff flows of unskilled manual workers into non-employment is three

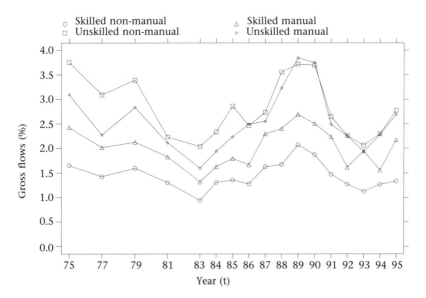

Figure 6.6   Gross job-to-job flows split by skill groups

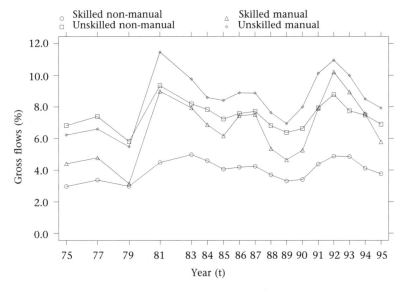

Figure 6.7 Gross job-to-nonemployment flows split by skill group

times greater than flows of skilled non-manual workers. Perhaps more surprisingly, Figure 6.6 shows that more-skilled workers are also less mobile between sectors. This may reflect the fact that these workers have higher levels of sector-specific human capital, as suggested earlier.

The increased inequality between skilled and unskilled workers, as observed in the UK and US over that last 20 years, may therefore be related to differential patterns of sectoral and employment turnover between these groups. Unskilled workers have much higher exit rates into non-employment, as well as higher job-to-job turnover. As we have seen, both are likely to cause relative declines in wages.

5   Conclusions and policy responses

Fundamental to most trade models of an economy's response to external shocks is the reallocation of factors of production between sectors. These often make extreme assumptions either that factor reallocation is frictionless (as in the Heckscher-Ohlin model) or very slow (as in the specific factors model).[18] In this chapter we have drawn together evidence on two important questions. First, has the rate of sectoral transformation in the UK increased, for whatever reason? Second, how difficult is it for labour to move between sectors, and has it become more difficult?

There is some evidence that the rate of sectoral transformation was greater in the UK in the 1970s and 1980s than in any other post-war decade. However, changes in employment shares across time disguise massive flows from declining to expanding sectors and in the reverse direction, as well as enormous flows within sectors. Although there is some evidence for the US that gross flows declined during the 1970s and 1980s, we find that gross flows in the UK are basically procyclical with no secular trend. We argue that gross flows are not in themselves indicative of the amount of sectoral reallocation occurring, because a sectoral shock can be accommodated by any amount of gross flows. Rather they are useful as an indicator of the costs of moving between sectors. In Section 4 a number of pieces of evidence were surveyed that suggest that sectoral reallocation is costly, particularly in terms of aggregate unemployment and unemployment duration.

If the process of adjustment between sectors is costly and unevenly distributed, then there may be a case for intervention. Policies can broadly be described as having one of two objectives: either to reduce the costs of adjustment, or compensate losers. The first is based on an efficiency argument. For a given amount of reallocation, there will be a smaller loss of output if the transition process involves less-frictional unemployment. 'An obvious policy to deal with this type of unemployment [i.e. mismatch] is to speed up the process of adjustment by reducing the impediments to intersectoral labour mobility' (Nickell (1991)). However, this begs the question as to why the market fails to reduce adjustment costs. For example, why do individuals fail to retrain to find jobs in the expanding sector or in more skilled occupations?

The second objective is based directly on an equity argument and indirectly on an efficiency argument. 'Government programmes are often justified on the grounds that society should compensate the losers for structural changes that benefit us in the aggregate' (Fallick (1996)). It is of course this perspective which underpins broadly-based social adjustment regimes, such as unemployment insurance. As a result, one might question the rationale for specific trade-related adjustment programmes. On this front there may be an efficiency dimension if potential losers have an incentive to lobby against adjustment. It seems plausible, for example, that trade adjustment assistance programmes in the US are implemented to compensate organised labour with the political power to lobby against increased adjustment.

In the US, programmes targeted specifically at displaced workers have offered income replacement, re-employment and retraining services for some limited period. More recently, support has also included the requirement of advance notification for plant closures or mass-layoffs. However, empirical evidence on the efficacy of these programmes is, at best, mixed. As income losses following displacement are often long-lived (e.g. Jacobson, LaLonde and Sullivan (1993)), it seems unlikely that temporary income replacement will fully compensate for this loss. The impact of retraining programmes has been subject to widespread empirical study – see Heckman, LaLonde and Smith (1999) for a recent survey. The consensus is that expenditure often outweighs benefits in terms of increased employment probabilities or earnings. Evidence is also emerging that the benefits of receiving advance notice are 'modest at best' (Kletzer (1998)).

Trade-related adjustment policies targeted specifically at displaced workers are less common in Europe than the US. This is in part a reflection of the presence of more general social safety nets in the form of unemployment assistance and insurance. Sapir (2000) suggests that the adjustment costs of globalisation have tended not to fall on the median voter in Europe, and that organised labour has therefore voiced less opposition to the adjustment and reallocation of labour. In the UK, attention has focused most on regional mobility. Compensation has often taken the form of regional assistance programmes rather than payments to displaced individuals. Some have argued that rigidities in the housing market contribute to immobility, although for different reasons. Hughes and McCormick (1981) argued that social housing prevents individuals moving, while Oswald (1996) argues that high levels of home ownership have contributed to aggregate unemployment because of the high costs of moving. An attempt to revive the private rented sector may therefore suggest itself as a remedy. Many have looked to the education system and human capital formation as an explanation for the inability of workers to adjust to changing patterns of demand. For example, Nickell and Bell (1996) suggest that 'The very high level of education and training embodied in the vast bulk of the German labour force enables them to respond in a flexible manner to demand shifts.'

Some have dismissed sectoral reallocation as a suspect in the search for the causes of high levels of unemployment and increasing skilled–unskilled wage differentials observed in some OECD countries over the last 30 years. We feel that this may be premature, for three reasons. First, industrial turbulence in the UK peaked in the 1970s and 1980s, and has subsequently returned to post-war levels. Second, net flows of labour between sectors have been largely facilitated by movements in and out of the labour force rather than directly from job to job. Third, microeconometric evidence suggests that movements between sectors are associated with longer unemployment spells than movements within sectors.

Notes

1   Intra-industry trade refers to the simultaneous import and export of products from a given industry; inter-industry trade arises when imports and exports originate in different industries. It has long been presumed that the former results in factor reallocation within rather than between industries, thereby resulting in smoother adjustment. See Greenaway and Torstensson (1997) for a review of the literature.

2   Abraham (1991) notes that since the indices are based on realised rather than desired changes in employment, they might fail to capture the full extent of reallocation shocks. Information on vacancies may be used to assess the extent of desired demand.

3   The data source used in this study is the UK Labour Force Survey (LFS) from 1975 to 1995. This is an annual (biennial from 1975 to 1983; quarterly from 1992 onwards) survey of 60,000 households comprising about 120,000 adults. In every year of the

survey, individuals are asked about their current labour force status (working, unemployed, out of the labour force) and their current industry, if employed. Individuals are also asked about their status and industry twelve months previously.

4   This relationship might occur if some sectors have high turnover whilst others have low turnover, and not because inflows and outflows are positively correlated. Although some sectors do have higher turnover than others, OLS regressions of inflows on outflows separately for each sector reveal a significant positive correlation *within* sectors.

5   Proportionate net flows are closely related to changes in employment shares measured by the turbulence index (1). Net flows are greater than changes in employment shares if adjustment comes about via movements of labour into and out of employment.

6   The two aggregate sectors are 'declining' and 'expanding', defined on the basis of the change in employment share in the data. The ten 1-digit sectors are based on UK 1980 SIC definitions. Gross flows between firms cannot be calculated from G directly because we do not know the identity of each firm at t and $t - 1$. However, we do know whether individuals are working for the same firm at t as at $t - 1$.

7   Net flows between firms cannot be calculated without identifying firms across time periods.

8   It is well known from the literature on flows of workers between labour market states that quits are procyclical (Blanchard and Diamond (1990)).

9   Non-employment is defined to include both unemployment and 'not in the labour force' (NILF). This grouping is necessary because a proportion of individuals who classify themselves as NILF do in fact move into and out of employment.

10   For example, Pissarides and Wadsworth (1989) and Jackman and Savouri (1992); Pissarides (1978) is an exception.

11   Evidence for this comes from the large (mainly US) literature on displacement. Kletzer (1998) provides a summary. Wage loss following displacement is also consistent with a number of other theories of worker compensation, such as screening or signalling theories (Weiss (1995)).

12   As discussed earlier, this methodology picks up unemployment due to cyclical impacts as well as structural impacts because of its use of an annual turbulence index.

13   For a recent survey, see Matusz and Tarr (2000).

14   Note also that the proportion of spells that are censored is higher in the UK (0.433 as opposed to 0.297). This occurs because the average duration of spells in the UK is longer.

15   It is longest for those which do not end before the end of the sample period.

16   This interpretation does not necessarily imply that potential wages in the original sector are greater than in any other sector.

17   These groups are based on aggregations from the 1980 Standard Occupational Classification.

18   In contrast, the labour economic literature has primarily been concerned with the movement of labour between labour market states rather than between sectors.

References

Abraham, K. (1991) 'Mismatch and Labour Mobility: Some Final Remarks', in F. Padoa Schioppa (ed.), *Mismatch and Labour Mobility* (Cambridge: Cambridge University Press), pp. 453–80.

Abraham, K. and L. Katz (1986) 'Cyclical Unemployment: Sectoral Shifts or Aggregate Disturbances?', *Journal of Political Economy*, vol. 94(3), pp. 507–22.

Altonji, J. and N. Williams (1997) 'Do Wages Rise with Job Seniority? A Reassessment', *NBER working paper* no. 6,010.

Blanchard, O.J. and P. Diamond (1990) 'The Cyclical Behaviour of the Gross Flows of U.S. Workers', *Brookings Papers on Economic Activity 2*, pp. 85–153.

Blanchflower, D. and R. Freeman (1994) 'Did the Thatcher Reforms Change British Labour Market Performance?' in R. Barrell (ed.), *The UK Labour Market: Comparative Aspects and Institutional Developments* (Cambridge: Cambridge University Press), pp. 51–92.

Brainard, S. and D. Cutler (1993) 'Sectoral Shifts and Cyclical Unemployment Reconsidered', *Quarterly Journal of Economics*, vol. 108(1), pp. 219–43.

Burgess, S. and H. Rees (1996) 'Job Tenure in Britain 1975–92', *Economic Journal*, vol. 106, pp. 334–44.

Davis, S. and J. Haltiwanger (1992) 'Gross Job Creation, Gross Job Destruction and Employment Reallocation', *Quarterly Journal of Economics*, vol. 107(3), pp. 819–63.

Fallick, B.C. (1993) 'The Industrial Mobility of Displaced Workers', *Journal of Labor Economics*, vol. 11(3), pp. 302–23.

Fallick, B.C. (1996) 'A Review of the Recent Empirical Literature on Displaced Workers', *Industrial and Labor Relations Review*, vol. 50(1), pp. 5–16.

Greenaway, D. and J. Torstensson (1997) 'Back to the Future: Taking Stock on Intra-Industry Trade', *Weltwirtschaftliches Archiv*, vol. 133(2), pp. 249–69.

Gregg, P. and J. Wadsworth (1995) 'A Short History of Labour Turnover, Job Tenure and Job Security, 1975–93', *Oxford Review of Economic Policy*, vol. 11(1), pp. 73–90.

Haskel, J. and M. Slaughter (1999) 'Trade, Technology and UK Wage Inequality', Centre for Research on Globalisation and Labour Markets Research Paper no. 99/2, University of Nottingham.

Haynes, M., R. Upward and P. Wright (2000) 'Smooth and Sticky Adjustment: A Comparative Study of the US and UK', *Review of International Economics*, vol. 8(3), pp. 517–32.

Haynes, M., R. Upward and P. Wright (2002) 'Estimating the Wage Costs of Inter- and Intra-Sectoral Adjustment', *Weltwirtschaftliches Archiv* (forthcoming).

Heckman, J., R. LaLonde and J. Smith (1999) 'The Economics and Econometrics of Active Labor Market Programs', in O. Ashenfelter and D. Card (eds), *Handbook of Labor Economics* (Amsterdam: North-Holland), pp. 1,865–2,097.

Hughes, G. and B. McCormick (1981) 'Do Council House Policies Reduce Migration between Regions?', *Economic Journal*, vol. 91, pp. 919–37.

Jackman, R. and S. Savouri (1992) 'Regional Migration in Britain: An Analysis of Gross Flows using NHS Central Register Data', *Economic Journal*, vol. 102, pp. 1,433–50.

Jacobson, L., R. LaLonde and D. Sullivan (1993) 'Earnings Losses of Displaced Workers', *American Economic Review*, vol. 83(4), pp. 685–709.

Jovanovic, B. (1979) 'Job Matching and the Theory of Turnover', *Journal of Political Economy*, vol. 87(5), pp. 972–90.

Jovanovic, B. and R. Moffitt (1990) 'An Estimate of a Sectoral Model of Labor Mobility', *Journal of Political Economy*, vol. 98(4), pp. 827–52.

Kletzer, L. (1996) 'The Role of Sector Specific Skills in Post-displacement Earnings', *Industrial Relations*, vol. 35(4), pp. 473–90.

Kletzer, L. (1998) 'Job Displacement', *Journal of Economic Perspectives*, vol. 12(1), pp. 115–36.

Lilien, D. (1982) 'Sectoral Shifts and Cyclical Unemployment', *Journal of Political Economy*, vol. 90(4), pp. 777–93.

Matusz, S. and D. Tarr (2000) 'Adjusting to Trade Policy Reform', mimeo, Michigan State University.

Mortensen, D. and C. Pissarides (1994) 'Job Creation and Job Destruction and the Theory of Unemployment', *Review of Economic Studies*, vol. 61(3), pp. 397–415.

Murphy, K. and R. Topel (1987) 'The Evolution of Unemployment in the United States 1968–1985', in S. Fischer (ed.), *NBER Macroeconomics Annual* (Cambridge MA: MIT Press), pp. 11–58.

Neal, D. (1995) 'Industry-Specific Human Capital: Evidence from Displaced Workers', *Journal of Labour Economics*, vol. 13(5), pp. 653–77.

Nickell, S. (1991) 'Mismatch and Labour Mobility: Some Final Remarks', in F. Padoa Schioppa, (ed.), *Mismatch and Labour Mobility* (Cambridge: Cambridge University Press), pp. 481–5.

Nickell, S. (1996) 'Sectoral Structural Change and the State of the Labour Market in Great Britain', The Labour Market Consequences of Technical and Structural Change Discussion Paper no. 2, Centre for Economic Performance.

Nickell, S. and B. Bell (1996) 'Changes in the Distribution of Wages and Unemployment in OECD Countries', *American Economic Review (Papers and Proceedings)*, vol. 86(2), pp. 303–8.

Oswald, A. (1996) 'A Conjecture on the Explanation for High Unemployment in the Industrialised Nations: Part I', mimeo, Department of Economics, University of Warwick.

Pissarides, C. (1978) 'The Role of Relative Wages and Excess Demand in the Sectoral Flow of Labour', *Review of Economic Studies*, vol. 45(3), pp. 453–67.

Pissarides, C. and J. Wadsworth (1989) 'Unemployment and the Inter-Regional Mobility of Labour', *Economic Journal*, vol. 99, pp. 739–55.

Sapir, A. (2000) 'Who is Afraid of Globalisation?', Paper presented at IEA conference on Globalisation and Labour Markets, University of Nottingham, July 2000.

Thomas, J.M. (1996) 'An Empirical Model of Sectoral Movements by Unemployed Workers', *Journal of Labour Economics*, vol. 14(1), pp. 126–53.

Weiss, A. (1995) 'Human Capital vs. Signalling Explanations of Wages', *Journal of Economic Perspectives*, vol. 9(1), pp. 133–54.

7

What Drove Relative Wages in France? Structural Decomposition Analysis in a General Equilibrium Framework, 1970–92

Sébastien Jean
Centre d'Etudes Prospectives et d'Informations Internationales (CEPII), Paris, France

Olivier Bontout
Ministry of Labour and Social Affairs, Paris, France

1 Introduction

Various causes have been invoked to explain the recent evolutions of skilled to unskilled relative wages in industrialised countries. The five most important ones are probably: changes in factor supplies, modifications of consumption patterns, institutional changes, technical change and international trade. In spite of the abundant literature on the subject, it remains difficult to know the precise contribution of each of these determinants.

Their impact is in most cases studied separately, using *ad hoc* methods (factor content of trade calculations, for example) or econometric analysis based on reduced forms. Informative as they are, these kinds of studies only tell part of the story. The residual, unexplained variations in relative wages are then often attributed to the causes not taken into account. Such an assessment does not account for the possible interactions between the various causes, and does not check the consistency of the overall explanation.

Other studies adopt a radically different approach, based on general equilibrium modelling. Recent examples include Rowthorn (1995), Cortes and Jean (1996, 1998), Cardebat and Teiletche (1997), Lawrence and Evans (1996), Bontout and Jean (1999) and Francois and Nelson (1998). These works are useful in clarifying the prevailing mechanisms. It is difficult, however, to understand how well these models explain observed trends. They generally

* The authors are grateful to Adam Blake, Jean-Lois Guérin, Nanno Mulder, Laurence Nayman, Geoff Reed, Rod Tyers and Pierre Villa for helpful comments. They also benefited from comments of participants to the CEPR/CSLA Workshop on International Trade and Wage Inequality: Theory and Measurement, Università Bocconi, Milan, October 1999, and to the IEA Conference in Nottingham, July 2000, where preliminary versions of this chapter were presented. The usual disclaimers apply.

focus on part of the possible causes, and they either rely on stylised databases or adopt a prospective standpoint.

As emphasised by Abrego and Whalley (2000, p. 473), the choice of a structural model has strong implications for the interpretation of given observations. They stress that 'it is important to explicitly explore the properties of particular structural models when contemplating decompositions, rather than only appealing to them as theoretically consistent models for reduced-form analyses'.

In this chapter, we confront a computable general equilibrium (CGE) model with observed trends in France between 1970 and 1992, using a structural decomposition analysis. We first choose the structural model assuming that the elasticities of substitution, both in the utility function and production function, are constant over time. Given these parameters (chosen from existing econometric studies), the structural equilibrium of the economy is determined by four categories of parameters and exogenous variables, which form a set of state variables: share coefficients in the production function, reflecting the productivity for each factor within each sector; factor supplies, assumed to be exogenous; share coefficients in the utility function, reflecting consumers' preferences; and, for each sector, the relative price of imports, as a proportion of domestic output price.

We assume the labour market to be perfectly competitive, so that wage rigidities and institutional changes are not accounted for. This is a problem, since structural unemployment rose steadily in France during the period considered. In 1970, structural unemployment was negligible: we therefore assume that the database corresponds to a full-employment equilibrium (frictional and cyclical unemployment are not accounted for). In 1992, in contrast, structural unemployment was significant: some 7 per cent of the labour force. From the 1992 database, and given this observed structural unemployment, we therefore compute an underlying full-employment equilibrium, assuming that relative wages adapt in order to remove this unemployment. As a consequence, the benchmark used for 1992 is not the initial database, but the equilibrium thus computed. We then analyse the causes of evolution of the French economy between these two full-employment equilibria, assuming that wages are perfectly flexible. This is most of all a way to avoid addressing the questions of changes in wage rigidities and institutional aspects of the labour market, for which CGE models are not well suited.

The structural change of the French economy between 1970 and 1992 can thus be summarised through changes in these four categories of state variable. To analyse their role, we build a database for 1970 and for 1992, and calibrate the model for each of these two dates. For each good and each factor, the physical unit used is the same for the two calibrations. The total change over the period can then be decomposed in order to determine the contribution of each category of state variable.

This procedure makes it possible to estimate the contributions of technical change, factor supply variations, shifts in the sectoral consumption pattern, and shifts in trade intensities in the variation of welfare and of each factor's real reward.

The model used is briefly presented in Section 2. In Section 3 we describe the methods used and carry out a decomposition analysis in Section 4. In Section 5 we study the importance of the possible endogenous effect of trade on productivity, as suggested in some recent studies. In Section 6 we analyse how the results differ if we assume different elasticities of substitution between factors, in order to examine the robustness of the results.

2 The model

The CGE model presented in this section has been conceived with the objective of providing a rough analysis of the structural change of the French economy. It is built on the basis of the model used in Jean and Bontout (1999), which is in many respects similar to those developed by Gasiorek, Smith and Venables (1992) and Mercenier (1992) for the assessment of European economic integration, as well as to the one proposed by Cortes and Jean (1996, 1998) for dealing with the emergence of low labour cost countries. This model uses an Armington hypothesis, but it also incorporates, for industrial sectors only, horizontal product differentiation, monopolistic competition and increasing returns to scale.

The model focuses on France, including its trade flows separately with a Southern and a Northern area.[1] Nine sectors are distinguished, eight of which belong to agriculture and industry. Services are gathered in a single sector. We consider three production factors: unskilled labour, skilled labour, and capital.

The demand side

Final consumption and intermediate consumption are modelled in the same way. For each, the demand function is homothetic, and the behaviour of a representative consumer is modelled in three stages (see Figure 7.1). The first stage describes the distribution of demand between industries. It is represented by a CES utility function with an elasticity of substitution σ_1 equal to 0.5. The share of an industry in total expenditure thus increases with its relative price.

This is the only stage the service sector enters, where goods are assumed to be homogeneous and non-tradable. Within each other sector, in contrast, we use an Armington hypothesis: the choice between products from different geographical origins (France, North and South) is modelled through a CES function, with an elasticity of 1.2 for the high-differentiation sectors, and 1.6 for the low-differentiation ones (see Table 7.1). A third tier is modelled, for French products only, corresponding to a Dixit-Stiglitz formulation: the consumer chooses between horizontally differentiated varieties of each good, with a constant elasticity of substitution equal to 4 in high-differentiation sectors and 8 in low-differentiation ones.

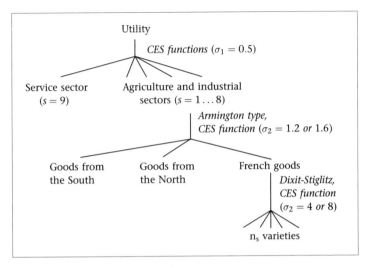

Figure 7.1   Structure of the utility function

Table 7.1   Sectoral parameters (elasticity and fixed costs)

	σ_2 (Armington elasticity)	σ_3 (Elasticity of substitution between French varieties)	Fixed costs, as a proportion of total cost
Agriculture	1.6	8	0.15
Agro-food industry	1.2	4	0.30
Energy	1.6	8	0.15
Intermediate goods	1.6	8	0.15
Productive equipment goods	1.2	4	0.30
Household equipment goods	1.6	8	0.15
Transport materials	1.2	4	0.30
Current consumption goods	1.6	8	0.15
Services and construction	–	–	–

The supply side

The production function involves intermediate consumption and the three types of production factor. It comprises two nested functions, shown in Figure 7.2. First, intermediate goods and value added are assumed to be perfectly complementary, as reflected by the use of a Leontief function. The service sector is assumed to exhibit constant returns to scale. For all other sectors, however, we take into account the presence of fixed costs, inducing economies of scale.

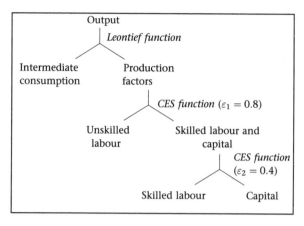

Figure 7.2 Structure of the production function

These fixed costs correspond to 15 per cent of the initial output in low-differentiation sectors (where the elasticity of substitution between French varieties is 8, and the Armington elasticity is 1.6), and 30 per cent in high-differentiation ones (with elasticities in demand of 4 and 1.2). This percentage is assumed to hold both in 1970 and in 1992.

The combination of production factors is represented in two stages, both with a CES form. The first stage distinguishes unskilled labour and an aggregate of skilled labour and capital, and the second stage distinguishes skilled labour and capital with a lower elasticity of substitution. This captures the relative complementarity of capital and skilled labour.

We set the elasticity of substitution between unskilled labour and the aggregate skilled-capital at 0.8. This value may seem fairly low, as surveys such as those by Freeman (1986) and Hamermesh (1986, 1993) suggest that it is not clear whether this elasticity should be greater or less than 1. However, Wood (1994, 1995) argues that commonly used values are overestimated, mainly because they are calculated using a very high level of aggregation for sectoral data. Consequently, the variations measured in factor intensities not only correspond to changes within firms, but also to structural effects linked to changes in the product mix. Only the first effect should be taken into account in the context of a CGE model, where uniform factor intensity is assumed within each sector. Legendre and Le Maître (1997) confirm that allowing for inter-firm heterogeneity leads to a lower estimate of capital–labour substitutability, and estimates by Steiner and Wagner (1997) with disaggregated data for Germany point in the same direction. Nonetheless, in Section 6 we also consider the possibility that this elasticity is greater than 1.

The service sector is assumed to be perfectly competitive, while industrial sectors are in monopolistic competition *à la* Cournot (see Appendix A for details). Given the substantial length of the period considered, and the fact that we focus on structural equilibria, the number of firms is assumed to be variable, and set by a zero-profit condition. Knowing fixed costs and the elasticity of substitution between goods, this zero-profit condition also enables the number of firms to be calibrated.

Trade flows

The French demand for imports does not require specific modelling: it is set via consumer demand as a result of utility maximisation. The demand for French exports, in contrast, has to be modelled in an *ad hoc* way. We assume that export intensity depends on the relative price of exports to imports with a constant elasticity, equal to the Armington elasticity of substitution used in the sub-utility index of the sector:[2]

$$\frac{Y_{Fr,s,j}}{Y_{Fr,s}} = CFC_s \left(\frac{p_{Fr,s,j}}{p_{j,s,Fr}} \right)^{-\sigma_{2,s}}. \tag{1}$$

The subscript Fr refers to France, j to another area (North or South), and s to an industrial sector ($s = 1$ to 8). $Y_{Fr,s,j}$ is the French output of sector s sold in area j as a final consumption, $p_{Fr,s,j}$ is the corresponding price, and $p_{j,s,Fr}$ is the price of French imports in the sector s, from area j. $Y_{Fr,s}$ is the total French output of sector s. CFC_s is a constant, calibrated on the basis of the French export flow of final consumptions in sector s. A similar equation can be written for intermediate consumptions, with a specific constant, CIC_s. $\sigma_{2,s}$ is the Armington elasticity of sector s.

Prices of imports ($p_{j,s,Fr}$) are given in the database. Two closing rules are possible with regard to foreign trade. The first is to consider import prices as exogenous, leading to an endogenous trade balance. The second is to consider the trade balance as exogenous, and to allow import prices to vary by the same proportion for all sectors, which is equivalent to assume the exchange rate to be endogenous. Except where otherwise stated, this second closure rule will be adopted.

Production factor markets

The rise in unemployment, in particular among unskilled workers, has been one of the main features of the French economy during the last decades. However, it is difficult to account for this in a CGE model. Since we are concerned only with structural equilibrium, frictional and cyclical unemployment are irrelevant here. Only structural unemployment could be studied in this framework, but even in this case, some important problems arise. Let us assume, for example, that the unskilled labour market can be described through a wage-bargaining model (as in Bontout and Jean (1999) for example). The problem is that many aspects of the bargaining (such as reservation wages, bargaining powers or unions' objectives) may have changed during the period studied, and that we cannot account explicitly for the determinants of this shift.

We therefore choose not to model explicitly unemployment. Instead, we try to account for the structural full-employment equilibrium underlying the benchmark. According to the OECD, the unemployment rate in France rose from 2.5 per cent in 1970 to 10.4 per cent in 1992. We will assume that in terms of structural unemployment only, this rate rose from 0 per cent in 1970 to 7 per cent in 1992. Consequently, we consider the 1970 database to describe a full-employment equilibrium. For 1992, we assume that this unemployment hurts only unskilled workers, due to a misadjustment in relative wages. We then recalculate the 1992 equilibrium, assuming that wages adjust in order to allow for full employment. Thus, all the changes we try to account for are expressed in terms of relative wages.

In this context, we can assume all factor markets to be perfectly competitive, with perfectly flexible prices, included the wages of unskilled labour. The supply of each production factor is assumed to be exogenous, and full employment of each factor is met through wage adjustment.

3 Decomposition analysis in a general equilibrium framework: methodology

Structural model and state variables

In order to describe the state of the economy at a given date, we initially need a database covering output, value added, production factors, intermediate consumptions and trade flows for each sector, plus the prices of goods and production factors. This database is described in the first part of Section 4 and in Appendix B.

Once the structural model is chosen, however, the state of the economy can be summarised more simply. Indeed, we assume constant over time the parameters which are not calibrated, that is, the elasticities of substitution between goods and the elasticities of substitution between factors, as well as the magnitude of fixed costs as a proportion of total costs in industrial sectors. We also suppose that there are no trade barriers.

In this context, the state of the economy is fully determined by two categories of calibrated parameters and two categories of exogenous variables. The calibrated parameters are:

1. The share coefficients in the production function;
2. The share coefficients in the utility function.

The exogenous variables are:

1. The sector structure of relative import prices (i.e. $p_{i,s,Fr}/p_{i,s',Fr}$), plus the level of exchange rate (i.e. the *level* of one import price, relative to the domestic price in the same sector) or the level of trade balance;
2. Factor supplies (in physical units, not in values).

From state variables to decomposition analysis

Once the structural model is chosen, these four sets of values constitute a set of state variables for the whole economy. If the structural model is assumed to be unchanged, the structural change of the economy between two dates can be summarised through the changes in these state variables. We can then relate the suggested determinants of changes in wage inequalities to changes in these state variables:

1. Technical change is summarised through the changes in the share coefficients in the production function;[3]
2. Changes in the sectoral distribution of consumers' demand are reflected in the changes in the share coefficients in the upper tier of the utility function;
3. Trade evolutions are the consequence of both changes in import prices relative to domestic prices (and in the value of trade balance), and evolutions of the share coefficients in the Armington tier of the utility function (which reflect the geographical distribution of consumers' demand, for given prices);
4. Changes in factor supplies are directly accounted for.

This enables the contribution of each of these four main shocks to be determined: it is equal to the impact of the change in the corresponding set of state variables. However, the problem remains that this impact depends on the initial state of the economy. The effect of the sum of these four shocks is known (it corresponds to the structural change observed between 1970 and 1992), but the impact of each of them is not the same if it is assumed to occur first (from the 1970 benchmark) or after other shocks. One way to overcome this problem would be to divide the period in many sub-periods, since the shorter the period, the weaker the dependence between the impact of a single shock and the order in which shocks are considered to occur. However, this method would require far more complex data. For the sake of simplicity, we adopt the following proxy. The impact of each shock (i.e. each change in a set of state variables) is computed assuming it occurs first, on the basis of the 1970 benchmark, and then assuming that it occurs after the three other shocks. In this case, the shock leads, from an intermediary state of the economy, to the 1992 benchmark.[4] The proxy is the average of these two impacts.[5]

This procedure is fairly straightforward to implement in the case of factor supplies and of technical progress. It is somewhat more difficult, however, for the sectoral consumption pattern and international trade. The first reason is that they modify the utility function of consumers, and therefore the dual price index. In this case, we use as a price index the geometric average of the dual price indexes of the initial and final utility functions. The second problem is the linkage between the various tiers of the utility function.

Accounting for changes in international trade intensities

To determine the contribution of trade to the structural change of the French economy, we simulate the impact of a shock corresponding to the modification of the state variables reflecting the evolution of trade intensities (export intensity and import penetration rate) by sector.

For export intensity, the change is due to the evolution of French export prices with respect to foreign prices (the latter are assumed to be equal to import prices), but also to the changes in the function of demand addressed to French exports, namely in the constant CFC_s (for final consumption, in sector s) and CIC_s (for intermediate consumption), which are changed from their 1970 value to their 1992 value.

In order to account for the changes in the import penetration rate, we first change the Armington tier of the utility function, moving from the share coefficients calibrated in 1970 to those obtained in 1992, both for final and intermediate consumptions. In fact, these coefficients summarise many things: possible changes in consumers' tastes, trade barriers, transport costs, access of importers to distribution networks, and supply effects (for example, an increase in the number of varieties offered by importers). We do not try to disentangle these various effects.

Changing these Armington coefficients means that the composition of the sector baskets used in the upper tier is changed. In this context, the same share coefficients in the upper tier of the utility function would lead to a different distribution of consumption between sectors, simply because these coefficients apply to baskets the definition of which has changed. It is therefore necessary to recalibrate the share coefficients in the upper tier, in order to make sure that the sectoral distribution of consumption is not changed, for given prices. Once this is done, we take into account changes in import prices.

To summarise, the trade intensity shock corresponds to a change in a set of state variables which induces a shift of export intensities and import penetration rates, for each sector, from their 1970 level to their 1992 level. The following state variables are changed:

1. Import prices with respect to domestic prices (as import prices are set, trade balance is supposed to be endogenous);
2. Constants in the function of demand addressed to French exports;
3. Share coefficients in the Armington-type sub-utility function of each industrial sector (with a recalibration of the coefficient of the upper tier in coherence with the change in the composition of each sector's goods basket).

Accounting for changes in the sectoral distribution of consumption

In order to account for the changes in the sectoral distribution of consumption, we change the value of the share coefficients in the upper tier of the utility function from their 1970 level to their 1992 level. But the definition of the baskets of goods concerned is not the same in both cases. It is therefore inconsistent to change the coefficients of the upper tier without taking into account the shift that occurred at the lower tier.

To overcome this problem, we assess the global effect of trade and the sectoral distribution of consumption taken together, by changing the whole utility function from its 1970 expression to its 1992 expression, and taking into account the changes in coefficients of demand addressed to exports, and in import prices. The effect of the shift in the sectoral distribution of consumption alone is then obtained by subtracting the effect of changes in trade intensities.[6] Note finally that, by definition, this shift has no effect on welfare, as it is thought of as a change in the welfare function. For the sake of coherence, we therefore recalculate the dual price index in order to make sure that the variation of the real income is indeed zero.

4   The results

Stylised facts

The data used are drawn from French National Accounts (see details in Appendix B). For each good and for each production factor, the physical unit used is the same in both databases (the evolutions expressed in volumes are set on the basis of 1980 prices).[7] The prices are all set to unity in the calibration of the 1970 benchmark, as usual, but this is not the case for the calibration of the 1992 benchmark, as we account for variations in prices. Note however that only real values are relevant here so the numeraire can be chosen freely in the second calibration.[8]

The main trends are summarised in Table 7.2. Note in particular that the real wage[9] for unskilled workers[10] has been rising faster (+51 per cent over the period) than the real wage for skilled workers (+33 per cent). But, as mentioned above, we do not use the 1992 database directly as the final benchmark: we first compute an underlying full-employment structural equilibrium, assuming that the economy (and in particular wages) adjusts in order to remove the 7 per cent structural unemployment. Once this is done, we observe that the relative competitive wage[11] of skilled to unskilled workers hardly changed over the period: it slightly increased, from 2.23 in 1970 to 2.24 in 1992, and the real wage is found to have increased by about 40 per cent for both categories. This evolution may seem surprising, and one may wonder whether it is indeed useful to study the causes of evolution of relative wages in these conditions. But, first, this relative stability does not necessarily mean that relative wages did not experience several counteracting influences during this period. Second, shedding some light on this equilibrium of influences over relative wages in France would be useful in order to put the different forces in international perspective. And, third, this result is due to the period of observation (the choice of which was constrained by questions of data), but the observed trend in wage inequalities has not been constant: they have been declining until the mid-1980s, and rising since then.[12]

Table 7.2 Descriptive analysis from the 1970 and 1992 databases

	Sector's share in national VA		Sector's share in national production		Sector's share in national consumption		Prices in 1992, compared to GDP price (1970 = 1)		
	1970	1992	1970	1992	1970	1992	Prod.	Exports	Imports
1 Agriculture	7.0	2.9	7.8	4.4	8.0	4.1	0.63	0.60	0.53
2 Agro-food industry	4.4	3.0	9.2	6.8	9.1	6.6	0.76	0.63	0.56
3 Energy	4.9	4.6	5.0	5.0	5.7	5.6	1.25	1.52	1.52
4 Intermediate goods	8.2	5.4	12.5	8.5	12.8	8.6	0.87	0.74	0.69
5 Productive equipment goods	5.6	4.5	7.3	6.6	7.2	6.3	0.89	0.75	0.59
6 Household equipment goods	0.6	0.3	0.8	0.6	0.9	0.7	0.44	0.58	0.38
7 Transport materials	2.4	2.1	3.6	3.9	3.1	3.7	1.07	1.06	1.11
8 Current consumption goods	7.6	5.3	11.2	9.1	10.8	9.3	0.92	0.74	0.68
9 Services and construction	59.3	71.9	42.6	55.2	42.4	55.1	1.09	–	–
Total	100.0	100.0	100.0	100.0	100.0	100.0	1.00	0.78	0.76

	Penetration rate of imports from the South (%)		Penetration rate of imports from the North (%)		Export intensity toward the South (%)		Export intensity toward the North (%)	
	1970	1992	1970	1992	1970	1992	1970	1992
1 Agriculture	4.9	3.4	4.2	6.0	1.2	4.3	5.6	10.5
2 Agro-food industry	3.4	3.7	3.0	7.8	1.3	3.1	5.3	10.4
3 Energy	11.8	10.5	3.9	5.0	0.6	1.6	2.7	3.6
4 Intermediate goods	2.5	5.7	15.0	22.6	4.5	7.0	10.9	19.7
5 Productive equipment goods	0.5	5.8	20.1	31.9	9.1	15.8	11.7	24.2
6 Household equipment goods	0.4	9.8	13.8	25.9	2.2	6.8	5.4	21.3
7 Transport materials	0.3	8.0	11.6	21.6	7.1	10.6	16.2	23.5
8 Current consumption goods	0.8	6.0	6.3	12.0	2.8	5.1	7.2	11.0
9 Services and construction	0.0	0.0	0.0	0.0	0.0	0.0	0.0	0.0
Industrial sectors (1–8)	3.2	6.1	9.3	15.8	3.6	6.8	8.2	14.9
Total	1.8	2.7	5.4	7.1	2.1	3.0	4.7	6.7

Table 7.2   (Continued)

	Value added at constant prices (1970 = 1000)	Capital income/VA (%)		Skilled wage bill/VA (%)		Unskilled wage bill/VA (%)		Partial productivity (1970 = 100)		
		1970	1992	1970	1992	1970	1992	Capital	Skilled	Unskilled
1 Agriculture	113.4	24.1	23.4	23.4	21.6	52.5	55.1	135.0	228.4	228.6
2 Agro-food	155.6	24.1	23.4	21.0	19.8	54.9	56.8	111.5	184.2	191.3
3 Energy	129.4	69.2	75.3	12.2	12.8	18.6	11.9	60.4	100.4	188.9
4 Intermediate goods	129.7	33.9	37.2	15.3	19.6	50.8	43.2	86.2	119.4	204.2
5 Productive goods	158.0	25.2	26.4	28.7	39.0	46.1	34.7	88.9	110.1	226.8
6 Household goods	203.1	32.0	31.6	27.9	40.2	40.1	28.1	190.2	210.2	490.9
7 Transport materials	141.4	10.7	32.9	20.6	22.7	68.6	44.5	25.1	112.6	217.4
8 Current consumption goods	133.7	27.0	33.1	15.8	24.7	57.1	42.2	73.2	92.6	223.1
9 Services and construction	193.1	20.8	26.4	31.8	37.8	47.4	35.8	59.6	102.0	183.2
Total	173.7	25.2	29.5	26.7	33.7	48.1	36.8	70.2	105.0	197.6

Sources: see Appendix B.

Employment growth has been very different for the two categories of labour. Skilled employment increased by 65 per cent, unskilled employment declined by 12.1 per cent before adjustment for unemployment and by 2.4 per cent after. As computed from the evolution of global income of capital and from the very strong increase in the net fixed capital stock (+147 per cent), the real cost of capital is found to have decreased by 18 per cent before adjustment for unemployment, and by 13 per cent after the adjustment.

Meanwhile, trade intensities have risen sharply in the tradable sectors. The average import penetration rate from the South nearly doubled, while it rose from 9.3 to 15.8 per cent for imports from the North. The average export intensity went up from 3.6 to 6.8 per cent toward the South, and from 8.2 to 14.9 per cent toward the North. Of course, given the increasing weight of services, the trends are less impressive for the economy as a whole, but still the average import penetration rate rose from 7.2 to 9.8 per cent, and the export intensity increased from 6.8 to 9.7 per cent.

The initial data set also enables the evolution of partial productivities to be observed. Their average over the whole economy reflects mostly the rhythm of accumulation of each factor relative to GDP growth. It is no surprise, in this context, to observe a sharp fall in the average partial productivity of capital (−30 per cent), while skilled-labour partial productivity slightly increases

(+5 per cent), and the average partial productivity of unskilled workers almost doubles (+98 per cent).

Results of the decomposition analysis

The results of the decomposition analysis are reported in Table 7.3. Note first that the global change (a), obtained by changing all state variables from their 1970 value to their 1992 value, and taking into account the change in the trade balance, differs from the changes described above. This is due mainly to differences in price measures. The model measures price variations through dual price indexes, instead of the chained Laspeyres indexes used in the national accounts. Moreover, we use a consumer price index in the model instead of a GDP deflator in the data mentioned above, and the former increased less than the latter. As a result, the consumer price index increase measured over the period is around 10 per cent lower following the model than in the data. Consequently, the global changes observed in the simulation for real values are around 10 per cent higher than in the benchmark.[13]

Applying the methodology described above makes it possible to decompose this global change, with a fairly good global fit: the residual between the resulting effect of the four shocks and the global effect is less than 2.5 per cent for each variable. Technical change and variations in factor supplies appear to be by far the most important contributors, in terms of welfare or real and relative wages. These two shocks have had a strong positive impact on welfare, but its distribution among factors is very different. Not surprisingly, variations in factor supplies seem to have been very favourable to unskilled real wages (the only factor whose stock decreased) and very unfavourable to the real reward for

Table 7.3 Decomposition analysis for France, 1970–92

	Welfare	Variation in real factor rewards			Variation in skilled/ unskilled relative wage
		Unskilled labour	Skilled labour	Capital	
Global change (a)	98.3	52.0	54.6	−6.9	1.7
Contribution of:					
Technical change (b)	19.3	−19.3	22.4	111.9	51.7
Factor supplies (c)	58.3	82.5	19.0	−57.3	−34.8
Trade (d)	6.2	4.6	5.6	4.5	1.0
Consumption (e)	0.0	0.0	2.9	2.6	2.9
Resultant effect (f)	100.6	54.0	58.4	7.8	2.9
Residual (g)	−1.2	−1.3	−2.4	1.0	−1.1

Note: All figures are variations in percentages. The resulting effect is calculated as: (f) = (1 + (b)) × (1 + (c)) × (1 + (d)) × (1 + (e)) − 1, and the residual is (g) = (1 + (a))/(1 + (f)) − 1.

capital, whose accumulation was rapid. The effect on skilled real wages is intermediate, so that this shock has had a strong negative effect (−34.8 per cent) on the skilled to unskilled relative wage. This effect is approximately counter-balanced by the impact of technical change, which increased the relative wage of skilled workers by more than 50 per cent, with a strong negative effect (−19.3 per cent) on unskilled real wages.

The variation in the sectoral distribution of demand corresponds mainly to a shift towards services. As services are more skilled-intensive and less capital-intensive than the average, this shock is unfavourable to capital (−2.6 per cent), but it has a positive effect on skilled real wages (+2.9 per cent), while the impact on unskilled real wages is negligible. This shock thus brought a positive contribution to the evolution of the skilled to unskilled relative wage.

Trade is the only shock to have a positive effect on the real cost of each of the three production factors, including unskilled labour (+4.6 per cent). There are gains linked to product differentiation and economies of scale, but the Stolper-Samuelson effect is largely dominated by the strong improvement in terms of trade (nearly +20 per cent). This is problematic, however. It is true that import prices rose less rapidly than domestic production prices, but we do not take into account here the other side of the coin: export prices rose even less rapidly. As long as we equate export prices to production prices (with only a small difference linked to markups), we cannot account for this stylised fact.

Trade increases the skilled to unskilled relative wage by 1 per cent, but this effect is small compared to the other impacts mentioned above. It is possible that the weak sectoral breakdown used here underestimates the variations in specialisation, in particular concerning trade with Southern countries.

5   The link between trade and productivity

The decomposition analysis presented above assumes that the different shocks studied above are independent, although their consequences are not, as we have emphasised. In particular, we assumed that technical change is independent from variations in trade intensities. This is not what some recent studies argue. Be it through defensive innovation, through decreasing X-inefficiencies, through technological catch-up or through firm selection, an increase in trade intensity may modify the production function of the representative firm of each industry, spurring productivity and inducing skill upgrading. Empirical evidence supporting this link has been found by Hine and Wright (1998), Feenstra and Hanson (1996),[14] Cortes and Jean (1997, 2002) and Greenaway, Hine and Wright (1999). The model enables us to clarify the importance of this relationship.

If trade intensity affects productivity, changes in factor productivities can be split into two components: one that is linked to trade, and the other that is autonomous. Only the latter should be counted as the contribution of technical change in the decomposition analysis. The joint impact of trade and technology is unchanged, but the respective contributions of these two shocks may change.

In order to modify the model, we use the empirical results of Cortes and Jean (1997). They show that a one-point increase in the import penetration rate in a given industry induces a 1.3 per cent increase in the partial productivity of labour in this industry if imports come from the South, and a 0.7 per cent increase if they come from the North. They also find an effect on labour skill: a one-point increase in the import penetration rate induces a 0.4 per cent increase in the skilled to unskilled ratio in the industry concerned. In other words, the effect is stronger on the partial productivity of unskilled labour than on the productivity of skilled labour. Formally, this effect is modelled through an endogenous impact of the import penetration rate variations on the parameters of the production function of the representative firm, industry by industry. We assume, in addition, that import penetration variations have the same impact on the productivity of capital than on the productivity of skilled labour (see Appendix C for further details).

The results of the reassessment of the contributions of trade and technology are reported in Table 7.4. The impact of trade is strongly increased when an effect on productivity is assumed to hold. It even induces a welfare increase (+20.9 per cent) larger than that obtained for technical change (+4.8 per cent).

Table 7.4 Contributions of trade and technical change, with and without trade-induced effect on productivities

		Variation in real factor rewards			Variation in skilled/ unskilled relative wage
	Welfare	Unskilled labour	Skilled labour	Capital	
Combined effect of trade and technical change	26.7	−15.6	29.3	121.4	53.2
Separate contributions:					
(a) Without trade-induced effect on productivities					
Trade	6.2	4.6	5.6	4.5	1.0
Technical change	19.3	−19.3	22.4	111.9	51.7
(b) With trade-induced effect on productivities					
Trade	20.9	17.1	25.4	18.1	7.1
Exogenous technical change	4.8	−27.9	3.1	87.5	43.0

Note: All figures are variations in percentages. The composition of both effects is exactly equal to the combined effect in the case 'with trade-induced effect on productivities', by construction. It is not the case for the contributions 'without ...', because the contributions have been calculated as in the previous section (average of the effects obtained assuming that the shock is the first/the last to occur).

This surprising result suggests that the trade-induced effect taken into account here may be somewhat overestimated. Once again, trade appears in this case to have had a positive impact on the real cost of each production factor, including unskilled workers (+17.1 per cent).

However, the influence of international trade on the skilled to unskilled relative wage is positive and substantial (7.1 per cent). Of course, this effect is weak compared to the impacts of exogenous technical change and factor supplies variations. But this direct comparison is not necessarily the most relevant. It is normal, according to secular trends, to observe an increase in the skilled to unskilled relative supply, and a parallel decrease in the partial productivity of skilled workers, compared to that of unskilled workers. An evolution in wage inequalities occurs when these trends turn out not to be 'parallel'. In this perspective, the 7.1 per cent impact of trade on relative wages is far from being negligible.

6 Sensitivity to the substitutability between production factors

The decomposition analysis presented above depends on the parameters chosen in the model on the basis of external information. These parameters include the magnitude of fixed costs in French industrial sectors, the elasticities of demand for French exports and the elasticities used in the utility function describing the substitution between sectors, between products from different geographical origins, and between French varieties. The most sensitive, however, are the elasticities of substitution between factors of production.

In particular, we know *a priori* that the effect of a given factor bias of technical change depends on whether the elasticity of substitution between the factors concerned is greater or less than 1 (see for example Cotis, Germain and Quinet (1997)). In the analysis thus far the elasticity of substitution has been set to 0.4 between capital and skilled labour, and to 0.8 between their aggregate and unskilled labour. Table 7.5 presents results from the same decomposition analysis assuming these two elasticities to be equal to 0.8 and 1.2, respectively.

Note first that the global change (a) is not exactly the same as previously. This is not surprising, because we assume first that relative wages adapt in order to remove structural unemployment. The corresponding adjustment is less important when the substitutability between production factors is higher. Here, it involves an 8.8 per cent increase in the skilled to unskilled relative wage (instead of a 14.3 per cent increase previously). As a consequence, the variation to be explained in this relative wage is a slight decrease (−3.4 per cent).

Compared to the previous results, the outcome of the decomposition analysis is not fundamentally changed. The contributions of both factor supplies and technical change is weakened, but they remain important and of the same order of magnitude. The consequences of the shift in the sectoral distribution of consumption are of the same nature, but their magnitude is halved. The contribution of trade does not change much, but its effect on relative wages is reduced.

Table 7.5 Decomposition analysis for France, 1970–92, with a high substitutability between factors ($\varepsilon_1 = 1.2$ and $\varepsilon_2 = 0.8$)

		Variation in real factor rewards			Variation in skilled/ unskilled relative wage
	Welfare	Unskilled labour	Skilled labour	Capital	
Global change (a)	98.3	56.3	51.0	−7.6	−3.4
Contribution of:					
Technical change (b)	20.1	−0.8	34.9	43.1	36.1
Factor supplies (c)	57.1	52.0	6.1	−37.8	−30.2
Trade (d)	6.2	4.6	5.3	4.7	0.6
Consumption (e)	0.0	0.0	1.6	−1.3	1.6
Resultant effect (f)	100.4	57.8	53.1	−8.0	−3.0
Residual (g)	−1.1	−1.0	−1.4	0.3	−0.4

Note: All figures are variations in percentages. The resulting effect is calculated as: (f) = (1 + (b)) × (1 + (c)) × (1 + (d)) × (1 + (e)) − 1, and the residual is (g) = (1 + (a))/(1 + (f)) − 1.

This robustness with respect to factor substitutability is perhaps surprising, especially in relation to the impact of technical change. It is due mainly to the fact that the definition of the corresponding shock has to be changed to be consistent with the new elasticities. The share coefficients in the production function are not the same when the elasticities of substitution used in the function change. It is necessary to recalibrate in order to recalculate the value of these coefficients both in 1970 and in 1992.

7 Conclusions

In this chapter we confronted a CGE model with observed evolutions in France between 1970 and 1992 using a decomposition analysis. We started by observing that, once the structural model is chosen, and assuming elasticities of substitution to be constant over time the change of the economy between two equilibria can be summarised through the changes in a set of four types of state variables: share coefficients in the production function, reflecting the productivity for each factor within each sector; factor supplies, assumed to be exogenous; share coefficients in the utility function, reflecting the preferences of consumers; and, for each sector, the relative price of imports, as a proportion of domestic output price, as well as the parameters characterising the foreign demand for French exports.

The separate simulation of the impact of the change observed in each of these four sets of state variables then provides an assessment of the specific contribution of each underlying cause: technical change, changes in factor supplies, shifts in consumption patterns, and international trade. These various causes are then assessed in a unified and consistent framework, with the constraint of explaining the whole observed data.

The ratio of skilled to unskilled competitive wage barely changed between 1970 and 1992 in France. However, we conclude that technical change had a strong positive effect on skilled relative wage, counterbalanced by the negative effect of changes in factor supplies. These two effects are by far the most important, and they mainly reflect the secular skill upgrading of industrialised economies.

The shift in consumption patterns away from industrial goods towards services increased the skilled relative wage. International trade also increased wage inequalities, but its effect is weak, at least with a standard formulation. Moreover, trade has a positive impact on the real reward of each factor, including unskilled labour, mainly because import prices decreased compared to domestic output prices. Nevertheless, if we take into account the trade-induced effect on productivity measured in some recent studies, we find that trade substantially increased the relative wage of skilled to unskilled workers. This suggests that, through its influence on technical change, the indirect effect of trade on wage inequalities is likely to be far from negligible.

These results should be viewed as a first attempt to apply a decomposition analysis method in a general equilibrium framework. Although this method is computationally complex, many extensions and applications are possible which are likely to be helpful in better understanding the recent trends of relative wages in industrialised countries.

Appendix A: Modelling imperfect competition in industrial sectors

In the French industrial sectors ($s = 1$ to 8), firms compete *à la* Cournot, and their markup ratio on a given market is defined by, omitting the index for the market:[15]

$$p_i \left(1 - \frac{1}{EP_i} \right) = Cm_i \tag{A1}$$

where p_i is the selling price and Cm_i the marginal cost of firm i. The firm's perceived price-elasticity EP_i depends on its market share (s_i) as follows:

$$\frac{1}{EP_i} = \frac{1}{\sigma_3} + \left(\frac{1}{\sigma_2} - \frac{1}{\sigma_3} \right) \frac{1}{n_{Fr}} + \left(1 - \frac{1}{\sigma_2} \right) \frac{p_i Y_i}{pp_s US_s} \tag{A2}$$

where σ_2 is the Armington elasticity of substitution, and r_3 is the elasticity of substitution between French varieties in the industry.[16] n_{Fr} is the number of French firms in the industry (we assume a one-to-one correspondence to hold between firms and varieties), Y_i is the output of firm i, and $pp_s US_s$ is the amount of consumption in sector s, in the market concerned. The last term is omitted for the foreign market, which is equivalent to assuming that the market share of French exporters on foreign markets is negligible.

Appendix B: The data

Most of the data (I/O tables, in particular) are drawn from French national accounts. 1992 is chosen as the last year because sectoral data for value added, intermediate consumption and labour compensation are not available for more recent years.

Some hypotheses have to be made for the sake of simplicity and coherence. Stocks variations and investments are considered as final consumptions. Trade flows in services are not taken into account, implying a correction in the final consumption for the service industry. Moreover, the data concerning factor intensities in the national accounts are not fully satisfactory. Some corrections have been made on the basis of the factor intensities given in the database built by the Observatoire Français des Conjonctures Economiques (OFCE) for its model MOSAIC.

The geographical distribution of trade is drawn from the Centre d'Etudes Prospectives et d'Informations Internationales (CEPII) *Chelem database*, keeping the value of total trade for each sector equal to its value in the national accounts.

The data concerning labour skill are taken from the Institut National de la Statistique et des Etudes Economiques (INSEE) survey, *Enquête sur la structure de l'emploi*. The labour cost for skilled labour and for unskilled labour are built on the basis of the net earnings from the Direction de l'Animation de la Recherche et des Etudes Statistiques (DARES) and INSEE *Déclaration Annuelles de Données Sociales*, adding social premiums.

Appendix C: Modelling the trade-induced effect on productivity

The aggregate of production factors (see also Figure 7.2) is expressed as follows, omitting the index for the firm:

$$PF = \left[\gamma_{UL} UL^{\frac{\varepsilon_1 - 1}{\varepsilon_1}} + \gamma_{SLK} SLK^{\frac{\varepsilon_1 - 1}{\varepsilon_1}} \right]^{\frac{\varepsilon_1}{\varepsilon_1 - 1}} \tag{C1}$$

where PF is the aggregate of production factors used by the firm, UL is the input in unskilled labour, SKL the input in the aggregate of skilled labour and capital. The γ are the share coefficients of these two inputs.

Cost minimisation then leads to:

$$\frac{VA}{UL} = p_{FP} \gamma_{UL}^{-\varepsilon_1} \left(\frac{w_{UL}}{p_{FP}} \right)^{\varepsilon_1} \tag{C2}$$

where p_{FP} is the dual index price of the aggregate FP, and w_{UL} is the unskilled wage. A similar relationship could be written for SKL, the aggregate of skilled labour and capital, instead of unskilled labour.

For given prices, the partial productivity of skilled labour is thus proportional to $\gamma_{UL}^{-\varepsilon_1}$. This makes it possible to include the empirical results of Cortes and Jean (1997) in the model. Formally, this effect is modelled as the following endogenous setting of the parameters γ:

$$-\varepsilon_1(\ln(\gamma_{UL}) - \ln(\gamma_{UL}^{ini})) = \left(0.013 + 0.004\,\frac{SKL}{SKL + UL}\right)(MP_{South} - MP_{South}^{ini})$$

$$+ \left(0.007 + 0.004\,\frac{SKL}{SKL + UL}\right)(MP_{South} - MP_{South}^{ini})$$

and

$$-\varepsilon_1(\ln(\gamma_{SLK}) - \ln(\gamma_{SLK}^{ini})) = \left(0.013 + 0.004\,\frac{SKL}{SKL + UL}\right)(MP_{South} - MP_{South}^{ini})$$

$$+ \left(0.007 + 0.004\,\frac{SKL}{SKL + UL}\right)(MP_{South} - MP_{South}^{ini})$$

where MP refers to the penetration rate of imports from the zone indicated by the subscript. The superscript '*ini*' refers to initial values.

Notes

1   This Northern area includes the countries the GDP in PPP per capita of which was greater than 80 per cent of the French one in 1980: USA, Canada, Switzerland, Japan, Australia, Norway, New Zealand, and EU-15, except Spain, Greece, Portugal and Ireland. The Southern area corresponds to the rest of the world.

2   This modelling of the demand addressed to exports is based on export intensity, not on exports, basically because we want to take into account the growth of foreign markets. Through this formula, we assume that foreign markets grow at the same rate as the domestic market. To put it another way: were we to choose a 'norm' for exports evolution, we would define it as a constant export intensity, not as a constant volume of exports.

3   This does not take into account changes in quality or the appearance of new products.

4   In practice, we start from a 1992 benchmark, and assume that the state variables concerned take back their 1970 value. This gives the 'intermediary state' of the economy mentioned above.

5   If Δ_{ini} is the variation observed on a variable for the first simulation, and Δ_{fin} the variation observed for the second simulation, then the average will be $[(1 + \Delta_{ini})(1 + \Delta_{fin})]^{1/2} - 1$.

6   This is a proxy, because it assumes that changes in the sectoral distribution of consumption always occur after changes in trade. As we will see, however, the impact of trade is rather low. As a consequence, assuming it to occur after changes in trade does not change too much the impact of variations in the sectoral distribution of consumption.

7   For capital stock, we use the estimates made by the French national statistical institute (INSEE) of the net, fixed capital stock by industry.

8   This is only a particular way to choose the physical unit, for each good and for each factor.

9   In this descriptive comment, real values are calculated on the basis of GDP deflator.

10 'Employés' and 'ouvriers', in the French classification. Skilled workers, in contrast, are those classified as intermediate and superior professions.

11 In fact, the data refer to labour cost, not to net or gross wages.

12 In future research, studying these two sub-periods separately could be an interesting way to extend the present work.

13 Even taking this into account, the matching between the global results and observed variations is not perfect, but the difference is always inferior to 2 per cent. These differences are linked to the treatment of monopolistic competition, because fixed costs have been set at the same share of total cost in both benchmarks. This should probably be further examined in future research.

14 Feenstra and Hanson focus on foreign outsourcing, but their results also show an impact of import penetration rate on the share of unskilled workers in the wage bill.

15 We assume zero conjectural variations, and we do not take into account any Ford effect.

16 For more details on equation (A2), see Gasiorek, Smith and Venables (1992), or Cortes and Jean (1996).

References

Abrego L. and J. Whalley (2000) 'The Choice of Structural Model in Trade-Wages Decompositions', *Review of International Economics*, vol. 3, pp. 462–77.

Bontout, O. and S. Jean (1999) 'Wages and Unemployment: The Impact of Trade and Technology under Different Labour Market Paradigms', Centre for Research on Globalisation and Labour Markets Research Paper no. 99/6, University of Nottingham.

Cardebat, J.-M. and J. Teiletche (1997) 'Salaires relatifs, commerce Nord-Sud et progrès technique: un modèle stylisé d'équilibre général calculable', in J. de Melo and P. Guillaumont (eds), *Commerce Nord-Sud, migration et delocalisation – Conséquences pour l'emploi et les salaires* (Paris: Economica).

Cortes, O. and S. Jean (1996) 'Pays émergents, emploi déficient?', *Document de travail* no. 96-05, CEPII.

Cortes, O. and S. Jean (1997) 'Commerce international, emploi et productivité', *Travail et emploi*, no. 70, pp. 61–79.

Cortes, O. and S. Jean (1998) 'Does Competition of Emerging Countries Threaten the European Unskilled Labour? An Applied General Equilibrium Approach', in P. Brenton and J. Pelkmans (eds), *Global Trade and European Workers* (London: Macmillan).

Cortes, O. and S. Jean (2002) 'Trade Spurs Productivity', in J. Francois, D. Roland-Holst and D. van der Mensbrugghe (eds), *Globalisation and Employment Patterns* (Oxford: Oxford University Press).

Cotis, J.-Ph., J.M. Germain and A. Quinet (1997) 'Les effets du progrès technique sur le travail peu qualifié sont indirects et limités', *Economie et Statistique*, no. 301–2, pp. 23–44.

Feenstra, R.C. and G.H. Hanson (1996) 'Globalization, Outsourcing and Wage Inequality', *American Economic Review*, vol. 86(2), pp. 240–5.

Francois, J. and D. Nelson (1998) 'Trade and Wages: General Equilibrium Linkages', *Economic Journal*, vol. 108, pp. 1483–99.

Freeman, R.B. (1986) 'Demand for Education', in O.C. Ashenfelter and R. Layard (eds), *Handbook of Labor Economics Volume 1* (Amsterdam: North-Holland), pp. 357–86.

Gasiorek, M., A. Smith and A. Venables (1992) '1992 Trade and Welfare: A General Equilibrium Model', in L.A. Winters (ed.), *Trade Flows and Trade Policies* (Cambridge: Cambridge University Press), pp. 35–63.

Greenaway, D., R.C. Hine and P. Wright (1999) 'An Empirical Assessment of Impact of Trade on Employment in the UK', *European Journal of Political Economy*, vol. 15(3), pp. 485–500.

Hamermesh, D.S. (1986) 'The Demand for Labor in the Long Run', in O.C. Ashenfelter and R. Layard (eds), *Handbook of Labor Economics Volume 1* (Amsterdam: North-Holland), pp. 429–71.

Hamermesh, D.S. (1993) *Labor Demand* (Princeton, NJ: Princeton University Press).

Hine, R.C. and P. Wright (1998) 'Trade with Low-Wage Economies, Employment and Productivity in UK Manufacturing', *Economic Journal*, vol. 108, pp. 1500–10.

Jean, S. and O. Bontout (1999) 'Sensibilité des salaires relatifs aux chocs de commerce international et de progrès technique: une évaluation d'équilibre général', *Revue d'économie politique*, vol. 109(2), pp. 241–71.

Lawrence, R.Z. and C.L. Evans. (1996) 'Trade and Wages: Insights from the Crystal Ball', *NBER Working Paper* no. 5,633.

Legendre, F. and P. Le Maître (1997) 'Le lien emploi-coût relatif des facteurs de production: quelques résultats obtenus à partir des données de panel', *Economie et statistique*, no. 301–2, pp. 111–27.

Mercenier, J. (1992) 'Can "1992" Reduce Unemployment in Europe? On Welfare and Employment Effects of Europe's Move to a Single Market', CRDE Discussion Paper no. 2,292, Université de Montréal.

Rowthorn, R. (1995) 'A Simulation Model of North–South Trade', UNCTAD Discussion Paper no. 104.

Steiner, V. and K. Wagner (1997) 'Relative Earnings and the Demand for Unskilled Labour in West German Manufacturing', *ZEW Discussion Paper*, no. 97–17, Mannheim.

Wood, A. (1994) *North South Trade, Employment and Inequality* (Oxford: Clarendon Press).

Wood, A. (1995) 'How Trade Hurt Unskilled Workers', *Journal of Economic Perspectives*, vol. 9(3), pp. 57–80.

8
International Trade and Labour Market Adjustment in Developing Countries

Augustin Kwasi Fosu *
African Economic Research Consortium, Nairobi, Kenya

1 Introduction

The current school of thought in the growth literature appears to favour openness as the appropriate strategy for generating sustainable growth in developing countries. Correspondingly, the import-substituting (IS) paradigm that seemed to dominate much of the 1950s and 1960s has now given way to export-promoting (EP) strategies.[1] Policies based on these trade-related modes of development are credited with promoting the relatively spectacular growth especially in East Asian economies. More recently, in the mid-1980s, many developing economies have engaged in trade liberalisation programmes, and there appears to be some evidence that such programmes have aided growth. What remains unclear, however, is the role of labour market adjustments in transmitting growth to improving the welfare of the population, at least in the short run. Such transmission has become particularly important as the current focus of the debate seems to have shifted from just economic growth to poverty reduction in developing countries.

The neoclassical approach, *à la* Heckscher-Ohlin-Samuelson (HOS), suggests that trade based on comparative advantage is welfare-improving for all countries. However, the relative gains would accrue to the factor used more intensively in the exportable sector. Since developing countries tend to exhibit unskilled-labour abundance relative to the rest of the world, these countries would thus benefit from trade through the expanded use of their unskilled labour in the exportable sector, according to HOS.

As is well understood in the literature, however, there are several reasons why this neoclassical story must be modified, given the nature of developing countries. First, it is a 'long-run' framework; second, factor markets are presumed to be 'integrated', in that factors may move rather freely across sectors; and third, externalities and other market imperfections are assumed to be non-existent. Conditions prevailing in developing countries, however, hardly satisfy the conditions of this traditional neoclassical model. Consequently, more

* This chapter has benefited from discussions at the Nottingham Conference.

recent studies have internalised these criticisms and have proposed frameworks that take into account the realities of developing economies.

This chapter reviews both the theoretical and empirical literature on labour market adjustments in the presence of increased international trade, as in the case of trade liberalisation in developing countries. In Section 2 we begin by reviewing the implications of the neoclassical framework. This starting point is important for three reasons. First, given the heterogeneity of developing countries, the assumptions of the neoclassical model may actually approximate the conditions of some of these economies. Second, the framework sets the parameters toward which we should expect developing countries to converge in the 'long run', and thus provides a standard for interpreting the observations from developing countries. Third, and perhaps most important, such information should shed light on the shadow price associated with the various constraints prevalent in the economies of the developing world.

Section 3 reviews recent three-sector models on labour market adjustment in the presence of trade liberalisation. Both the short- and long-run results are considered. Implications for overall wages and employment are delineated in Section 4, and Section 5 pays special attention to aggregate unemployment. Section 6 considers the nature of supply response in developing countries and its importance in distinguishing between the relevance of short- versus long-run analysis. Implications of labour market adjustment for inequality, in the presence of trade, are also discussed in Section 7.

To assess the applicability of theory to actual labour markets of developing countries, the characteristics and functioning of these markets are outlined in Section 8. Section 9 concludes the chapter by discussing the realities and implications of the nature of developing countries' labour markets for trade theory.

2   The neoclassical framework and labour markets

Within the HOS framework, derived demand for labour increases in the exportable sector, in response to trade liberalisation, raising both wages and employment. In contrast, output in the importable sector contracts, resulting in a decrease in the sectoral labour demand and, hence, wages (initially) and employment. Wages subsequently rise in the importable sector, though, as labour supply decreases in this sector to accommodate expansion in the exportable sector. Thus, the wage rises in both sectors. Whether or not economy-wide employment expands, however, depends on the net effect across the two sectors.

Testable predictions from HOS are: (1) the exportable sector in trade-oriented developing countries would be more labour-intensive than the importable sector; (2) labour in the former sector would be relatively unskilled and grow faster; and (3) the relative wage of the unskilled would increase with trade liberalisation. In addition, the model suggests that trade reforms leading to a more liberalised economic regime that results in the elimination of distortions, especially in the labour market, would result in increased employment.

Several studies have attempted to test the above implications of the neoclassical model. For example, an NBER project directed by Bhagwati (1978) and Krueger (1978) dealt with, though in a rather general way, the question of the consequences of trade reforms in ten countries. Both authors concluded that the country-specific observations were consistent with neoclassical predictions. Krueger (1978), for example, observes that employment grew more rapidly under the more liberalised external sector, characterised as Phases IV and V regimes.

Another NBER study directed by Krueger (1981) attempted to assess the long-run relationship between trade orientation and employment creation, based on the experiences of ten developing countries: Brazil, Chile, Colombia, Indonesia, Ivory Coast, Korea, Pakistan, Thailand, Tunisia and Uruguay. This study appears to have uncovered evidence in favour of the predictions of the neoclassical HOS framework. It observes, for example, that in most countries, exportable industries tended to be more labour-intensive than the import-competing industries, and that the use of unskilled labour was relatively intensive in the export sector. The study further finds that employment tended to grow faster in outward-oriented economies, while employment creation was aided by the removal of both factor market distortions and trade restrictions in most of the developing countries.

Another World Bank study directed by Balassa (1982) also attempted to assess the long-term implications of trade liberalisation. Based on the analysis of eleven countries (Argentina, Brazil, Chile, Colombia, India, Israel, Korea, Mexico, Singapore, Taiwan and Yugoslavia), Balassa observes that tariff reduction will tend to benefit employment, since both exportable primary and manufacturing production activities are relatively labour-intensive.

3 Recent theories and the labour market

The traditional HOS theory is essentially long-run in nature, in that market rigidities and friction are assumed to be non-existent. Hence, the theory does not apply to the bulk of developing countries whose conditions differ substantially from what is theoretically posited. For example, these economies are characterised by very high unemployment, whether open or disguised, which cannot exist in the traditional neoclassical framework of flexible wages. In addition, there are several enduring sectors in developing countries, of which the exportable and importable sectors constitute only a part. To remedy some of these incongruities, several sector-specific models have been introduced into the literature, for example Mussa (1978), Neary (1978). Typically, these models allow for sector-specific fixed capital in the short run, mobility of labour across sectors, and inelastic aggregate labour supply.

More recently, Edwards (1988) has examined labour market adjustments, in both the long and short runs, for a small open economy with two factors

Table 8.1   Sectoral (employment, wage) changes after trade liberalisation

	No wage rigidities		Wage rigidities	
	Short run	**Long run**	**Short-run**	**Long-run**
Exportables	$(+, -)$	$(+, +)$	$(+, +)$	$(+, ?)$
Importables	$(-, -)$	$(-, +)$	$(-, +)$	$(-, +)$
Non-tradables	$(?, -)$	$(?, +)$	$(?, -)$	$(+, ?)$

Notes: The table is adapted from Edwards (1988); see also Milner and Wright (1998). 'Wage rigidities' refers to the case of minimum wages. The first and second coordinates in $(\cdot, \cdot)$ denote changes in employment and wages, with '+', '−' and '?' indicating positive, negative and indeterminate directions, respectively. For example, $(+, -)$ shows positive and negative directions of change for employment and wages, respectively. The wage is defined as the nominal wage relative to the price of non-tradables.

(labour L; capital K), and three goods (exportables X; importables M; non-tradables N). It is assumed that there is incomplete specialization, that factor supplies are fixed, and that production functions have the usual properties: positive but diminishing marginal products. The following rank-ordered relative factor intensities are also assumed: $(K/L)_M > (K/L)_N > (K/L)_X$. That is, relative to capital, the exportables sector is the most labour-intensive, followed by non-tradables, and the importables sector has the most capital-intensive production function. The modelling is conducted for labour market adjustment in response to trade liberalisation (import tariff reduction), with and without wage rigidities. The major findings are summarised in Table 8.1.

Case A: Absence of wage rigidities

Capital is assumed to be immobile across sectors in the *short run*, but labour is mobile. The following results emerge: The exportable sector experiences an expansion in employment in response to trade liberalisation, as both labour demand and supply increase. The wage rate will be lower, however, due to an increase in the supply of labour and a decreasing marginal product of labour in the light of fixed capital. Both employment and wages in the importable sector fall due to a decrease in output demand. While the wage in the non-tradable sector also decreases, the change in employment in that sector is indeterminate, the direction depending on the substitution relationship between non-tradables and tradables. For example, where importables and non-tradables are highly substitutable in consumption, a decrease in employment is likely, the reverse being the case where the relative substitutability is with the exportable.

The *long-run* impacts are similar to those predicted by the Stolper-Samuelson theorem. That is, a decrease in the tariff rate leads to a rise in the *relative* price of the exportable, an increase in both its quantity supplied and the use of its relatively abundant factor, labour, raising both employment and wages. In contrast, production in the importable sector shrinks, resulting in a decrease in the sector's employment. The wage, however, increases in response to a decrease in labour supply, as labour emigrates to the exportable sector in order to achieve inter-sectoral equilibrium. Demand for non-tradables increases in response to positive income effects from a tariff reduction and higher incomes. This raises the wage in the non-tradable sector and employment. Given the relative capital intensity of the non-tradable sector, however, capital deepening should occur, in response to the higher wage, thus reducing employment. Hence, the direction of employment in the non-tradable sector following liberalisation measure is indeterminate.

Case B: Presence of wage rigidities

It is assumed here that wage rigidity is in the form of a minimum wage in the importable sector. This assumption seems reasonable, given that in developing economies, minimum wages are usually imposed in the import-competing industry.[2] Hence the importable sector is the 'covered' sector, while the exportable and non-tradable sectors are 'uncovered'.

Both the employment and wage outcomes in the uncovered sectors in the *short run* are qualitatively identical to those under case A. That is, employment expands in the exportable sector but its direction of change is indeterminate in the non-tradable sector. Meanwhile, the wage decreases in both sectors. For the 'covered' importable sector, employment falls as in case A above. The wage rigidity in the sector ensures, however, that the real wage (in terms of non-tradables) rises.

As in case A, employment in the *long run* unambiguously rises in the exportable sector in response to an increase in the derived demand for labour. However, the direction of change of the wage rate is ambiguous. On the one hand, capital movement to the exportable sector should raise the wage. On the other hand, an increase in the sector's labour supply in response to additional unemployment created by a binding minimum wage in the importable sector should decrease the wage, so that the net change is indeterminate. Qualitatively, the employment and wage impacts in the importable sector are identical to case A. That is, employment falls, and the real wage increases, given the wage rigidities. Indeed, the tendency for capital to shift away from the importable sector in the long run, in the light of lower relative returns to capital, would exacerbate the unemployment problem in this sector. In the case of the non-tradable sector, employment expands in the long run as capital relocates from the importable sector. The increase in labour demand in the exportable sector means that the direction of the wage change in the sector becomes indeterminate, as it recovers from its fall in the short run resulting from labour supply increases.

4   Implications for overall wages and employment

In the absence of wage rigidities, *wages* (in terms of non-tradables) fall in all sectors in the short run. Thus, assuming that the non-tradable sector consists of the bulk of the consumption basket in a developing country,[3] consumers will generally experience a lower cost of living in the short run. The reverse is the case in the long run, however. The outcome with wage rigidities in the short run is similar, except that wages would be higher in the importable sector during the post-liberalisation period. However, if the subset of employed workers earning the mandated wage is small, as is probable in the bulk of developing countries, then it is quite likely that most of the population would experience a lower cost of living when compared to the pre-liberalisation period. In the long run, wages would be higher under trade liberalisation in all sectors in the absence of wage rigidities, consistent with HOS. However, this result need not hold, even in the long run, where there are wage rigidities, for the direction of the wage change becomes indeterminate in the non-covered exportable and non-tradable sectors.

The direction of change in overall *employment*, whether in the short or long run, apparently depends on the ability of workers to shift from the shrinking importable sector to the exportable and non-tradable sectors. With homogeneous labour, displaced workers should be easily absorbed and, consistent with HOS, overall employment would not decrease. However, the existence of labour market distortions (wage rigidities in the present model) is likely to prevent non-frictional mobility of labour across sectors, especially in the short run. Nevertheless, as the results in Table 8.1 indicate, even in the case of wage rigidities, employment need not decrease with trade liberalisation in the long run, as both the non-covered sectors (exportables and non-tradables) exhibit increases in employment at the expense of the importable sector. Thus, though unemployment might exist in the covered importable sector, overall employment could actually rise. The important point to stress here, however, is that the direction of economy-wide employment change with respect to trade liberalisation is ambiguous, especially in the short run, whether or not wage rigidities exist.

5   Emphasis on aggregate unemployment

A particularly vexing practical concern of developing countries is that trade liberalisation may lead to an increase in aggregate unemployment. In the absence of labour market restrictions, it is expected that there will be no involuntary unemployment, even in the light of decreased employment. However, there is much about the nature of developing countries to suggest that wage rigidities exist, so that there may be non-trivial adjustment costs in terms of increased unemployment. Besides, even where there are no such rigidities, adjustment may not be sufficiently rapid to prevent unemployment costs in the short run, especially when significant mobility costs exist. Unfortunately, theoretical modelling seldom deals with this very short-run scenario.[4]

Using a similar two-factor, three-good sector framework as Edwards (1988), Cox-Edwards and Edwards (1994) concentrate on the implications of structural adjustment reforms (import liberalisation) on overall unemployment in the presence of labour market distortions. Considering a sector-specific minimum wage (imposed in the importable sector), Cox-Edwards and Edwards reach similar conclusions as Edwards (1988) (see Table 8.1). That is, in the short run, employment would increase in the exportable sector, decrease in the importable sector, but be indeterminate in the non-tradable sector. In effect, aggregate unemployment could rise with liberalisation. A decrease in aggregate unemployment in the long run is still likely though. Considering an economy-wide minimum wage, Cox-Edwards and Edwards observe that, in the long run, 'starting from an initial condition of unemployment, a trade liberalisation reform will increase total employment in the economy' (1994, p. 119). In contrast, they find that overall unemployment would increase in the short run in response to trade liberalisation. They conclude that 'in the presence of labour market distortions, trade liberalisation policies usually considered to be beneficial may generate nontrivial (short-run) unemployment problems' (p. 124).

Perhaps the most ambitious study on the transitional employment effects of trade liberalisation is the World Bank project, Michaeli, Papageorgiou and Choski (1991), involving detailed analysis of data from a large number of countries. In this study, the authors distinguish between 'gross' and 'net' effects, with 'gross' akin to the sectoral changes, while 'net' refers to the aggregate change. The discussion above would imply a decrease in gross employment for the importable sector, but an increase for the exportable sector. The net employment effect then would be positive or negative as the exportable sector effect exceeded or fell short of that in the importable sector, assuming for now a neutral impact from the non-tradable sector. The results of this study were generally inconclusive. For some countries, there appeared to be increases in net unemployment after certain liberalisation periods but decreases following others. However, the authors generally attributed any increases to factors unrelated to liberalisation per se. They conclude that 'by and large, liberalisation attempts have not incurred significant transition costs by way of unemployment' (Michaeli *et al.* (1991, ch. 6, p. 80)).

There have also been several single-country studies, most of them involving Latin America. For example, Edwards and Cox-Edwards (1991) observe that the trade liberalisation in Chile generated unemployment in the order of 3.5 per cent. They attribute this to existing labour market rigidities. Corbo *et al.* (1986) report similar results for the southern cone of Latin America (see also Ramos (1986)). In addition, Rama (1994) observes a negative relationship between trade reform and employment (though no effect on wages) in Uruguayan manufacturing. Revenga (1997) finds that the reduction in tariffs during 1985–88 as part of trade liberalisation in Mexico resulted in a relatively small decrease in overall manufacturing employment, accompanied by an increase in wages.[5] The author also reports significant changes in the composition of employment across industries.

A more recent study (Milner and Wright (1998)) provides perhaps the most comprehensive test of the predictions of the Edwards-type model presented above, based on evidence for Mauritius. The study finds that employment of the exportables sector rose both in the short and long runs, but that wages fell in the short run and rose in the long run, consistent with the predictions of the model (see Table 8.1). As argued above, this phenomenon is likely attributable to the short-run effect being dominated by labour supply shifts between the importables and exportables sectors in response to liberalisation. In the longer run, however, the derived-demand effect kicks in. With respect to importables, Milner and Wright find that employment and wages increased together in both the short and long runs. The wage increase is generally consistent with the predictions of the Edwards-type model. However, the result on employment contrasts with the theoretical prediction of a fall in employment in both the short and long runs.[6] A plausible explanation is offered by the authors for this inconsistency. They argue that in an economy with an expanding labour supply (assumed fixed in the Edwards-type model), labour supply could have increased sufficiently to raise employment, despite the decrease in labour demand. In the case of Mauritius, the expanding labour supply was fuelled by increased labour force participation of women. Indeed, though not discussed by the authors, the decline in the positive wage impact of the output shock between the short and long runs (from .14 to .09; see Table 4 in Milner and Wright (1998)) is consistent with this interpretation, as the expansion of the labour force would increase the elasticity of the labour supply.

It is apparent from the Milner and Wright evidence then that, in response to trade liberalisation, net (aggregate) employment would increase in both the short and long runs, assuming an expanding labour force. These results are, therefore, consistent with the predictions of the neoclassical model based on fixed labour, *à la* HOS. As we have observed above, however, there is much evidence, especially from Latin America, that seems to be at variance with the neoclassical predictions, which might simply be attributable to the extent of wage rigidities in the Latin American economies.

6   How long are the short and long runs? The role of supply responsiveness and asymmetric response

The question of the length of the short or long run is, of course, important to policy makers in developing countries. After all, if long-run benefits are to be realised, it is important to know for how much longer the citizenry must wait, given non-trivial adjustment costs. The appropriate response to this issue depends in part on the question of product supply responsiveness. For example, a number of studies have bemoaned the relatively inelastic product supply that may have led to de-industrialisation of many developing countries following structural adjustment (e.g. Lall (1995)). The effect of trade liberalisation on the importable sector is almost immediate, as relatively inefficient firms are likely to wither quickly with increased foreign competition. In contrast, the response of the exportable sector is likely to occur with a considerable lag, as the product supply responsiveness tends to be rather small. This may occur for several reasons: poor infrastructure, imperfections in the capital market, institutional impediments such as onerous bureaucracy, and so on.

Unfortunately, an asymmetric supply response between the exportable and importable sectors is not captured in many of the existing models. Its implications for unemployment in the very short run can be profound, however. It means that unemployment would probably rise more than expected within the framework of the short-run models depicted above. Due to low product supply response, the wage elasticity of demand for labour would be low as well. Hence, if mobility costs are small, then the fall in wages may be large compared with the increase in employment. Thus wage income will tend to fall. This is likely to be the case in the very short run, at least, and to provide a major political challenge in many developing countries embarking on trade liberalisation.

7 Implications for inequality

There would, then, appear to be important implications for inequality resulting from adjustments in the labour market. This is more probable in the short rather than long run, and for sector-specific wage rigidities than for economy-wide wage rigidities or no wage rigidities. For example, under perfectly flexible wages and mobile labour, there should be no more wage inequality than prevailed prior to liberalisation. In addition, in the case of economy-wide wage rigidity, sectoral differences in wages following liberalisation should be minimal. In contrast, where sector-specific wage rigidities are present, the wage gap would increase between a shrinking covered sector (importables) and the non-covered sectors (exportables and non-tradables), in response to trade liberalisation. The inequality would be larger as the wage elasticity of demand for labour is smaller for these non-covered sectors. There appears to be a silver lining in the inequality story, however. In the long run, international trade should reduce the ability of agents such as labour unions and governments to continue to sustain rigidities. The extent to which international trade may succeed in weakening rigidities would, of course, depend on the sources of such rigidities.

By wage rigidity, we mean the existence of an above-equilibrium wage. This may result from several sources. The usual culprit is government, in the case of a mandated minimum wage, or labour unions in terms of monopoly rent-sharing arrangements. In either case, trade liberalisation should unleash competitive forces to whittle down the economic rent or compel a growth-maximising government to adopt a less binding minimum wage law.[7]

Wage rigidities could also result from efficiency wage-type behaviour. Profit-maximising conditions, in the presence of quasi-fixed costs, may imply that employers pay workers in excess of the equilibrium in order to minimise turnover costs, such as training, recruitment, hiring and firing costs. This form of wage rigidity should, in general, not be eroded by trade, except to the extent that trade succeeds in reducing quasi-fixed costs, as a result of increased competitiveness.[8]

8   Characteristics and functioning of labour markets in developing countries

To delineate appropriately which model predictions most suitably apply to which countries, this section delineates the characteristics and functioning of labour markets across developing economies. The discussion is intended to distil both commonalities and differences.

Although three classifications are usually provided in the literature, four sectors of the labour market are generally identifiable in developing countries: formal rural, informal rural, formal urban, and informal urban.[9] The *formal rural sector* is characterised in large part by medium- or large-scale commercial operations, agricultural and non-agricultural. It may entail proprietorship, partnership or corporation; however, most workers are unskilled. The agricultural sub-sector is likely to be more pervasive in Latin America than Africa generally (with East Africa a possible exception), and it usually involves exportable cash crops such as coffee, bananas, cocoa or tea.

In contrast, the *informal rural* sector consists mainly of small-scale operations involving self-employed persons and unpaid family members, most of whom are unskilled. Located in this sector are both the non-agricultural sub-sector of the proprietorship type, as well as small-scale operations producing (exportable) cash crops and non-tradable food. Labour productivity is usually quite low here.

The *formal urban sector* comprises medium and large enterprises producing both tradable and non-tradable goods, using a relatively sizeable amount of skilled as well as unskilled labour. Enterprises may either be private or state-owned. Wages and other forms of working conditions are usually subject to formal contracting and government regulations, such as fringe benefits and minimum-wage requirements, respectively. In addition, labour union activity is usually prevalent.

The *informal urban sector* is characterised by self-employed individuals and privately owned enterprises producing mainly services or other non-tradables. These include: small traders, bricklayers, carpenters, tailors, cobblers, taxi drivers and food vendors. This sector is generally unregulated,[10] wages and job security are low, and fringe benefits such as health insurance, life insurance, or pension are usually non-existent. Union activity is rare, legal minimum wages do not apply, and wages are flexible. There is also high underemployment in the sector.

Table 8.2 presents a summary of the characteristics of these sectors. The present classification expands the three-sector scheme of Mazumdar (1989). While

Table 8.2 Structure of the labour market for a developing country

Rural		Urban		Unemployed
Formal Sector	**Informal Sector**	**Formal Sector**	**Informal Sector**	
Wage labour on large plantations Non-agricultural workers in rural factories	Small-scale farming: (a) Workers in the small-scale farm sector (b) Owner, operational small-scale farm (c) Owner, including share croppers Non-agricultural workers in non-factories (a) Self-employment, full time (b) Self-employment, part time (c) Wage labour, part time (d) Landless, full-time wage labour	Public and large-scale firms Private (large enterprises)	Informal sector wage labour Self-employed workers Casual wage labour	

Source: Adapted from three-sector classification of Mazumdar (1989, p. 3). Note that the present four-sector scheme divides the rural sector into formal and informal components, unlike Mazumdar's.

the urban delineation is identical to that in Mazumdar, we subdivide Mazumdar's rural sector into its informal and formal components. The agricultural sector, for instance, is sub-classified into plantations and non-plantations labour. To the extent that the former is sufficiently regulated, it could be viewed as a 'formal rural' sector, given the classification criteria advocated by Kannappan (1985) and Mazumdar (1983), for example. Nevertheless, this sector is likely to be characterised by low wages; job security may be high, though *implicit* contracts tend to prevail. In addition, factories located in the rural setting would entail relatively formal working arrangements and other characteristics of non-agricultural formal sector employment.

Table 8.3   Distribution of the labour force in SSA (sectors with per cent share of employment in parentheses)

Industry	Services	Agriculture	Unemployed (6)
Wage industry (3)	Wage services (9)	Wage agriculture (6)	
Non-wage industry (6)	Non-wage services (15)	Non-wage agriculture (55)	

Source: World Bank (1995a).

The above sectors are of varying importance in terms of employment for different developing countries. The characteristics may also differ by region or development level. Nevertheless, the informal sector represents a sizeable share of the economies in most developing countries. For example, the share of the informal sector in non-agricultural employment was about 55 per cent in the early 1990s for Latin America, 60 per cent in the mid-1980s for India, and 64 per cent for Sub-Saharan Africa (SSA) in the early 1990s (World Bank (1995a)).

Table 8.3 reports data on the relative importance of the various sectors, classified above, in SSA provided in World Bank (1995a). It is apparent that agriculture is the dominant sector, employing over 60 per cent of the work force, followed by services at roughly 25 per cent. Industry, especially wage-paying, is rather minuscule, constituting less than 10 per cent.

The non-wage sub-sector, which approximates the informal sector, constitutes the bulk of the economy in SSA, according to Table 8.3. In agriculture, for example, it is roughly 90 per cent of the employed workforce. It is over 60 per cent in both industry and services. For the whole economy, the proportion engaged in the informal economy is roughly 80 per cent. Thus the informal sector constitutes a sizeable segment of the economy in a large number of developing countries. Its relative importance is likely to be country-specific, though. For example, there appears to be an inverse relationship between income per capita and the size of the informal sector (Turnham (1993)). However, even for upper middle-income developing countries, the informal sector still constitutes roughly 30 per cent of employment. The relative importance of the informal sector also appears to be increasing. In Latin America, for example, its share in non-agricultural employment increased from 40 per cent in 1980 to 47 per cent and 55 per cent in 1985 and 1993, respectively.

Another important characteristic of the labour market of developing countries is the share of government employment, though this phenomenon is far from uniform. As Table 8.4 indicates, the share of public sector in non-agricultural employment has been large in SSA and Middle East–North African (MENA) regions compared with OECD countries. The shares in Latin America and Asia are comparable to that in OECD, though. Similarly, Kraay and van Rijckeghem (1995) find that central government employment in developing countries increased from 23 per cent over the 1972–80 period to 28 per cent in

Table 8.4 Share of public sector
in non-agricultural employment
by region (%)

Region	%
Asia	19.8
Latin America	17.7
MENA	31.7
SSA	32.9
OECD	20.6

Source: World Bank data reported in
Berthelemy *et al.* (1998).

1981–92; the respective shares for SSA were 28 per cent and 35 per cent. Similar observations have been made by Lindauer *et al.* (1988), who find that employment expanded faster in the public than private sector, especially for SSA.

Part of this pervasiveness of the public sector in employment might be attributable to the development strategies historically adopted in many countries, where the government was the major agent of development. Thus many existing firms were nationalised after independence, while government sought and retained majority shares in new enterprises. In many cases, however, the lack of sufficient private investment meant that government has had to serve the role of 'employer of last resort'. In addition, public sector employment has historically been attractive, particularly in terms of benefits relative to those in the private sector: job security, subsidised housing, pension, enhanced social status, and opportunities for further earnings through moonlighting and economic rent-earning (Gelb *et al.* (1991)).

The recent expansion of the public sector in the 1980s may further reflect the growing attractiveness of government jobs, especially given a declining import-substituting sector in response to increasing trade-liberalisation measures in many developing countries. Meanwhile, continued subsidisation of post-secondary education in the bulk of these countries has meant that there is a pervasive and increasing excess supply of the relatively educated. This has further expanded the government's role as employer of last resort. As the employment situation has become more precarious for the relatively educated, fringe benefits associated with public sector jobs have been rendered even more attractive. Stevenson (1992), for example, argues that while the attractiveness of government jobs was primarily based on their relatively high wages in the 1970s, the 1980s have witnessed job benefits as the major attraction.

Another distinguishing characteristic of the labour markets of developing countries is the presence of large 'underemployment', a 'disguised' form of unemployment where employed individuals work less than their desired hours of work at the going wage. Such pervasiveness clearly renders the open (official) unemployment rate, which includes only individuals looking for work in the formal sector, an inadequate gauge of effective unemployment in developing countries. For example, the officially reported unemployment rate in Ghana for 1988–89 was only 1.6 per cent, compared with 24.1 per cent underemployment (World Bank (1995b)). In some developing countries, combined open and disguised unemployment can be as high as 60 per cent (Turnham (1993)). As in developed economies, but more so in developing countries, procuring accurate data on disguised as well as open unemployment is important in studying the implications of international trade for unemployment. There is a tendency for workers displaced in the formal sector to enter the informal sector, where they may remain underemployed. If such workers were to become 'discouraged' due to the diminished likelihood of obtaining employment in the formal or modern sector and hence to discontinue job search, they would no longer be considered (officially) unemployed. Similarly, if job prospects improved and increased migration from rural to urban areas, then previously underemployed individuals would now become part of open unemployment. This phenomenon of employment 'fungibility' is precisely why there is the tendency in much of the empirical literature to concentrate on analysing employment rather than the (official) unemployment rate per se. Yet, in a growing economy, employment may increase as a result of an expanding labour force, which may be unrelated to trade. Hence, labour force expansion must be properly controlled in order to accurately reflect the implications of trade.[11]

Another important aspect of the labour market in many developing countries is the lack of integration of labour markets. On average, wages in the urban formal sector have typically exceeded those in other sectors. Part of the rationale is that skill levels have been higher in this sector. Another is that the formal urban sector is segmented from the others as a result of institutional barriers: minimum wage laws, unionisation, or the payment of efficiency wages, ratified by the existence of turnover costs: search, hiring, training, and severance.

Segmentation is likely to occur between the informal and formal sectors, especially the formal urban where government regulation and union rules hold sway. Such segmentation may help to explain why labour costs are considered to be quite high in many developing countries, especially in SSA, while at the same time there is plenty of unemployment, including underemployment, and most workers earn extremely low wages, even among relatively educated individuals. To the extent that segmentation is pervasive, increased trade may further exacerbate wage inequality problems in developing countries by increasing labour supply in the other sectors more than would have otherwise been the case. With more flexible wages in the informal sector, informal-sector earnings could be significantly eroded. As has been observed above, this outcome would pertain especially if the formal sector overlapped significantly with the importables sector.

Other sources of segmentation include mobility costs across regions due to transportation and other economic costs, and cultural and ethno-linguistic or religious differences might raise mobility costs,[12] which are likely to also pose frictional problems for both intra- and inter-sectoral adjustments.

The degree of market segmentation varies substantially across developing countries. Union activity, for instance, seems generally more effective in Latin America than in other regions (Agenor (1996, p. 284)). But even in other regions, such as SSA, the union premium is not insignificant. Schultz and Mwabu (1997), for example, estimate a union wage premium of 19 per cent for South Africa. Unfortunately, such estimates seldom include fringe benefits that can be substantial in large unionised firms, especially in the importables sector.[13]

9 Conclusion

Given the characteristics and functioning of developing countries' labour markets depicted above: what does existing trade theory imply for labour market adjustment in these economies? what are the implications of the realities for possible modifications in trade theory?

As is clear from the above account, despite a great deal of cross-country variation, the labour markets for developing countries typically consist of several sectors, are dominated by the informal sector, are likely to be segmented, and are subject to low derived labour demand elasticities. Trade liberalisation may indeed achieve at least the short-run results predicted within the framework of the Edwards-type capital-specificity models. Unfortunately, these short-run results are not very encouraging, for overall wages are likely to fall, while increases in aggregate employment need not occur.

Meanwhile, the inability to correctly measure effective unemployment (open plus disguised unemployment) suggests that an accurate empirical verification of the theory is dubious. Irrespective of the measurement problems associated with unemployment, however, the structure of the labour market depicted above has special implications for trade theory. For example, it suggests that a two-sector representation, that does not take account of the informal labour market, is problematic.[14] More recent models, however, have attempted to remedy this shortcoming (e.g. Komiya (1967), Edwards (1988), Cox-Edwards and Edwards (1994)).

It is also important to note that the direct implications of the three-sector framework with importables, exportables and non-tradables do not necessarily overlap sufficiently with the labour markets of developing countries. For example, the formal and informal (urban and rural) sectors consist of both tradables and non-tradables. To determine the implications of trade for the general economy, therefore, it is important to map these 'theoretical' (importables, exportables and non-tradables) sectors into the 'actual' (informal and formal) sectors depicted above. For example, the formal urban sector contains significant shares of both tradables and non-tradables. The dominant informal sector deserves special attention. The rural informal sector comprises mainly exportables and non-tradables.[15] Thus, in the short run, trade liberalisation is likely to benefit this sector in employment,[16] but not in wages.[17] Similarly, the urban informal sector primarily entails non-tradables. Hence, while wages are predicted to fall (in the short run), the direction of employment change is indeterminate. Any expected benefit for workers in this sector in terms of earnings, therefore, seems small. An important implication is also that the majority of the population, who are likely to be located in the informal sector, face the real possibility of a diminution in their standard of living in the short run.

The role of the public sector also requires special attention. Governments can influence the level of unemployment and inequality via their ability to set wages in the public sector. In addition, they should be able to affect the degree of imperfection in the economy that bears on labour market functioning and outcomes. Governments can also influence the horizon (short run versus long run). In effect, the government can play at least an important intervening role in the trade–labour market relationship. Unfortunately, this role is not well understood in the trade literature.

Furthermore, there is a need to incorporate asymmetries in responsiveness between labour demand decreases in the importable sector and increases in the exportable sector, into trade theory. This 'very short-run' horizon is likely to be characteristic of many developing countries. Indeed, political realities may be such that the short-run equilibrium may not even be politically feasible, unless the likely negative consequences associated with the very short run can be sufficiently mitigated.

Finally, there is need for more definitive empirical analyses of this important subject on the implications of trade for labour market adjustment. Such analyses would entail detailed data at the country level, but also a cross-country comparative analysis that would allow for better standardisation and generalisation.

Notes

1　See Bhagwati (1978) and Krueger (1978) for summaries of arguments in favour of EP strategies. While these two studies concentrate on country-specific data, a number of cross-country studies have also tended to support the EP thesis (Balassa (1985, 1978), Ram (1985), Feder (1982), Tyler (1981), Michaeli (1977), Maizels (1968), Emery (1967)). Edwards (1993) provides a recent summary of the literature on the role of openness and trade liberalisation in developing countries' growth. For African economies, in particular, see for instance Sachs and Warner (1997), Ghura (1995), Lussier (1993), and Fosu (1990).

2　Edwards (1988) also considers the case of an economy-wide minimum wage. The implication of this assumption for predictions of the model are discussed below.

3　The diversity of developing countries suggests that this assumption is not universal. For example, in the relatively high-income countries, the consumer basket is likely to comprise a large component of importables. Even in low-income countries, exportables may not constitute an insignificant share of the consumer basket, such as the case of tea in India. Nevertheless, most developing countries tend to rely rather heavily on staples, that are generally non-tradable.

4   For an example of a study based on imperfect mobility, see Agenor and Aizenman (1996). In their model, the authors assume a two-sector (exports and non-traded) small open economy, with imperfect mobility of labour across sectors; capital is fixed by sector. An above-equilibrium wage is paid in the exports sector in order to reduce turnover costs. The quit rate depends critically on the wage differential between sectors (Harris-Todaro assumption). The model predicts that the unemployment rate would decrease or increase, in response to trade liberalisation (reduction in tariffs), depending on the wage elasticity of the export relative to the non-traded goods sector, falling (increasing) as the elasticity is less (greater) than unity.

5   During this 1985–88 period, which constituted a relatively early part of the liberalisation process, the reduction in tariffs was about 10 percentage points, compared with a 2–3 percentage-point decrease in employment.

6   These results seem at variance with those recently reported by Greenaway *et al.* (1999) for the relatively developed UK economy. The authors find that increases in trade volumes, both in terms of imports and exports, result in reductions in employment via decreases in the levels of derived labour demand. They attribute these results to decreases in x-inefficiency caused by greater trade intensities.

7   'Minimum wage' here is being applied generally; it may entail other government mandates involving labour, including mandated fringe benefits, and even working conditions.

8   For example, Devarajan and Rodrik (1991) observe from Cameroon data that, under imperfect competition, liberalisation would lead to an expansion of the manufacturing (modern) sector, due to increased competition.

9   The three sectors generally identified in the literature are: the rural, urban formal, and urban informal (e.g. Mazumdar (1983, 1989), Rosenzweig (1988)). However, in some countries the formal rural sector may not be insignificant. In Kenya, for instance, formal sector wage earners are about equally divided between rural and urban areas (Riveros (1989)). Hence, we adopt here a finer classification to encompass this stylised fact, despite the traditional three-sector classification. Fields (1990) also provides a further distinction within the informal sector: 'easy-entry' and 'upper-tier', with the latter providing wages that are comparable to those in the lower rank of the formal sector. These relatively high wages are preserved by certain constraints, such as financial capital requirements.

10 For the use of regulation as the major basis for formal–informal sector classification see, in particular, Mazumdar (1983) and Kannappan (1985).

11 It is interesting to note from Milner and Wright's (1998) empirical evidence on Mauritius, for instance, that employment increased for the importable sector in the short run, contrary to the prediction of trade theory, a finding that the authors attribute to an expanding labour force. Note, however, that had the unemployment rate been used instead, the above contradiction might not have occurred, depending on if the increase in employment was proportional to the labour force expansion.

12 Recent religious-based incidents of violence in Indonesia and Nigeria, among many other countries, provide a vivid example of the perils that might await those who venture to live and work in communities that are relatively alien to them. Even in the US, where labour mobility is rather rapid, there is still evidence of 'social economy' that may result in regional idiosyncratic differences (Fosu (2000)); see also Ward and Dale (1992)).

13 The union fringe benefit effect has been found to be significant in developed countries such as the US (Freeman (1981)). For an exposition on the union impact on fringe benefits see, for example, Fosu (1993).

14 The early trade theory of the HOS type, as indicated above, assumes only exportable and importable sectors, though Komiya (1967) presents a three-good, two-factor model that captures the realism of an additional non-tradable sector. A more recent two-sector theory of the HOS type is applied to a small country with unemployment by Choi and Beladi (1998), for example, who observe that trade is likely to cause the price of the importable to fall below the autarky equivalent price, resulting in reductions in employment and production in the importable sector. For more recent models that simulate the labour market conditions of developing countries but use two-sector (exportable and non-tradable) modelling see, for instance, Agenor and Aizenman (1996).

15 The exportable sector is likely to consist primarily of small-scale export producers, such as cocoa farmers in West Africa and tea and coffee producers in East Africa.

16 Note that the direction of employment change for the non-tradable sub-sector is predicted to be indeterminate (see Table 8.1).

17 For the large majority of developing countries, the short-run phenomenon may be relatively typical for two reasons. First, capital mobility across sectors is likely to take a long time; second, the experience of policy reversals in many developing countries in the past is likely to generate expectations that are short run in nature.

References

Agenor, Pierre-Richard (1996) 'The Labour Market and Economic Adjustment', *IMF Staff Papers*, vol. 43(2), pp. 261–335.

Agenor, Pierre-Richard and Joshua Aizenman (1996) 'Trade Liberalization and Unemployment', *Journal of International Trade and Economic Development*, vol. 5(3), pp. 265–86.

Balassa, Bela (1978) 'Exports and Economic Growth: Further Evidence', *Journal of Development Economics*, vol. 5, pp. 181–9.

Balassa, Bela (1982) *Development Strategies in Semi-industrial Economies* (New York and London: Oxford University Press).

Balassa, Bela (1985) 'Exports, Policy Choices, and Economic Growth in Developing Countries after the 1973 Oil Shock', *Journal of Development Economics*, vol. 18, pp. 23–35.

Berthelemy, Jean-Claude, P.A. Pissarides and A. Varoudakis (1998) 'Human Capital in Economic Development', paper presented at the Seminar on Economic Growth and Its Determinants, The Hague, Netherlands (March 1998).

Bhagwati, Jagdish (1978) *Foreign Trade Regimes and Economic Development: Anatomy and Consequences of Exchange Control Regimes* (Cambridge, MA: Ballinger Publishing Co. for NBER).

Choi, Kwan E. and Hamid Beladi (1998) 'Welfare Reducing Trade and Optimal Trade Policy', *Japan and the World Economy*, vol. 10(2), pp. 187–98.

Corbo, Vittorio, Jaime de Melo and James Tybout (1986) 'What Went Wrong in the Recent Reforms in the Southern Cone', *Economic Development and Cultural Change*, vol. 34(3), pp. 607–40.

Cox-Edwards, Alejandra and Sebastian Edwards (1994) 'Labour Market Distortions and Structural Adjustment in Developing Countries', in Ravi Kanbur, Susan Horton and Dipak Mazumdar (eds), *Labour Markets in An Era of Adjustment* (Washington, DC: The World Bank), pp. 105–46.

Devarajan, Shantayanan and Dani Rodrik (1991) 'Pro-Competitive Effects of Trade Reform: Results from a CGE Model of Cameroon', *European Economic Review*, vol. 35, pp. 1157–84.

Edwards, Sebastian (1988) 'Terms of Trade, Tariffs, and Labour Market Adjustment in Developing Countries', *World Bank Economic Review*, vol. 2(2), pp. 165–85.

Edwards, Sebastian (1993) 'Openness, Trade Liberalization, and Growth in Developing Countries', *Journal of Economic Literature*, vol. 31, pp. 1,358–93.

Edwards, Sebastian and Alejandra Cox-Edwards (1991) (eds) *Monetarism and Liberalization: The Chilean Experiment Reviewed* (Chicago: University of Chicago Press).

Emery, Robert F. (1967) 'The Relation of Exports and Economic Growth', *Kyklos*, vol. 20(2), pp. 470–86.

Feder, Gershon (1982) 'On Exports and Economic Growth', *Journal of Development Economics*, vol. 12, pp. 59–73.

Fields, Gary S. (1990) 'Labour Market Modelling and the Urban Informal Sector: Theory and Evidence', in David Turnham, Bernard Salome and Antoine Schwarz (eds), *The Informal Sector Revisited* (Paris: Development Centre of the Organization for Economic Cooperation and Development).

Fosu, Augustin K. (1990) 'Exports and Economic Growth: The African Case', *World Development*, vol. 18(6), pp. 831–5.

Fosu, Augustin K. (1993) 'Nonwage Benefits as a Limited-Dependent Variable: Implications for the Impact of Unions', *Journal of Labour Research*, vol. 14(1), pp. 29–43.

Fosu, Augustin K. (2000) 'Labour Force Participation of Married Women: Do Regions Matter?' *American Economist*, vol. 44(1), pp. 70–80.

Freeman, Richard B. (1981) 'The Effect of Unionism on Fringe Benefits', *Industrial and Labour Relations Review*, vol. 34(4), pp. 489–509.

Gelb, Alan, J.B. Knight and Richard Sabot (1991) 'Public Sector Employment, Rent Seeking and Economic Growth', *Economic Journal*, vol. 101, pp. 1186–99.

Ghura, Dheneswar (1995) 'Macro Policies, External Forces, and Economic Growth in Sub-Saharan Africa', *Economic Development and Cultural Change*, vol. 43(4), pp. 759–78.

Greenaway, David, Robert C. Hine and Peter Wright (1999) 'An Empirical Assessment of the Impact of Trade on Employment in the United Kingdom', *European Journal of Political Economy*, vol. 15, pp. 485–500.

Kannappan, Subbiah (1985) 'Urban Employment and the Labour Market in Developing Nations', *Economic Development and Cultural Change*, vol. 33, pp. 699–730.

Komiya, Ryutaro (1967) 'Nontraded Goods and the Pure Theory of International Trade', *International Economic Review*, vol. 8, pp. 132–51.

Kraay, Aart and Caroline van Rijckeghem (1995) 'Employment and Wages in the Public Sector – A Cross-Country Study', *IMF Working Paper* 95–70 (Washington, DC: International Monetary Fund).

Krueger, Anne O. (1978) *Foreign Trade Regimes and Economic Development: Trade Liberalization Attempts and Consequences* (Cambridge, MA: Ballinger Publishing Co. for NBER).

Krueger, Anne O. (1981) *Trade and Employment in Developing Countries* (Chicago: University of Chicago Press).

Lall, Sanjay (1995) 'Structural Adjustment and African Industries', *World Development*, vol. 23(12), pp. 2019–31.

Lindauer, David, Oeyastra Meesook and Parita Suebsaeng (1988) 'Government Wage Policy in Africa: Some Findings and Policy Issues', *World Bank Research Observer*, vol. 3, pp. 1–25.

Lussier, Martine (1993) 'Impacts of Exports on Economic Performance: A Comparative Study', *Journal of African Economies*, vol. 2, pp. 106–27.

Maizels, Alfred (1968) *Exports and Economic Growth in Developing Countries* (London: Cambridge University Press).

Mazumdar, Dipak (1983) 'Segmented Labour Markets in LDCs', *American Economic Review*, vol. 73, pp. 254–9.

Mazumdar, Dipak (1989) 'Microeconomic Issues of Labour Markets', Economic Development Institute Seminar Paper no. 40, The World Bank.

Michaeli, Michael (1977) 'Exports and Growth: An Empirical Investigation', *Journal of Development Economics*, vol. 4, pp. 49–53.

Michaeli, Michael, Demetris Papageorgiou and Armeane Choski (1991) *Liberalizing Foreign Trade: Lessons of Experience in the Developing World*, vol. 7 (Oxford and Cambridge, MA: Basil Blackwell).

Milner, Chris and Peter Wright (1998) 'Modelling Labour Market Adjustment to Trade Liberalization in an Industrializing Economy', *Economic Journal*, vol. 108, pp. 508–28.

Mussa, Michael L. (1978) 'Dynamic Adjustment in the Heckscher-Ohlin-Samuelson Model', *Journal of Political Economy*, vol. 86(5), pp. 775–91.

Neary, P. (1978) 'Short-Run Capital Specificity and the Pure Theory of International Trade', *Economic Journal*, vol. 88, pp. 448–510.

Ram, Rati (1985) 'Exports and Economic Growth: Some Additional Evidence', *Economic Development and Cultural Change*, vol. 33(2), pp. 415–25.

Rama, Martin (1994) 'The Labour Market and Trade Reform in Manufacturing', in Michael Connolly and Jaime de Melo (eds), *The Effects of Protectionism on a Small Country: The Case of Uruguay* (Washington, DC: World Bank Regional and Sectoral Studies), pp. 108–23.

Ramos, Joseph (1986) *Neoconservative Economics in the Southern Cone of Latin America* (Baltimore: Johns Hopkins University Press).

Revenga, Ana (1997) 'Employment and Wage Effects of Trade Liberalization: The Case of Mexican Manufacturing', *Journal of Labour Economics*, vol. 13(3, Part 2), pp. S20–43.

Riveros, Luis A. (1989) 'International Differences in Wage and Nonwage Labour Costs', Policy, Planning, and Research Working Paper no. 188 (Washington, DC: The World Bank, Country Economics Department).

Rosenzweig, Mark (1988) 'Labour Markets in Low-Income Countries', in Hollis Chenery and T.N. Srinivasan (eds), *Handbook of Development Economics*, vol. 1 (Amsterdam: North-Holland), chapter 15.

Sachs, Jeffrey and Andrew Warner (1997) 'Sources of Slow Growth in African Economies', *Journal of African Economies*, vol. 6(3), pp. 335–76.

Schultz, T. Paul and Germano Mwabu (1997) 'Labour Unions and the Distribution of Wages and Employment in South Africa', Discussion Paper No. 776, Economic Growth Center, Yale University.

Stevenson, Gail (1992) 'How Public Sector Pay and Employment Affect Labour Markets: Research Issues', Policy Research Working Paper no. 944 (Washington, DC: The World Bank).

Turnham, David (1993) *Employment and Development: A New Review of Evidence* (Paris: Development Centre of the Organization for Economic Cooperation and Development).

Tyler, William G. (1981) 'Growth and Export Expansion in Developing Countries', *Journal of Development Economics*, vol. 4, pp. 121–30.

Ward, Clare and Angela Dale (1992) 'Geographical Variation in Female Labour Force Participation: An Application of Multilevel Modelling', *Regional Studies*, vol. 26(3), pp. 243–55.

World Bank (1995a) *Labour and the Growth Crisis in SSA: Regional Perspectives on World Development Report, 1995* (Washington, DC: The World Bank).

World Bank (1995b) 'Workers in an Integrating World', *World Development Report* (Washington: The World Bank).

9
Internationalisation of Japanese Manufacturing Firms and the Relative Demand for Skilled Labour*

Keith Head and John Ries
University of British Columbia, Canada

1 Introduction

Thirty years ago Japanese firms concentrated almost all of their production in Japan. Since then, firms such as Sony and Toyota have joined the list of the world's best-known multinational enterprises. Data on 1,052 Japanese manufacturing firms show that the overseas worker share of total employment rose from 5 per cent in 1970 to 30 per cent in 1989. Over the corresponding period, the nonproduction worker share of the wage bill for the median firm increased from 21 to 31 per cent. These figures suggest that the international activities of Japanese multinational enterprises (MNEs) shifted demand for labour in Japan towards nonproduction workers (including managers, product designers, and marketers) and away from less-skilled production workers. If true, one possible consequence would be increased wage inequality in Japan.

This chapter outlines different strategies of multinational enterprises and models the effect each strategy has on demand for production and non-production workers at home. Using firm-level data on Japanese manufacturing companies, we measure the effects that the scale of operations and the share of activity conducted overseas have on the ratio of production to nonproduction workers in Japan. We compare the results to the predictions of each alternative strategy.

The empirical literature presents mixed evidence on the effects of MNE activity on skill intensity. Slaughter (2000) fails to find a statistically significant relationship between the nonproduction share of the wage bill and MNE activity using US industry-level data. Using a similar specification with firm-level data, Head and Ries (2000) find a positive relationship for Japanese investment in countries with low levels of per capita income and no clear relationship when the investment occurs in wealthier countries. Feenstra and Hanson (1996) investigate the effect of foreign outsourcing in US industries,

* We thank Matthew Slaughter and Michelle Haynes for their helpful comments. We thank Meng Zhang for research assistance.

defined as the substitution of imported inputs for domestic inputs, on skill intensity. They find that outsourcing can account for up to 30 per cent of the increase in the nonproduction share of the wage bill.

The next section discusses the data we employ in the study and describes the main trends in the variables in question. Section 3 describes different strategies of MNEs and models the effects that each strategy will have on skill intensity at home. Section 4 introduces the econometric specification and presents the estimated results. The conclusion summarises our findings and their relationship to alternative multinational strategies.

2 Data

We match financial statement information for 1,070 publicly-traded Japanese manufacturing companies with data on foreign investment. The financial information (sales, materials purchases, components of wage bill, assets, employment) is for the 1965–90 period. However, firms enter the sample gradually and the full set of 1,070 is only attained in 1977. The data for many firms are not available in 1990. To maintain a constant sample, we sometimes restrict the sample to the 1,052 firms observed continuously from 1970 to 1989.

Toyo Keizai's *Japanese Overseas Investment* (1992) records information on the affiliates of Japanese companies existing in 1991. We retain only the sample of

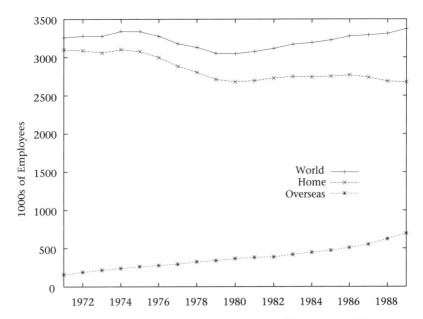

Figure 9.1 Employment at home and at overseas affiliates for 1,052 Japanese manufacturers

production affiliates (thus we exclude sales affiliates) that are at least 10 per cent owned by listed (i.e. publicly-traded) Japanese manufacturing firms. We convert the investment survey data into a time series using the dates each foreign affiliate started operations. For example, if in 1991 Mitsubishi has three foreign plants that began operations in 1985 with a total of 5,000 employees in 1991, we consider the stock of Mitsubishi foreign employment to have increased by 5,000 in 1985. This assumption makes sense if there is an efficient size for each investment and firms reach that level immediately. Head and Ries (2000) investigate alternative methods of imputing the growth in employment over time and show that the qualitative results are robust to different methods.

Figure 9.1 focuses on 1,052 firms for which we have data from 1971 to 1989 and shows employment abroad and at home for these firms. Employment abroad rises over time while employment at home falls, leaving these firms' overall employment roughly constant over this period. In 1989, foreign employment for these relatively large manufacturing firms stood at 697,000 while home employment totalled about 2.7 million. The figure suggests that these Japanese firms are substituting foreign employees for home employees.

Table 9.1 reveals that the 154 firms in the electronics industry, which employed 307,000 workers in foreign affiliates in 1989, account for over one-third of total overseas employment in our sample. The second and third biggest investors by industry were automobiles and machinery. The final column of the table shows the share of worldwide employment of the Japanese firms in

Table 9.1 World employment by industry ('000s)

	Firms	Overseas	Home	Share Overseas (%)
Electronics	154	307253	733868	30
Automobiles	53	91602	364114	20
Machinery	158	46850	210772	18
Chemicals	133	44887	214639	17
Textiles	80	41052	128827	24
Rubber	20	34786	49021	42
Precision machinery	30	26538	79487	25
Non-ferrous metals	90	24198	128059	16
Iron and steel	59	17743	216001	8
Foods	93	17726	150330	11
Glass and cement	57	16178	78986	17
Shipbuilding	10	10757	90480	11
Other manufacturing	40	9107	73792	11
Pharmaceuticals	34	6390	84367	7
Pulp and paper	31	2447	50910	5
Other transportation	18	1494	20158	7
Petroleum	10	109	15337	1

the industry accounted for by foreign affiliates. This often exceeds 20 per cent and ranges as high as 42 per cent in the case of rubber.[1]

The related empirical literature uses the nonproduction labour share of the wage bill as a measure of skill intensity. Berman, Bound and Machin (1997) present information for the US showing that nonproduction workers have higher levels of education than production workers. Head and Ries (2000) provide evidence that this is also true in Japan. Thus, the nonproduction labour share reflects skill intensity to the extent that skills increase with education levels.

Our financial information provides the selling, general and administration (SGA) payroll as well as the production payroll. Head and Ries (2000) show that the SGA share of total payroll matches closely with the nonproduction share compiled by the Japanese government statistical agencies. Thus, we will call the SGA share the nonproduction share and consider it a measure of skill intensity.

Figure 9.2 plots the nonproduction labour share of the total wage bill for each year for the median firm in our sample. This share rises from 0.21 in 1966 to 0.31 in 1989, indicating an important skill-upgrading trend.

One interpretation of the evidence presented so far is that overseas investment has shifted demand towards highly educated workers. If this hypothesis were correct, we would expect it to cause skilled-worker wages to rise and contribute to income inequality in Japan. Figure 9.3 shows that the wage

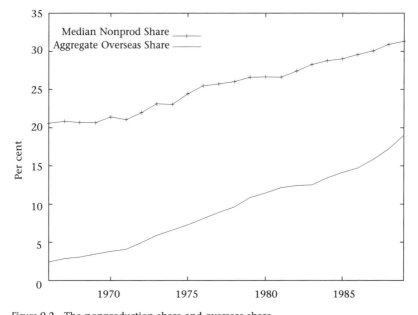

Figure 9.2　The nonproduction share and overseas share

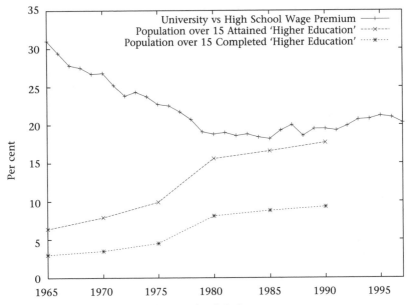

Figure 9.3 Relative wages and education levels in Japan
Sources: Wage data from Japan's *Basic Survey of Wage Structure* and education levels from Barro and Lee (1996).

premium for university versus high school educated workers actually *declined* until 1985. The premium then stabilised at around 20 per cent, considerably lower than the premium found in countries such as the US and UK.

If MNE activity did cause an increase in relative demand for educated workers, this appears to have been more than offset by a relative supply increase for these workers. Indeed, an alternative explanation for the greater use of nonproduction workers in Japan is that a fall in their relative wage induced companies to employ them more intensively. As shown with the two lower lines in Figure 9.3, education levels in Japan increased markedly during the period of our study. The portion of the population over 15 that had completed higher education more than tripled over the 1965–90 period in Japan. However, even in 1990, only 9.3 per cent had completed a higher degree in Japan, compared to 21.8 per cent in the United States.[2]

The subsequent analysis investigates how foreign investment has influenced skill intensity in Japan. We move away from aggregate patterns to a consideration of the activities of individual firms. In the next section, we model the effect of overseas operations on the use of high- and low-skilled workers at home. We show that both skill upgrading and skill downgrading are possible outcomes depending on the parameters. The subsequent empirical analysis investigates the statistical relationship between overseas activities and the ratio of skilled workers to unskilled workers at home.

3   The international task allocation model

Our purpose is to derive an estimable relationship specifying how overseas employment affects skill intensity at home from assumptions about how firms divide tasks among workers.

To provide some intuition on how production activities abroad influence those at home, consider Figure 9.4 which portrays three canonical configurations for foreign direct investment. To make things as simple as possible, we consider only two countries, home and foreign, and two production activities, 'U' for *upstream* and 'D' for *downstream*. The thin arrows represent flows of intermediate inputs from upstream to downstream units, while the thick arrows show shipments of final goods from the downstream stage to final consumers. We assume that there is a single final good and that its attributes are not affected by the location of production.

The *replication* configuration depicts a multinational enterprise that creates the mirror image of home activities in the foreign country. No exporting occurs in this case due to the assumption of a single product. The replication configuration makes sense when transportation costs or tariffs are high enough to make it uneconomical to ship intermediate or final goods across borders.

The *branching* configuration concentrates the upstream activity at home (in the tree metaphor, this is the 'trunk') and replicates the downstream activity at home and in the foreign market (the 'branches'). Upstream inputs

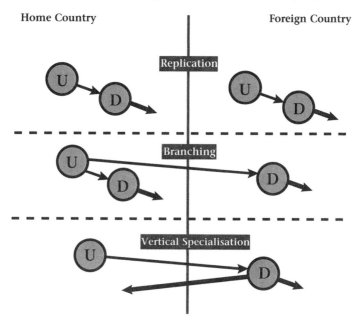

Figure 9.4   Alternative configurations for two-stage MNEs

produced at home are transmitted to both downstream plants. If 'U' represents headquarter services, this configuration is consistent with Carr, Maskus and Markusen (2001) who posit that MNEs transmit headquarter services to production plants at home and abroad. The non-rival nature of these services makes replicating them in multiple markets undesirable. Carr *et al.* refer to multinationals of this type as 'horizontal'. However, it is actually a hybrid, since there is clearly a vertical component: the flow of upstream services to the downstream production units.

The third configuration depicts *vertical specialisation*. Each activity is conducted in a single site and located in a different country. While Figure 9.4 shows the downstream activity in the foreign market, concentrating the upstream activity in the foreign market is also plausible. However, in the Carr *et al.* framework, the upstream is headquarter services and therefore defines the home of the MNE. If the upstream were overseas, it would become a foreign MNE.

Each configuration has a different implication for skill intensity in the parent country. Replication has no direct effect on home production and skill intensity. Assume that the upstream activity embodies relatively more skilled labour than the downstream activity. Branching causes foreign 'D' activities to displace 'D' at home. The fall in employment of low-skilled labour then raises skill intensity. The effect of vertical specialisation on skill intensity depends on which activity moves overseas. Relocation of downstream activities abroad raises skill intensity. However, a shift of skill-intensive upstream activities to the foreign country would lower skill intensity at home.

The preceding discussion indicates that overseas activities may exert a variety of effects on home skill intensity. To test for these effects, we develop a model that generates a nested decision structure that is compatible with the configurations discussed above. The model generalises the configurations depicted in Figure 9.4 by allowing for a continuum of tasks rather than just two ('U' and 'D'). Our model bears some resemblance to that proposed by Feenstra and Hanson (1996). Production of one unit of output requires the execution of a continuum of tasks, indexed by $z \in [0, 1]$. We assume that tasks are defined so narrowly that each task is executed by a single worker. Unit costs of task z are given by $c_i(z)$ where i is a discrete variable that identifies the type of worker who completes the task. This differs from Feenstra and Hanson's approach of requiring both skilled and unskilled workers to contribute to the production of each intermediate input. Our approach reflects the observation that production and nonproduction workers (the usual proxies for low and high skill) usually work separately, that is, the production workers at the factory and the nonproduction workers at the head office.

Examples of tasks would include riveting two pieces of metal together, placing memory chips on a computer motherboard, designing an application-specific semiconductor, cleaning apparatus after use, moving fabric from a textile factory to the location where it will be sewed into clothing, and faxing blueprints. As suggested by the final two examples, tasks may involve transportation or communication. Furthermore, some tasks require complementary inputs such as machinery or structures. They also differ in their requirements for education and experience.

Unit costs of finished goods are given by the sum of the costs for each individual task, weighted by the relative importance of the task to final costs, $\alpha(z)$:

$$c = \int_0^1 \alpha(z)c_i(z)\,dz.$$

The additive separability of this function implies that total costs can be minimised by choosing the individual of type i who is able to accomplish each task z at lowest cost. There are four types of workers who might complete any given task z:

1. H: High-skilled workers in the home country.
2. L: Low-skilled workers in the home country.
3. H^*: High-skilled workers at foreign affiliates.
4. L^*: Low-skilled workers at foreign affiliates.

Let P_i denote the proportion of tasks that can be completed at lowest cost by type-i workers. This will be equivalent to choosing the i that maximises $-c_i(z)$. Thus we imagine a discrete choice problem in which each individual task z selects the worker type who maximizes $-c_i(z)$. We represent the costs of task z as $-c_i(z) = \mu_i + \varepsilon_i(z)$. In this decomposition μ_i represent observable attributes of of workers that will be included in the empirical specification and $\varepsilon_i(z)$ is a random unobservable term capturing the nature of a task z and how suitable it is for a worker of type i. From this point we will focus on a representative task and suppress the z from our notation.

We consider different nested structures that specify distributions of the multivariate density structure governing ε_i. Each nest corresponds to a configuration described previously. We assume McFadden's generalisation of the Gumbel extreme value distribution, which is also known as the double exponential. The cumulative multivariate density function is given by $F(\varepsilon_H, \varepsilon_{H^*}, \varepsilon_L, \varepsilon_{L^*}) = \exp(-\exp(\rho I_1) - \exp(\rho I_2))$, where $I_s \equiv \ln \sum_{i \in \beta_s} \exp(\mu_i)$ is termed the 'inclusive value' for subset s. β_s is the subset of choices at the lower level of a nest (sometimes referred to as the 'twigs' connected to a particular 'branch'). Parameter ρ measures the relative strength of correlations within and between subsets. This parameter, which is restricted to be positive, takes a maximum value of 1, at which the nesting structure disappears and all choices become equally close substitutes.

Figure 9.5 represents graphically three different correlation structures for ε_i that correspond to the FDI configurations in Figure 9.4. In case 1, worker types nest according to locations. The branch subsets are therefore $\beta_1 = \{H, L\}$ and $\beta_2 = \{H^*, L^*\}$. Intuitively, the MNE first decides whether to do the task at home

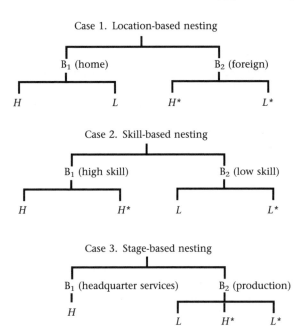

Figure 9.5 Alternative nesting structures

or abroad and then decides which skill type to employ. This structure makes sense if transport and communication costs are high and thus the firm prefers to locate activities close to the market where the output is destined. This nesting structure corresponds to the replication configuration.

Case 2 in Figure 9.5 groups workers by their skill levels rather than locations. The branch subsets are therefore $\beta_1 = \{H, H^*\}$ and $\beta_2 = \{L, L^*\}$. This structure corresponds to the case where tasks differ primarily according to their skill requirements. Thus if an activity is skill intensive, then it is likely to be low cost for workers of type H or H^*. This case reflects vertical specialisation.

The final case depicts stage-based nesting. Suppose that the upstream activity is 'headquarters' services and that high-skilled home workers (type H) are the only ones suitable for generating and disseminating these knowledge-based services. The implicit reason could be that such activities involve large indivisibilities and are non-rival. Thus it becomes wasteful to replicate headquarter activities. The first level of the nest structure reflects whether a randomly selected task is part of headquarter services. If so, it is produced by high-skilled workers at home. Otherwise, it is a production task and may be completed by low-skilled home workers or either type of foreign worker. This structure is closely related to the 'knowledge-capital' model of the MNE that has been advanced by Carr, Maskus and Markusen (2001) and corresponds to the branching configuration.

Given these alternative nested structures, we can derive expressions for the relative probability of choosing either high-skilled or low-skilled home workers for a randomly selected task, P_H/P_L. This ratio is an appealing measure of skill intensity of home production and gives the *odds* that a randomly selected task can be executed at lowest cost by a high-skilled domestic worker. To analyse these probabilities, we start by determining the probability of each type *within* a nest, that is the conditional probability. Then we multiply by the probability of the nest itself. The conditional probability of choice i in subset s is simply $\exp(\mu_i - I_s)$. The probability of choosing nest s is $\exp(\rho I_s - \langle I \rangle)$, where $\langle I \rangle \equiv \ln[\exp(\rho I_1) + \exp(\rho I_2)]$. Armed with these formulae, we can now determine the odds ratios for each nesting structure.

Consider first the case of location-based nesting.

$$\frac{P_H}{P_L} = \frac{\Pr(H \mid \beta_1)\Pr(\beta_1)}{\Pr(L \mid \beta_1)\Pr(\beta_1)} = \exp(\mu_H - \mu_L). \tag{1}$$

This result illustrates a key aspect of nested logit decision structures. The relative odds of choice within a nest is independent of the attributes of choices in other nests. Intuitively, if $\mu_H{}^*$ or $\mu_L{}^*$ were to increase, then the probability of choosing both types of domestic factors (H and L^*) would decline but in a proportional way, leaving the odds unaffected. This independence is *not* a feature of case 2, skill-based nesting. This is because L moves out of branch 1 and P_H/P_L is now an odds ratio taken across nests.

$$\frac{P_H}{P_L} = \frac{\Pr(H \mid \beta_1)\Pr(\beta_1)}{\Pr(L \mid \beta_2)\Pr(\beta_2)} = \exp(\mu_H - \mu_L + (1 - \rho)(I_2 - I_1)). \tag{2}$$

Note that this odds formulation reverts to the one obtained in case 1 as ρ approaches unity. The reason is that $\rho = 1$ corresponds to a non-nested logit structure in which odds ratios are all independent of each other. However, for $0 < \rho < 1$, we now have an odds specification that depends on the attributes of foreign workers. In particular, a positive shock to the productivity of foreign low-skilled workers, that is an increase in $\mu_L{}^*$, will raise the inclusive value of the low-skill subset (β_2), raising $I_2 - I_1$ and therefore also increasing P_H/P_L. The intuition is simple: low-skilled foreign workers are close substitutes for low-skilled home workers. Thus when L^* workers become more efficient at executing tasks, they will mainly 'steal' tasks from the L workers. Conversely, improving the productivity of foreign high-skilled workers lowers P_H/P_L.

Finally, consider the nesting structure based on stages of production. This case maintains H in subset 1 and L in subset 2. Thus we can use the same expression, with the modification that now $\Pr(H \mid \beta_1) = 1$. The resulting odds ratio is given by

$$\frac{P_H}{P_L} = \exp(\rho\mu_H - \mu_L + (1 - \rho)I_2). \tag{3}$$

As before $\rho = 1$ reverts to the odds formula of case 1. However, there is an important difference between cases 2 and 3 for intermediate values of ρ:

increases in *either* μ_H* or μ_L* will result in rises in P_H/P_L. Intuitively, foreign workers are substitutes first and foremost for domestic production workers and have relatively small impacts on domestic headquarter workers.

4 Empirical implementation

The dependent variable we will use in the regressions is the log of the ratio of nonproduction worker pay (selling, general and administration) to production pay. These data are available for our sample of 1,070 manufacturing firms. As noted earlier, following the literature, we consider nonproduction workers to be high skilled and production workers low skilled and denote their pay as $w_H E_H$ and $w_L E_L$. We assume that there is a very large number of tasks, $E_H/E_L = P_H/P_L$. Therefore, our dependent variable can be expressed as

$$\ln\left(\frac{w_H E_H}{w_L E_L}\right) = \ln(P_H/P_L) + \ln(w_H/w_L).$$

Substituting equations (1), (2), and (3) in for the first term yields three specifications, each corresponding to one nest structure:

$$\ln\left(\frac{w_H E_H}{w_L E_L}\right) = \mu_H - \mu_L + \ln(w_H/w_L) \tag{4}$$

$$\ln\left(\frac{w_H E_H}{w_L E_L}\right) = \mu_H - \mu_L + (1 - \rho)(I_2 - I_1) + \ln(w_H/w_L) \tag{5}$$

$$\ln\left(\frac{w_H E_H}{w_L E_L}\right) = \rho\mu_H - \mu_L + (1 - \rho)I_2 + \ln(w_H/w_L). \tag{6}$$

We represent the determinants of costs as

$$\mu_i = \alpha_i + \gamma_i \ln k_i + \eta_i \ln q - \theta_i \ln w_i.$$

The accounting data do not apportion the capital stock (structures, machinery, equipment and vehicles) between SGA and production activity. As a result we assume that $k_H = k_L = k \equiv K/(E_L + E_H)$, where K is the firm's stock of depreciable assets. That is, each domestic worker has an equal share of the firm's domestic capital. Using this specification to substitute for μ_H and μ_L in equations (4), (5) and (6) yields

$$\ln\left(\frac{w_H E_H}{w_L E_L}\right) = a_1 + b_1 \ln k + c_1 \ln q + d_1 \ln w_L - e_1 \ln w_H \tag{7}$$

$$\ln\left(\frac{w_H E_H}{w_L E_L}\right) = a_2 + b_2 \ln k + c_2 \ln q + d_2 \ln w_L - e_2 \ln w_H + (1 - \rho)(I_2 - I_1) \tag{8}$$

$$\ln\left(\frac{w_H E_H}{w_L E_L}\right) = a_3 + b_3 \ln k + c_3 \ln q + d_3 \ln w_L - e_3 \ln w_H + (1 - \rho)I_2 \tag{9}$$

where the estimated parameters relate to structural parameters as follows:

$$a_1 = a_2 = \alpha_H - \alpha_L \quad \text{and} \quad a_3 = \rho\alpha_H - \alpha_L,$$
$$b_1 = b_2 = \psi_H - \psi_L \quad \text{and} \quad b_3 = \rho\psi_H - \psi_L,$$
$$c_1 = c_2 = \eta_H - \eta_L \quad \text{and} \quad c_3 = \rho\eta_H - \eta_L,$$
$$d_1 = d_2 = \theta_L - 1 \quad \text{and} \quad d_3 = \theta_L - 1,$$
$$e_1 = e_2 = \theta_H - 1 \quad \text{and} \quad e_3 = \rho\theta_H - 1.$$

We capture the first term (a) with a firm-specific constant (fixed effect). We measure k as depreciable assets per employee. The sign of the coefficient on capital depends on whether the firm's stock of capital has a greater productivity-enhancing effect on average on its high- or low-skilled workers. The US industry-level literature suggests that we should expect great capital intensity to increase relative demand for skill, thus leading to a positive coefficient. However, it is theoretically possible for capital equipment to have a greater effect on lower-skilled workers.

We do not have any reliable data on worldwide production. As a result, we use the firms' worldwide employment as a proxy for q. Finally we use year-specific dummy variables to capture movements in Japanese factor prices (w_H and w_L) common to all firms in the manufacturing sector.

We have now specified $a_h + b_h \ln k + c_h \ln q + d_h \ln w_L - e_h \ln w_H$ for each nesting structure h, but have yet to account for the terms $(1 - \rho)(I_2 - I_1)$ and $(1 - \rho)I_2$. Recall that I_1 and I_2 are inclusive values that reflect costs of using workers represented in the subset. Thus, these terms include the costs of foreign workers. Our empirical strategy will be to introduce proxies for μ_H^* and μ_L^*, which are the sources of shifts in I_2 and I_1 that are orthogonal to μ_H and μ_L. Note that the 'foreign' country in practice consists of many countries with vastly different factor abundances. We will use changes in the share of a firm's employees in low-income countries (LICs) as a measure of shocks to μ_L^* and the share of a firm's employees in high-income countries (HICs) as a measure of shocks to μ_H^*.[3] We add these variables to the specification to generate the following equation to be estimated:

$$\ln\left(\frac{w_H E_H}{w_L E_L}\right) = a = b\ln k_{it} + c\ln q_{it} + D_t + f HIC_{it} + g LIC_{it} \tag{10}$$

where the subscripts i and t denote firm and year.

The specification provides us with a simple way to discriminate across the three nesting structures and the corresponding MNE configurations. Under replication (location-based nesting), domestic skill intensity (P_H/P_L) should not be affected by shares of employees in HICs or LICs. Under vertical specialisation (skill-based nesting), increases in the LIC share should be positively associated with skill intensity at home while changes in the HIC share should have the opposite effect. Finally, under branching (stage-based nesting) both HIC and LIC shares should have positive partial correlations with skill intensity.

5 Results

Table 9.2 displays the results for our sample 1,070 firms over 25 years. All specifications include firm fixed effects; thus the estimates are based on time-series variation in the data. In the first column, we estimate equation (10) without including the variables measuring overseas employment. There is no significant relationship between capital intensity and skill intensity. However, scale as measured by the number of worldwide employees exerts a strong negative effect on skill intensity. This result is consistent with the Carr, Maskus and Markusen (2001) hypothesis that skill-intensive headquarter services are partially non-rival. Thus, high-skilled workers need not be increased as much as production workers when firms expand output. This leads to a negative scale effect. The estimate, however, is at odds with those from US industry-level studies – Berman, Bound and Griliches (1994), Feenstra and Hanson (1996) and Slaughter (2000) – that report positive effects of scale on skill intensity. The 'residual change' measures the average increase in skill intensity across the firms over the sample period that is 'unexplained' by the included variables. It is positive and significant.

In column (2), we add the foreign affiliate share of total employment to the specification. The estimate is positive and significant indicating a strong association between skill intensity and the overseas activities of firms. Our

Table 9.2 Log SGA-production ratio regressions

	Dependent Variable: ln[P(H)/P(L)]					
	(1)	(2)	(3)	(4)	(5)	(6)
Log assets per	0.012	−0.003	−0.004	−0.008	−0.070[a]	0.069[a]
employee	(0.007)	(0.007)	(0.007)	(0.009)	(0.009)	(0.016)
Log worldwide	−0.279[a]	−0.320[a]	−0.317[a]	−0.303[a]	−0.314[a]	−0.063[a]
employment	(0.007)	(0.007)	(0.007)	(0.011)	(0.014)	(0.020)
Foreign employment		0.772[a]				
share		(0.039)				
Employment share			0.914[a]	0.889[a]	1.310[a]	0.549[a]
in LICs			(0.055)	(0.068)	(0.092)	(0.078)
Employment share			0.619[a]	0.512[a]	0.250[a]	0.254[b]
in HICs			(0.057)	(0.092)	(0.074)	(0.098)
Residual change	0.536[a]	0.498[a]	0.50[a]	0.271[a]	0.289[a]	−0.106
	(0.034)	(0.034)	(0.034)	(0.027)	(0.012)	(0.097)
Sample:	All	All	All	1965–79	1980–90	Elec.
N. observations	25108	25108	25108	13573	11535	3605
R^2 (within)	0.286	0.297	0.298	0.205	0.19	0.228

Note: Standard errors in parentheses. a and b indicate significance in a two-tail test at the 1% and 5% levels. Each regression is estimated with a fixed firm effect. Year effects are included but not reported in each regression.

model, however, posits that investment in low-income countries has different effects on skill intensity from investment in high-income countries. Accordingly, the last three columns contain estimates based on regressions that include variables measuring the share of employees in HICs and LICs. Column (3) reflects the whole period and the ensuing two columns contain results when the sample is split into two time periods, 1965–79 and 1980–89. Column (3) reveals that investment in both LICs and HICs is associated with increased skill intensity at home. The LIC effect is stronger than the HIC effect. This pattern holds in each of the two sub-samples as well. These results are inconsistent with the replication configuration which predicts no effect. The positive coefficient for LIC makes sense for vertical specialisation with low-skill activities going to low-income countries. However, we expected that vertical specialisation would involve moving skilled activities to high-income countries resulting in lower skill intensity in Japan. The *positive* coefficient on HICs refutes this proposition and suggests that relatively low-skilled production is also moving to high-income countries. Our results are strongly supportive of the branching configuration where MNEs shift relatively unskilled-labour-intensive downstream production abroad while servicing these downstream plants with skill-intensive headquarter services at home.[4]

Introducing the HIC and LIC variables into the specification does not alter the result that increased scale leads to lower skill intensity. The results for capital intensity are mixed-negative for the 1965–79 subperiod but positive in the 1980–89 subperiod. The residual change variable indicates that much of the skill upgrading that occurred in this period is unexplained by the variables used in this study.

6   Conclusion

We depict three alternative configurations of the multinational enterprise and build nested discrete choice models that are consistent with each configuration. This allows us to derive a regression specification to test the effect that overseas employment has on skill intensity at home and distinguish the configuration that is most consistent with the data.

We find that investment in both low-income and high-income countries is associated with skill-upgrading at home. These results are consistent with the branching configuration of the MNE and inconsistent with replication where no effect is predicted. They are also at odds with vertical specialisation involving the movement of skill-intensive activities from home to a foreign country. The results shown here are similar to those we find in Head and Ries (2000) using a translog regression specification. The main difference in that study is that HIC investment had no consistent effect on skill intensity. These results from Japanese data are very different to those contained in Slaughter (2000) who finds positive scale effects and insignificant effects of overseas production activities.

Over the past few decades, there has been a strong increase in the overseas presence of Japanese firms and a rapid rise in the share of nonproduction workers in the wage bill in Japan. We find that increases in overseas employment is a small but significant factor in observed skill-upgrading in Japan.

Notes

1 The rubber industry comprises 20 firms. The high overseas affiliate share reflects major acquisitions by Bridgestone (Firestone) and Sumitomo Rubber (Dunlop).
2 It is an interesting puzzle that Japan should have both a relative scarcity of college-educated workers and yet pay them a smaller premium than in the United States. It suggests that the US has higher relative demand for skill or that there are important differences in the structure of labour markets in the two countries.
3 Low-income countries are those with per capita income less than half that of Japan. See Head and Ries (2000) for details.
4 The strong positive and significant coefficient in this study arises because here we control for *worldwide* scale. Head and Ries (2000) use a translog specification that controls for *domestic* output. That paper obtains mainly insignificant coefficients on the HIC share. The difference is that in the current specification an increase in employment in HICs raises the HIC share and raises worldwide employment. These two changes have offsetting effects on skill intensity, leading to no net effect in a regression that controls for domestic scale rather than worldwide scale.

References

Barro, Robert and J.W. Lee (1996) 'International Measures of Schooling Years and Schooling Quality', *American Economic Review (Papers and Proceedings)*, vol. 86(2), pp. 218–23.

Berman, Eli, John Bound and Zvi Griliches (1994) 'Changes in the Demand for Skilled Labor within Manufacturing: Evidence from the Survey of Manufacturers', *Quarterly Journal of Economics*, vol. 109(2), pp. 367–98.

Berman, Eli, John Bound and Stephen Machin (1997) 'Implications of Skill-Biased Technological Change: International Evidence', *NBER Working Paper* no. 6,166.

Carr, David, Keith Maskus and James Markusen (2001) 'Estimating the Knowledge-Capital Model of the Multinational Enterprise', *American Economic Review*, vol. 91, pp. 693–708.

Feenstra, Robert C. and Gordon H. Hanson (1996) 'Foreign Investment, Outsourcing, and Relative Wages', in Robert Feenstra and Gene Grossman (eds), *Political Economy of Trade Policy: Essays in Honor of Jagdish Bhagwati* (Cambridge, MA: MIT Press), pp. 89–127.

Head, Keith and John Ries (2000) 'Offshore Production and Skill Upgrading by Japanese Manufacturing Firms', mimeo, University of British Columbia.

Slaughter, Matthew J. (2000) 'Production Transfer within Multinational Enterprises and American Wages', *Journal of International Economics*, vol. 50(2), pp. 449–72.

Toyo Keizai, Inc. (1992) *Japanese Overseas Investment: A Complete Listing by Firms and Countries 1992/93* (Tokyo: Toyo Keizai).

10
Are there Regional Spillovers from FDI in the UK?*

Sourafel Girma and Katharine Wakelin
Centre for Research on Globalisation and Labour Markets, University of Nottingham, UK

1 Introduction

One of the aims of attracting FDI to the UK through incentives is to improve regional development. Having firms locate in depressed regions, or regions with relatively low activity, will provide a direct impact in terms of employment and capital creation – assuming there were under-utilised resources prior to entry and a potential indirect effect via spillovers to local firms. A recent example of such intervention is the aid package given to Siemens to locate in the North East of England, an underdeveloped region with Assisted Area status. State investment included a $30 million grant which, along with other benefits, totalled $76 million (UNCTAD (1996)). The assumption behind such packages is that the long-term economic impact on the region will exceed the cost of the subsidies. We aim to examine whether spillovers from foreign to domestic firms occur at the level of the region. We look at whether domestic firms gain from foreign firms only if they locate in the same region, or whether all firms in a sector gain regardless of location.

Examining the evidence for spillovers is important, as it is the existence of spillovers, that is benefits for which the receiving firm does not pay the full price, which provides the rationale for government incentives. If spillovers occur, then the social rate of return to an investment will exceed the private rate of return, justifying government intervention. Such incentives are allowed under EU competition regulations when the aim is to promote economic development in underdeveloped regions (there are some restrictions on the level). In addition, assessing the level of spillovers is one way of judging the level of technology transfer from MNEs, a topic that has received much attention from both economists and policy makers. The evidence relating to the existence and

* The authors acknowledge financial support from the Leverhulme Trust under Programme Grant number F114/BF and a grant from the European Commission through the 5th Framework Programme (contract HPSE-CT-1999–00017). We are grateful for comments from the CEPR meeting 'Labour Market Effects of European Foreign Investments', Madrid, 20–21 October 2000.

extent of spillovers is mixed. Aggregate empirical evidence for the UK (Barrell and Pain (1997)) indicates that spillovers may be an important source of productivity improvements in the UK. In contrast, Girma, Greenaway and Wakelin (2001) find no evidence of national *intra-sectoral* spillovers using firm-level data, although more detailed analysis indicated that some firms gain while others lose from the presence of foreign firms in the same sector. We wish to extend that work by adding a regional dimension.

Some studies have explicitly concentrated on regional spillovers, but to our knowledge this is the first UK study using firm-level data. Firm data allow us to control for sector characteristics that may influence spillovers. We also explicitly take account of other features, including the source country of FDI, the level of competition in the sector and the role of incentives in influencing the level of spillovers from FDI.

The structure of the chapter is as follows. Section 2 gives a summary of why we would expect regional spillovers. Section 3 sets out the model to be estimated and gives some information on the data set used. Section 4 outlines the results. Section 5 briefly concludes.

2   Regional spillovers from FDI

The theoretical basis for the expectation of spillovers from foreign firms is the level of firm-specific assets that MNEs are assumed to have in order to overcome the higher costs they face in foreign markets (Hymer (1976); Dunning (1977)). These higher costs arise as the foreign firm is unfamiliar with the market, demand characteristics, supplier links, and so on, that are known to the domestic firm. These firm-specific assets are often of a technological nature – more than 80 per cent of royalty payments for international technology transfers were made by affiliates to their parent companies (UNCTAD (1997)). They also have public-good characteristics: excluding other (in this case local) firms from obtaining the knowledge can be difficult. The empirical evidence as to the actual extent of spillovers from MNEs is mixed (Blomström and Kokko (1996); Blomström *et al.* (1999)); the evidence for a productivity differential between foreign and domestic firms in favour of MNEs is more convincing (Girma *et al.* (2001); Djankov and Hoekman (2000)).

Why would spillovers have a regional dimension? That is, why would firms geographically close to MNEs particularly benefit from their presence? There are a number of possible explanations. First, direct contacts with local suppliers and distributors (i.e. upward and downward linkages) may be local in nature in order to minimise transport costs and facilitate communication between the supplier/distributor and the MNE. Second, the training of employees by MNEs and subsequent turnover of labour is another avenue for spillovers (Haacker (1999)). As regional labour mobility in the UK is relatively low (Greenaway *et al.* (2000)), many of the benefits in terms of a better-skilled workforce with tacit technical knowledge gained from MNEs will be experienced by local employers. Third, demonstration effects may also be local if firms only closely observe and imitate other firms in the same region (Blomström and Kokko (1996)). Fourth, knowledge flows may be regional in character. Jaffe *et al.* (1993) have found that knowledge-flows in the US have a regional component. The spread of new ideas is most intense in the area close to the innovation. These factors may lead to significant regional benefits from spillovers.

An alternative hypothesis is that if MNEs locate in less-developed regions to take advantage of subsidies, spillovers may be reduced, as local firms in these areas do not have the technological capacity to benefit from the MNEs. There is some evidence that a certain level of technological ability or 'absorptive capacity' (Cohen and Levinthal (1989)) is needed for domestic firms to benefit from MNEs (Girma *et al.* (2001); Aitken and Harrison (1999)). Spillovers may be maximised by allowing MNEs to choose locations according to location advantages rather than influencing that choice through incentives. This would indicate that spillovers were lower in regions that have been subject to such incentives.

Within the EU, government assistance to industry is limited by the European Commission under competition regulations first set up under the Treaty of Rome (UNCTAD (1996)). These regulations apply to aid offered both to domestic and to foreign firms. One of the main exceptions to these regulations is through aid to promote development in underdeveloped regions (termed 'Assisted Area' status in the UK). Such regional exceptions explain 50 per cent of aid to manufacturing granted within the European Union in 1996 (UNCTAD (1996)). Even with this form of assistance there are regional ceilings to the level of aid; in the UK these vary between 20 per cent and 30 per cent. There is some evidence (Wren and Taylor (1999)) that these regional incentives have had an impact on UK industrial structure.[1] In particular, there is evidence that such incentives influence the choice of location of MNEs within a country (see for instance Head *et al.* (1999) for the US).

In the UK, Taylor (1993) indicates that the Assisted Area status of a county was a significant predictor for the level of Japanese investment. Only 24 per cent of Japanese manufacturing affiliates (up to 1992) had chosen to locate in UK regions without Assisted Area status. A counter-factual estimation indicated that around two-thirds of the location choices were influenced by a region having Assisted Area status (Taylor (1993)). This may have reduced the potential for spillovers from MNEs as they are located in regions with low absorptive capacity.

So far we have concentrated on positive spillovers from MNEs. However, spillovers may also be negative if they increase competition in the sector. Aitken and Harrison (1999) found that increased FDI lowered the productivity of domestically owned firms in Venezuela, presumably as a result of increased competition. Through superior technology and economies of scale, MNEs may be able to produce lower down their average cost curve, increasing competition for domestic firms. At the most extreme, indigenous firms may leave the market as a result of increased competition from MNEs. Girma *et al.* (2001) also found that some firms lost out as a result of MNE presence in the UK. In particular, firms located in low-skill sectors, with low levels of import competition and a large technology gap between the domestic and foreign firms experienced negative spillovers.

At the regional level, Driffield (1999) has examined the role of productivity spillovers from inward investment in the UK using sector-level data. The data set covers ten regions, 20 manufacturing sectors and the period from 1984–92. The results indicate that there are positive productivity spillovers from FDI in the same sector and region, and more generally at the regional level, but that these effects are small. FDI in the sector as a whole (but not in the region) actually has a negative impact on productivity. This is assumed to be because of the increased competition at the sector level.

In contrast, Sjöholm (1998), using firm-level data for Indonesia, finds evidence of *intra-industry* spillovers at the national level, but *not* at the level of the province or the district. He interprets this as indicating there are no extra benefits from being geographically close to foreign firms. He does, however, find some evidence for *inter-industry* spillovers at the regional level. This gives some support for the idea of local linkages to neighbouring sectors. Aitken and Harrison (1999) test to see if spillovers are local in the case of Venezuela. They find no significant impact of region and sector-specific FDI on domestic firms' productivity. They conclude that there is no regional element to spillovers. In fact, the only evidence of spillovers they find is to firms that are partly foreign owned (i.e. in joint ventures); wholly domestic firms experience negative spillovers from FDI at the national level.[2]

A number of firm and sector characteristics have been suggested as possible influences on the level of spillovers (Blomstöm *et al.* (1999); Sjöholm (1998)). Domestic firms with low levels of technology may not be able to benefit from spillovers as they lack the necessary absorptive capacity (Lapan and Bardhan (1973)). This may also be the case for small domestic firms that cannot compete in terms of economies of scale (Dunning (1993)) and as a result may experience negative spillovers from MNEs. Competition has also been suggested as an important influence on the extent of spillovers. MNEs may need to bring more advanced technology to the host country when competition in that country is high, increasing the possibility of spillovers (Blomstöm *et al.* (1999)). Some of these hypotheses have found confirmation at a national level (Girma *et al.* (2001); Kokko (1994)). Both studies found the degree of spillovers from FDI to increase as the technology gap between foreign and domestic firms *decreased*. The results cover both developing and developed countries: the former study is for the UK and the latter for Mexico. In contrast, Sjöholm (1998) found some evidence that *sectors* characterised by large technology gaps between foreign and domestic firms gained more from the foreign presence than sectors with smaller gaps in Indonesia. He also found a positive relationship between competition at the sector level and spillovers from FDI confirmed by Kokko (1994). We also test to see if these characteristics are important at the regional level.

The existing literature highlights a number of hypotheses that we investigate in our econometric analysis:

- Are spillovers from multinationals to domestic firms larger when the MNE is located in the same region (as well as the same sector) as the domestic firm? Or is it only the sector in which the MNE is located that is important?
- Does the nationality of the MNE influence the level of spillovers to domestic firms?
- Do the characteristics of the domestic firm and sector influence the level of spillovers? Characteristics include the level of intangible assets of the firm and the competition in the sector.
- Does the presence of government incentives to locate in the region influence the impact of spillovers?

The next section outlines how these hypotheses may be tested in an econometric model.

3   The model

In order to identify the role of FDI in firm productivity, we estimate total factor productivity equations for our sample of firms including additional terms to account for the level of FDI in the sector and region. As we measure the impact of spillovers on total factor productivity, measures for both labour and capital employed at the firm level are included. The relationship to be estimated is given by:

$$Q_{it} = f(L_{it}, K_{it}, FDI1_{srt}, FDI2_{st}, FDI3_{s2rt}, FDI1^*_{srt}X) \tag{1}$$

where:

Q_{it} is log of output in firm i at time t;

L_{it} is log of employment in firm i at time t;

K_{it} is log of fixed assets in firm i at time t;

$FDI1_{st}$ is the level of employment by foreign affiliates in each firm's four-digit sector s and in the same region r at time t;

$FDI2_{st}$ is the level of employment by foreign affiliates in each firm's four-digit sector s outside its own region r at time t;

$FDI3_{srt}$ is the level of employment by foreign affiliates in each firm's two-digit sector $s2$ in the firm's region r, less $FDI1$ at time t.

X is a vector of firm and sector characteristics including at time t:

$ASSETS_{it}$ the level of intangible assets in firm i relative to employment;

$CONC_{srt}$ the Herfindhal concentration index for the four-digit sector s in the region r; as concentration increases, we assume local density of competition in the sector is reduced;

AA_r a dummy variable taking the value of one if a region r has Assisted Area status.

The three FDI variables are designed to capture spillover effects from within the industry and the same region (FDI1), from outside the region but within the sector (FDI2) and from neighbouring sectors in the same region (FDI3). Neighbouring sectors are defined as those not in the same detailed four-digit classification as the firm, but who form part of the wider two-digit definition. The first two variables measure intra-sectoral spillovers, while the third is inter-sectoral. FDI1 and FDI3 both represent spillover sources within the region, while FDI2 is outside. If regional spillovers from FDI within the sector are important, we would expect FDI1 to be significant, from outside the sector FDI3 is the relvant variable. As discussed earlier, spillovers can be either negative or positive.

In order to check the role of firm and sector characteristics, FDI is also interacted with a number of characteristics. We expect FDI interacted with local concentration to have a negative impact on firm output: firms in less competitive (i.e. highly concentrated) local sectors will benefit less from spillovers as MNEs bring less technology with them, reducing the potential for spillovers. In addition, the low density of local competition (shown by high regional and sectoral concentration) indicates fewer local interactions between firms. We expect the firm-specific assets of the domestic firm (measured by intangible assets of the firm ASSETS) to increase the possible spillovers from foreign firms as it proxies the absorptive capacity of the firm. Finally, we expect regions that have Assisted Area status to benefit less from spillovers than other regions, as attracting FDI through incentives may reduce the potential benefits from MNEs. In our sample, firms located in Assisted Areas have significantly lower total factor productivity than firms in other regions, by around 6 per cent. This lower average productivity may mean they do not possess the necessary absorptive capacity to benefit from foreign firms.

We estimate possible productivity spillovers using the following equation:

$$y_{it} = \delta_1 FDI1_{srt} + \delta_2 FDI2_{st} + \delta_3 FDI3_{s2rt} + \delta_4 FDI1^*_{srt}AAr + \delta_5 FDI1^*_{srt}CONC_{srt}$$
$$+ \delta_6 FDI1^*_{srt}ASSETS_{it} + \beta_1 L_{it} + \beta_2 K_{it} + D_{sic} + D_i + D_r + \varepsilon_{it} \qquad (2)$$

where i and t are index firms and years respectively and s and r are sector and region; D_{sic} is a four-digit SIC92 dummy for fixed industry effects. D_t are time dummies that account for aggregate shocks. D_r are regional dummy variables, they account for agglomeration effects at the regional level. Some regions may have particular advantages that attract firms to those areas, in order to take account of those factors we have included these dummy variables. ε denotes a possible heteroscedastic random noise term with unrestricted (within-firm) serial correlation structure. The dependent variable y is the log of output, and L and K are labour and capital respectively. All the FDI terms are as described earlier. Exact definitions of the variables are given in the Appendix.

The regressions are run on data for domestic firms alone. Since industry fixed-effects are included, we are only exploiting within-sector variations. If the regressions were run without the industry dummies, we would have been able to exploit the between-sector FDI variations as well. However, with that modelling framework a positive coefficient on the FDI variable can simply reflect the fact that foreign firms invest in industries that pay higher wages and enjoy higher productivity rather than the existence of any genuine spillovers to domestic firms, that is, there is a sector selection problem. This is the same at the regional level, explaining why we have also included regional dummy variables.

Database construction and sample characteristics

We use a large firm-level panel data set of over 3,400 domestic firms in UK manufacturing for the period 1988–96.[3] The data set is highly disaggregated and there are no reasons for supposing the period is in any way unrepresentative. The primary source of information on firms is the OneSource database of private and public companies. Firms are defined as foreign if the country of origin of their ultimate holding company is not the UK; these are not included in the estimations but are used to assess the level of FDI in the sector.[4] Only domestic firms are included as we wish to estimate the spillovers to these firms.

This data set has a number of attractions. First it covers a recent period. Second, we use highly disaggregated price deflators (at the five-digit SIC92 level) which allow us to avoid many of the problems associated with more aggregate price deflators. Third, we have been able to match firm-level data with industry variables such as concentration. Finally, the use of a firm-level data set mitigates aggregation biases by allowing us to control for a number of observable and unobservable firm-level characteristics.

We have a number of criteria for selecting our sample. First, we chose domestic *subsidiaries* that have not experienced a change of ownership between 1988 and 1996. Subsidiaries are chosen as parent companies may have consolidated accounts leading to double counting. In addition, recent work on the impact of acquisition on wages and productivity (Conyon *et al.* (1999)) found that acquisition by a foreign firm leads to higher productivity and wages. We wish to abstract from this, by concentrating on affiliates that have not experienced a change in ownership over the period. Second, the resulting firms are screened for data availability on wages, employment, value added and fixed assets; firms are included if they have at least three consecutive years of data. Third, to mitigate the impact of outliers we excluded the top and bottom five percentile firms in terms of value added and wages. We also excluded firms with annual wages or value-added growth exceeding 100 per cent, as we have doubts about the reliability of these extreme data points. This leaves us with a panel of 3,408 domestic affiliates.[5]

For the analysis we divide firms into 14 regions. Clearly the choice of a 'region' is always fairly arbitrary. We have chosen this division partly for reasons of tractability, but also because it corresponds to areas with definite regional identities.[6] Summary statistics are provided for those 14 regions in Table 10.1 for all manufacturing industry. An asterisk designates a region with Assisted Area (AA) status.[7]

Table 10.1 Summary statistics regional means and deviations

Region *AA status	Employment	Wages (£'000)	Output/ Employment (£m)	MNEs (no.)	MNE share of emp. (%)
Central London	254 (455)	16.6 (4.9)	21.3 (42.9)	478	15.8
Central South	198 (341)	15.8 (4.2)	15.1 (39.7)	447	25.1
East Anglia	160 (306)	15.0 (4.0)	11.7 (23.2)	212	35.0
East Midlands	212 (289)	13.6 (3.9)	11.7 (17.9)	278	24.8
Home Counties	168 (243)	16.2 (4.2)	11.9 (20.1)	126	47.7
North East*	239 (345)	14.2 (3.8)	16.1 (27.4)	494	28.6
North Scotland*	115 (126)	12.8 (4.6)	11.2 (25.5)	22	22.9
North West*	191 (316)	14.1 (3.9)	13.2 (24.2)	470	22.3
Outer London	204 (374)	17.0 (4.7)	20.5 (64.6)	213	19.8
South East	140 (196)	15.5 (4.0)	8.9 (15.6)	146	37.2
South West	124 (149)	14.5 (3.7)	8.5 (12.7)	91	12.3
South Scotland*	236 (356)	13.8 (3.9)	14.6 (22.6)	128	26.0
Wales*	164 (234)	14.3 (3.7)	13.6 (40.2)	100	40.0
West Midlands*	219 (305)	13.9 (3.6)	13.9 (24.8)	544	34.3

Note: Employment, wages and labour productivity are averages over all the firms in the region and over time. MNE share of employment is measured as the level of multinational employment in the sector and region over the sector and region total averaged over time.

As can be seen from Table 10.1, wages and average employment by firm do show some variation across regions. The lowest average wages are seen in Scotland and the Midlands (both East and West) while the highest are in Central and Outer London. In terms of average firm size, the lowest average seems to be in rural areas (North of Scotland, East Anglia) and highest in industrial areas (South of Scotland, West Midlands), reflecting industrial structure in those regions. There is also considerable variation in labour productivity, with particularly high rates found in the two London regions and low labour productivity in the South East and South West. As the high standard deviations indicate, there is also a great deal of variation within regions as well as between them. The distribution of multinational companies across regions is also very uneven. The highest share of foreign-owned firms in employment is in the south – the Home Counties and East Anglia – and in Wales and the West Midlands (both regions containing areas with Assisted Area status). The lowest foreign share (for manufacturing, obviously it would be high in services) is in Central London and the South West. Scotland generally has a low share of foreign employment.

4 Results

The results after estimating equation (2) are given in the second column of Table 10.2. In order to test if the country of origin of the FDI is important,

Table 10.2   The basic model (dependent variable: log of output)

	Total FDI	FDI by nationality
Capital	0.17 (19.28)***	0.17 (19.26)***
Labour	0.79 (65.77)***	0.79 (65.89)***
FDI1	0.14 (2.47)***	
FDI2	−0.13 (2.15)**	−0.13 (2.14)**
FDI3	0.04 (0.73)	0.05 (0.76)
FDI*ASSETS	0.008 (1.37)	0.008 (1.37)
FDI*CONC	−0.24 (2.51)***	−0.24 (2.57)***
FDI*AA	−0.14 (2.36)***	
FDI1 USA		0.14 (2.04)**
FDI1 USA * AA		−0.18 (2.11)**
FDI1 Japan		0.33 (2.10)**
FDI1 Japan * AA		−0.19 (0.51)
FDI1 Other		0.12 (1.83)*
FDI1 Other * AA		−0.09 (1.22)
Adjusted R^2	0.85	0.85
N	23756	23756
F (26, 23557)	780.21***	685.3***

Note: T-statistics are given in brackets; they are calculated with robust standard errors. *** indicates significant at 1%; ** at 5% and * at 10%.

a second estimation with FDI divided by nationality is also included. FDI is divided into that originating from the US, Japan and 'other'. The last category is mostly made up of FDI from other European countries such as Germany and the Netherlands. These results are presented in the third column of Table 10.2. Regional and sectoral dummy variables are not reported.

The results indicate that there is a regional spillover effect from having multinationals locate in the same sector and same region as the domestic firm (FDI1). It has a positive effect on output after controlling for capital and labour inputs. This positive effect is mitigated, as we expected, if the FDI is located in a region with Assisted Area status (FDI1*AA). In the case of assisted areas the impact of FDI in the same sector and region is negligible. Thus it may be that MNEs have been attracted to those sectors by incentives rather than location advantages, and that local firms do not have the absorptive capacity to benefit from spillovers. FDI in the same sector and region also has much less of an impact in sectors with low levels of competition. Higher levels of CONC indicate high concentration in the firm's sector locally, implying low levels of competition in the sector and region; this is negatively related to spillovers from FDI. This confirms that sectors with high local competition benefit more from foreign firms. This may be because the foreign firms introduce better technology as a result of the level of competition in the sector, increasing the potential for spillovers, and that the high density of local firms in the sector increases the potential for spillovers. The level of intangible assets of a firm (taken as a proxy for its own firm-specific assets, and therefore its ability to absorb new technologies) has the expected positive sign but is not significant. Overall, FDI has a positive impact at the regional level, but this effect is reduced in sectors with low competition and with Assisted Area status.

Other measures of FDI are also included. FDI2 is FDI in the same sector but outside the region has a negative impact on output. This implies a negative competition spillover, with foreign firms raising the level of competition in the sector. This confirms other results for the UK (Driffield (1999)) but is in contrast to evidence for developing countries (Sjöholm (1998); Aitken and Harrison (1999)). The last two papers either found negligible or positive spillovers at the sector level, but no regional dimension. It appears that there is a more *regional* dimension to spillovers in industrialised than developing countries. This negative sectoral effect does not seem to be compensated for by any positive learning effects unless the FDI takes place in the region as well as the sector. FDI in the region but outside the immediate sector (FDI3) has no significant impact.

When the positive region and sector-specific effect is broken down by nationality, the results are very similar across countries. FDI from Japan has a higher coefficient than FDI from either of the other two, indicating that the magnitude of the regional spillover is higher in the case of Japanese affiliates in the UK. The negative effect observed for FDI attracted to areas eligible for regional assistance seems to be due to US-owned firms rather than FDI from either of the other two categories. In the case of both FDI from Japan and from other countries no significant effect is found. However, US firms that locate in regions with Assisted Area status do seem to be associated with lower spillovers to domestic firms. Thus although Japanese firms appear to be attracted to less-developed regions (Taylor (1993)), this does not seem to reduce the level of spillovers from them to domestic firms.

Overall, the results confirm that spillovers seem to have a regional dimension. Domestic firms appear to gain only from firms locating in the same sector and region as them, while they simultaneously lose out from foreign firms locating in the same sector but not the same region. Positive information and demonstration spillovers appear to have a regional dimension, while negative competition effects are limited to the sector. Foreign firms locating in the wider two-digit sector in the same region appear to have no impact on productivity.

One of the hypotheses that we particularly wanted to investigate is whether firms with a large technology gap benefit more or less from the presence of foreign firms. In order to test this we split domestic sectors into three groups. First we calculate total factor productivity at the two-digit level separately for domestic and foreign firms in each sector. Then we measure the technology gap between foreign and domestic firms by:

$$GAP_s = \frac{TFP_{fs} - TFP_{ds}}{TFP_{fs}}$$

where *s* indicates the sector, *f* foreign firms, *d* domestic and *TFP* is total factor productivity growth. We then split the domestic firms into three groups:

- Low gap: those with a small gap between domestic and foreign firms in the sector (*GAP* is less than 15 per cent);
- Medium gap: those with a gap between 15 per cent and 33 per cent from foreign firms;
- High gap: when the gap from foreign firms is over 33 per cent.

Using this separation we repeat the basic model estimated in Table 10.2 for the three groups of firms. If firms closer to the technological frontier benefit more, we would expect to see significant spillovers for the group with a low gap, rather than for the other two groups. The results are given in Table 10.3.

It is clear from the results that the regional spillover variable FDI1 is only significant for the firms in sectors with a low technology gap between foreign and domestic firms. It is only in sectors in which domestic firms do not lag far behind foreign that positive spillovers are experienced. This confirms that domestic firms find it easier to learn from foreign firms when the technological gap between them is relatively small. As this gap increases domestic firms may find it harder to adopt the new technology brought by the foreign firms. However, it is only for firms in sectors with small technology gaps that experience negative spillovers from MNEs. The increased competition at the sector level (see the results for FDI2) appears to be more intense in sectors where the domestic firms lag only slightly behind the foreign firms. This negative effect is also insignificant for the other two groups of firms. Therefore, domestic firms that do not lag behind experience both positive spillovers – from foreign firms in the same sector and region – and negative spillovers at the sector level.

Table 10.3   Results split by technology gap

	Low gap	Medium gap	High gap
Capital	0.17 (13.4)***	0.16 (16.6) ***	0.16 (10.2)***
Labour	0.77 (44.5)***	0.80 (58.9) ***	0.82 (36.1)***
FDI1	0.18 (0.07)***	0.13 (1.62)	0.10 (0.78)
FDI2	−0.18 (0.09)**	−0.11 (1.24)	−0.16 (1.12)
FDI3	0.13 (1.59)	−0.06 (0.82)	0.18 (1.39)
FDI1*ASSETS	0.005 (0.59)	0.02 (3.75) ***	0.001 (0.26)
FDI1*CONC	−0.40 (3.42)***	−0.16 (1.19)	−0.21 (1.01)
FDI1*AA	−0.17 (2.40)***	−0.13 (1.72) *	−0.07 (0.58)
Adjusted R^2	0.84	0.85	0.85
N	9770	10657	3317
F	421.9***	607.1***	206.1***

Note: T-statistics are given in brackets; they calculated with robust standard errors. *** indicates significant at 1%; ** at 5% and * at 10%.

FDI from outside the immediate sector but inside the region remains insignificant for all groups.

Interestingly the interaction between a firm's intangible assets and FDI is significant only for the medium group. It may be that all firms in the low-gap group have high levels of intangible assets, so the marginal effect is small. However, in the medium group having intangible assets may distinguish one firm from others in the sector. Firms with high intangible assets in this group seem to benefit more from spillovers than other firms in the sector.

The competition result is again significant only for the group with the low gap, indicating that, among those sectors with low technology gaps, those that have high levels of competition still have higher spillovers. The level of competition has no significant influence in the other two groups of sectors.

Regions with Assisted Area status still appear to have lower spillovers for both firms in sectors with low and medium technology gaps. It is only those firms with high technology gaps that have no significant effect. For firms with medium to low technology gaps spillovers are still lower in regions that offer financial incentives to locate there.

5 Conclusions

Summarising our results, we do find evidence that positive spillovers from foreign firms occur only to domestic firms in the same sector and region as the foreign firms. We also find some evidence of negative spillovers at the sector level but outside the region. There clearly does seem to be a regional channel for spillovers – this may be through linkages to other firms, local information and demonstration effects or through the local labour market. The size of these spillovers varied only slightly over nationality, with larger local spillovers from Japanese firms.

We also found evidence that the characteristics of sectors and firms are important in influencing spillovers. Sectors with high local levels of competition and in regions without Assisted Area status gained more from the presence of foreign firms. It seems that attracting FDI through regional incentives may actually reduce the level of spillovers resulting from their location in the UK. However, using a dummy variable for Assisted Area status is a relatively crude way of measuring this effect. In future work we hope to use a more precise estimate for the level of regional incentives.

It also seems to be the case that domestic firms located in sectors characterised by low technology gaps between foreign and domestic firms gain more from spillovers. This is consistent with the idea that a certain level of absorptive capacity is needed in order to benefit from the superior technology introduced by many foreign firms.

To conclude, the expectation of regional spillovers from foreign to domestic firms appears reasonable. However, there is some evidence that in less-developed regions (i.e. those with Assisted Area status) the spillovers from foreign firms are lower than in other regions. This may partly be because other firms in those regions do not have the necessary knowledge and skills to benefit from the presence of foreign firms. Ironically, regional policies to attract FDI may limit exactly what they wish to attract.

Appendix

Output: total sales by the firm in the year (OneSource).
Employment: Average number of employees during the year including full-time and part-time workers (OneSource).
Wages: Average remuneration paid to employees in a year excluding tax, social security and pension payments (OneSource).
Fixed assets: Tangible fixed assets at their net book values (OneSource).
Producer Price Indices: Five-digit SIC92 level indices obtained from The Business Monitor MM 22.
FDI: The presence of foreign direct investment is estimated by the foreign share of manufacturing employment either at the level of the sector or region. These are calculated by considering the population of subsidiaries in OneSource.
CONC: Herfindhal index for each sector and region (calculated from One-Source).
ASSETS: Real intangible assets in the firm (OneSource).
AA: 1 if a region has Assisted Area status (taken from the DTI website).

Notes

1 See Young *et al.* (1994) for a review of the impact of FDI on regional development and Gillespie *et al.* (1999) for a regional computable general equilibrium analysis of the impact of FDI on the Scottish economy.
2 There is some evidence that high levels of regional FDI increased skilled wages for Mexico in the 1980s (Feenstra and Hanson (1997)).
3 We have price deflators for the five-digit sectors based on the 1992 Standard Industrial Classification.
4 In cases where the ultimate holding company is not known, the country of origin of the holding company it used. We do not know the extent of foreign ownership within the firm, but evidence indicates that is it not an important influence on spillovers (Blomstöm and Sjöholm (1999)).
5 Onesource claims to cover the population of UK firms. However, comparing the figures in Table 10.1 with published data sources indicates that it may be underestimating the level of foreign ownership.
6 Northern Ireland is not included in our database.
7 For part of the period the West Midlands was classified as an Intermediate Area. However, this separation was removed. We have treated it as an Assisted Area.

References

Aitken, B.J. and A.E. Harrison (1999) 'Do Domestic Firms Benefit from Direct Foreign Investment? Evidence from Venezuela', *American Economic Review*, vol. 89, pp. 605–18.

Barrell, R. and N. Pain (1997) 'Foreign Direct Investment, Technological Change and Economic Growth within Europe', *Economic Journal*, vol. 107, pp. 1770–86.

Blomström, M. and A. Kokko (1996) 'Multinational Corporations and Spillovers', *Stockholm School of Economics Working Paper Series in Economics and Finance*, no. 99.

Blomström, M., S. Globerman and A. Kokko (1999) 'The Determinants of Host Country Spillovers from Foreign Direct Investment: Review and Synthesis of the Literature', paper presented at the NIESR conference on 'Inward Investment, Technological Change and Growth: The Impact of Multinational Corporations on the UK Economy', British Academy, London, 29 September 1999.

Blomström, M. and F. Sjöholm (1999) 'Technology Transfer and Spillovers: Does Local Participation with Multinationals Matter?' *European Economic Review*, vol. 43, pp. 915–23.

Cohen, W.M. and D.A. Levinthal (1989) 'Innovation and Learning: The Two Faces of R&D', *Economic Journal*, vol. 99, pp. 569–96.

Conyon, M., S. Girma, S. Thompson and P. Wright (1999) 'The impact of Foreign Acquisition on Wages and Productivity in the UK', GLM Research Paper 99/8, School of Economics, University of Nottingham.

Djankov, S. and B. Hoekman (2000) 'Foreign investment and Productivity Growth in Czech Enterprises', *The World Bank Economic Review*, 14(1), pp. 49–64.

Driffield, N.L. (1999) 'Regional and Industry Level Spillovers from FDI', paper presented at the NIESR Conference on 'Inward Investment, Technological Change and Growth: The Impact of Multinational Corporations on the UK Economy', British Academy, London, 29 September 1999.

Dunning, J.H. (1977) 'Trade, Location of Economic Activity and MNE: A Search for an Eclectic Approach', in B. Ohlin, P.O. Hesselborn and P.M. Wijkman (eds), *The International Allocation of Economic Activity* (London: Macmillan), pp. 394–418.

Dunning, J.H. (1993) *Multinational Enterprises and the Global Economy* (Wokingham: Addison-Wesley).

Feenstra, R.C. and G.H. Hanson (1997) 'Foreign Direct Investment and Relative Wages: Evidence from Mexico's Maquiladoras', *Journal of International Economics*, vol. 42, pp. 371–93.

Gillespie, G., P.G. McGregor, J.K. Swales and P.Y. Ya (1999) 'A Regional Computable General Equilibrium Analysis of the Demand and "Efficiency-Spillover" Effects of Foreign Direct Investment', paper presented at the NIESR conference on 'Inward Investment, Technological Change and Growth: The Impact of Multinational Corporations on the UK Economy', British Academy, London, 29 September 1999.

Girma, S., D. Greenaway and K. Wakelin (2001) 'Who Benefits from Foreign Direct Investment in the UK?' *Scottish Journal of Political Economy*, vol. 48(2), pp. 119–33.

Greenaway, D., R. Upward and P. Wright (2000) 'Sectoral Transformation and Labour Market Flows', *Oxford Review of Economic Policy*, vol. 16, pp. 57–75.

Haacker, Markus (1999) 'Spillovers from Foreign Investment through Labour Turnover: The Supply of Management Skills', Centre for Economic Performance, London School of Economics.

Head, C. Keith, John C. Ries and Deborah L. Swenson (1999) 'Attracting Foreign Manufacturing: Investment Promotion and Agglomeration', *Regional Science and Urban Economics*, vol. 29, pp. 197–218.

Hymer, S.H. (1976) *The International Operations of National Firms: A Study of Direct Foreign Investment* (Boston, MA: MIT Press).

Jaffe, A., M. Trajtenberg and R. Henderson (1993) 'Geographic Localisation of Knowledge Spillovers as Evidenced by Patent Citations', *Quarterly Journal of Economics*, vol. 108, pp. 577–98.

Kokko, A. (1994) 'Technology, Market Characteristics and Spillovers', *Journal of Development Economics*, vol. 43, pp. 279–93.

Lapan, H. and P. Bardhan (1973) 'Localised Technical Progress and the Transfer of Technology and Economic Development', *Journal of Economic Theory*, vol. 6, pp. 585–95.

Sjöholm, Fredrik (1998) 'Productivity Growth in Indonesia: The Role of Regional Characteristics and Direct Foreign Investment', Stockholm School of Economics, Working paper no. 216.

Taylor, Jim (1993) 'An Analysis of the Factors Determining The Geographical Distribution of Japanese Manufacturing Investment in the UK, 1984–1991', *Urban Studies*, vol. 30(7), pp. 1209–24.

UNCTAD (1996) 'Incentives and Foreign Direct Investment', UNCTAD, Division on transnational corporations and investment, Series A, No. 30.

UNCTAD (1997) *World Investment Report: Transnational Corporations, Market Structure and Competition Policy* (New York: United Nations).

Wang, J-Y. and Blomström, M. (1992) 'Foreign Investment and Technological Transfer: A Simple Model', *European Economic Review*, vol. 36, pp. 137–55.

Wren, Colin and Jim Taylor (1999) 'Industrial Restructuring and Regional Policy', *Oxford Economic Papers*, vol. 51, pp. 487–516.

Young, Stephen, Neil Hood and Ewen Peters (1994) 'Multinational Enterprises and Regional Economic Development', *Regional Studies*, vol. 28(7), pp. 657–77.

11

Technology, Trade, Multinationals and Aggregate Employment: Evidence from UK Panel Data

Karl Taylor
Department of Economics, University of Leicester, UK

Nigel Driffield
Birmingham Business School, University of Birmingham, UK

1 Introduction

It is now well documented that over the past two decades there has been a substantial increase in the demand for skilled labour (Gottschalk and Smeeding (1997)). Moreover, the majority of such relative increases have occurred within industries and within groups of individuals with the same education and experience (Schmitt (1995); Taylor (1999)). A number of explanations exist which try to give reasons for the demand shock. In particular the two most common in the literature are that of technological change biased in favour of skilled labour and growing international trade (Levy and Murnane (1992); Gottschalk and Smeeding (1997)). There is some disagreement about whether technology or trade is the most important factor in causing increasing demand for skilled workers (Machin and Van Reenen (1998); Wood (1994, 1998); Taylor (1999); Desjonqueres *et al.* (1999)), and this is as much a theoretical issue as an empirical one (Haskel (1999); Slaughter (1999)). However, it is fair to say that the majority of research has focused upon trade and technology as the main causes of changes in labour demand.

Recently, the growing role of multinational activity has been forwarded as another avenue of technological change (Barrell and Pain (1997); Figini and Gorg (1999); Blonigen and Slaughter (1999)). The inference here is that MNEs demonstrate higher levels of labour productivity, and in turn greater demand for high-quality labour. Recent research has suggested that there are substantial differences between the domestic and foreign-owned sector and there is growing evidence for this in the UK (Driffield (1996); Conyon *et al.* (1999); Girma *et al.* (2001)). Entry by such firms therefore is expected to impact on domestic labour markets and linked to this is the likely effect on domestic firms of the inflow of new technology that is assumed to accompany FDI. Barrell and Pain (1997) find that, in the UK manufacturing sector, a 1 per cent rise in the FDI stock is estimated to raise technical progress by 0.26 per cent. The increasing demand for skilled labour, following foreign entry, is then assumed to be as a result of technology spillovers increasing the productivity of skilled workers in the domestic sector.

Although the majority of the literature has focused upon the *relative* impacts upon employment and wages following the increase in demand, the *aggregate* impacts (that is the change in overall employment, i.e. skilled plus unskilled jobs) have been largely neglected in the employment literature. Two exceptions are Hine and Wright (1998) and Greenaway *et al.* (1999) where both sets of authors consider how trade with low-wage countries has influenced employment. A large literature exists on how technological change and trade has influenced the demand for skilled and unskilled labour. However, the idea that technology or trade may in fact be labour-saving and may imply an aggregate reduction in the overall employment of both skilled and unskilled labour has been largely unexplored (Nickell and Bell (1995); Pianta and Vivarelli (2000)). Indeed Nickell and Bell (1995) report that there have been significant increases in both unskilled and skilled unemployment in most European countries.

The purpose of this chapter is to consider how technology, trade and multinational activity may have influenced total employment in the domestic sector over the period 1983 to 1992. In the next section we consider the evolution of employment in manufacturing, along with changes in technology, trade and FDI. Section 3 introduces the theoretical model and empirical analysis used to assess how technology, trade and FDI impact upon employment. Finally the results are presented in Section 4.

2   Employment and the evolution of technology, trade and FDI

The data used in this chapter are based at the three-digit industry level for UK manufacturing sectors (SIC, 1980 sectors 2–4) over the period 1983 to 1992. Most of the data used in this study are published in *The Annual Production Inquiry*, formerly *Report on the Census of Production*, UK Office of National Statistics (ONS), for various years. These data are used initially to consider the recent trends in employment, technology, trade and multinational activity.

Employment

Figure 11.1 shows the evolution of employment in the UK manufacturing sector over the period 1983 to 1992 (with 1983 indexed to 100). Clearly, there have been large falls in overall employment levels by around 15 per cent, from 5,092,000 jobs in 1983 to 4,351,000 by 1992. Splitting manufacturing into one-digit classifications shows that SIC2 (manufacture of metals, mineral products and chemicals) and SIC3 (metal goods, engineering and vehicles) experienced similar trends. Both industries saw employment fall by nearly 20 per cent (SIC2 717,300 in 1983 to 581,000 by 1992; for SIC3 over the same period, 2,314,200 to 1,862,600). However, employment in SIC4 (other manufacturing) only fell by just over 7 per cent from 2,060,300 to 1,908,700 by 1992. Looking at a more

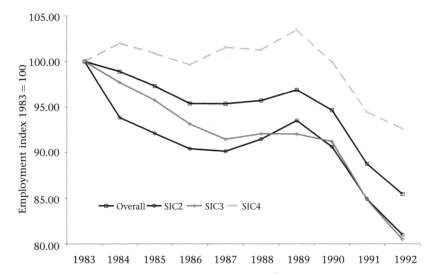

Figure 11.1   Changes in Manufacturing employment, 1983–92
(See *Notes* and *Source* for Figure 11.2)

disaggregated level, SIC483 (processing of plastics) actually experienced an overall employment increase of 40,000 jobs or 31 per cent, and SIC412 (slaughtering of animals and production of meat and by-products) an increase of 23,200 jobs (25 per cent).

The main reason as to why SIC4 employment escaped large cutbacks in employment can be seen from Figure 11.2, which shows the percentage change in skilled and unskilled employment over the period 1983 to 1992. Clearly in other manufacturing (SIC4) the fall in unskilled employment of 10 per cent was over half that of SIC2 and SIC3 and accounted for some 156,600 jobs, whilst the employment of skilled labour actually increased by 4,000 jobs or around 1 per cent.

Technology, trade and multinationals

As mentioned in the introduction, the majority of the literature has attempted to explain relative employment between the skilled and unskilled, rather than the impact of potential demand shocks upon aggregate employment. There is a broad consensus in the literature that demand has increased for higher-skilled labour at the expense of the lower-skill endowed, however, the impact upon aggregate employment is unclear. The following section looks at the evolution of the main potential factors (technology, trade) which could have caused such a demand shift and FDI.

Technological changes suggest that recent advances have favoured those workers with higher levels of skill. The possibility that such a relationship exists

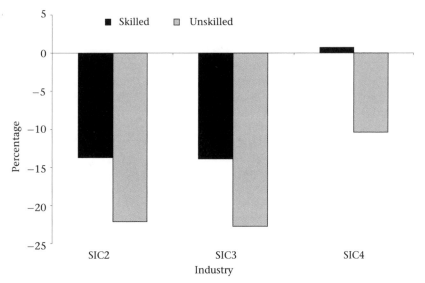

Figure 11.2   Evolution of skilled and unskilled employment by industry, 1983–92
Notes: In Figures 11.1 and 11.2 employment is for the domestic sector only. Our measure
of unskilled workers (operatives) includes all manual wage earners, for example operatives
in power stations, engaged in outside work of erecting, fitting etc., inspectors, main-
tenance workers and cleaners. Staff engaged in transport (including roundsmen) and
employed in warehouses, stores, shops and canteens are also included in the definition.
Source: Census of Production, ONS, for both Figures 11.1 and 11.2.

today has prompted the widely held conjecture that technology and skilled
labour are relative complements, whilst technology and less-skilled labour are
substitutes. Consequently, an increase in the rate of technological change can
be expected to raise the demand of the skilled relative to the less skilled.
Technology intensity is measured by the stock of research and development
expenditure over time, as is common in the literature (Machin and Van Reenen
(1998); Berman and Machin (2000)). Figure 11.3 shows that technology intensity actually fell in manufacturing by around 28 per cent over the period,
although in SIC4 (other manufacturing) intensity increased by 140 per cent.
If technology is biased in favour of skilled labour then this is prima facie
evidence of why skilled employment actually rose in SIC4 (see Figure 11.2).

   To the extent that the West's comparative advantage lies with skilled labour,
globalisation might be expected to benefit those workers relative to the less
skilled. Moreover, developed countries have become open to competition from
lower-wage developing economies, and firms have taken the opportunity to
gain from these lower costs by substituting unskilled intensive production
abroad. Under the HOS framework globalisation suggests a redistribution of
employment from the import sector towards the export sector, thus increased
imports reduce employment and increased exports increase employment. The

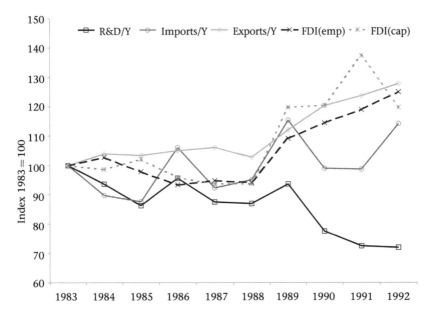

Figure 11.3 Technology, trade and multinationals, 1983–92
Notes: Our measure of technology intensity is the stock research and development expenditure as a proportion of output (R&D/Y), trade is measured by import and export intensity (Imports/Y) and (Exports/Y) respectively. Measures of the impact of FDI are the share of foreign employment (FDIemp) and the share of the capital stock accounted for by foreign firms (FDIcap).

role of growing competition from low-wage countries and the impact upon employment is proxied by import and export intensity (Anderton and Brenton (1999); Hine and Wright (1998)). Over the period import intensity increased by around 14 per cent with the largest increase in SIC2 (manufacture of metals, mineral products and chemicals), of nearly 23 per cent (although intensity in this sector was the lowest at around 10 per cent of output). The most import intensive sector was SIC4, other manufacturing, with imports around 23 per cent of output by 1992. The manufacturing sector as a whole became more export orientated over the decade with export intensity rising by 28 per cent with the largest increases in SIC3, metal goods engineering and vehicles, of around 33 per cent.

In addition to the role of technology and trade, concern has also been expressed that the actions of foreign-owned firms in Western economies have had the effect of reducing the relative demand for unskilled labour. The welfare implications of such effects are less than clear. For example, technological progress is universally regarded as beneficial, not to say essential to an economy. However, if technology is largely labour augmenting, then it is clear that technological progress will lead to a fall in the demand for unskilled labour, and, at least in the short to medium term, unemployment. However, at the same time, structural models of labour demand essentially assume that a reduction in the demand for unskilled labour, even as a result of FDI or trade, is evidence of technological progress. This clearly ignores the prospect of 'crowding out'; imports from low-wage countries may simply be able to replace domestic output, not because they are technologically superior, but simply because they are produced by firms with lower labour costs. Employment substitution from inward investment may be seen in the same light. Domestic employment may fall as a result of inward investment, not because of the introduction of new technology, but because of entry by foreign firms in receipt of subsidies, that have located low-wage parts of the UK.

Such empirical work as has been done in this area, suggests that inward investment does indeed lead to an increased demand for skilled workers, and that this occurs as a result of a combination of two effects. First, that the entry of MNEs, in possession of a technological advantage over domestic firms will offer rates of pay above current rates, and will increase the demand for skilled labour. The second effect is essentially a spillover effect, that the new (to the host country) technology which accompanies the FDI, is to a degree assimilated by the domestic sector. This increases the productivity of skilled workers still further *in the domestic sector*, resulting in increasing demand for skilled workers at the expense of unskilled workers. However, for the purposes of this chapter we are interested in how multinational activity has influenced overall employment. That is, have the employment gains of the skilled outweighed the employment losses of the unskilled or vice versa?

We use two measures of multinational activity, the first being the share of foreign employment to total manufacturing employment, and the second the share of net capital expenditure by foreign firms in the UK manufacturing. Figure 11.3 shows that both measures of FDI activity increased over the period by 25 per cent and 20 per cent respectively. By far the largest increases were experienced in SIC4 with the employment measure of FDI increasing by approximately 40 per cent and the capital measure of FDI increasing by 23 per cent.

Having described the factors that have been used in the literature to explain demand shocks and their recent trends, the following section introduces the model used to determine each potential effect on aggregate employment.

3   Theory and empirical methodology

To consider how technology, trade and FDI may have impacted upon aggregate employment we start from a simple static profit maximising model of firm behaviour. Assuming a Cobb-Douglas production function of the form:

$$Y_{it} = A_{it}^{\gamma} K_{it}^{\alpha} N_{it}^{\theta} \tag{1}$$

where Y is real output, K is the capital stock and N is the units of labour utilised. Rearranging to eliminate capital from the expression, it is trivial to show that a profit-maximising firm can be represented by:

$$Y_{it} = A_{it}^{\gamma} \left(\frac{\alpha N_{it}}{\theta} \times \frac{w_{it}}{r_{it}} \right)^{\alpha} N_{it}^{\theta} \tag{2}$$

where w is the wage rate, and r is the cost of capital. The parameter A is allowed to vary across time in the following way:

$$A_{it} = Tech_{it}^{\gamma_1} \times Trade_{it}^{\gamma_2} \times FDI_{it}^{\gamma_3} \times e^{\gamma_4 T} \tag{3}$$

where $\gamma_1, \gamma_2, \gamma_3, \gamma_4 > 0$ and T is a time trend. Rearranging equations (2) and (3) and taking a logarithmic transformation yields:

$$\ln N_{it} = \eta - \delta T - \phi \ln Tech_{it} + \lambda \ln Trade_{it} + \psi \ln FDI_{it}$$
$$+ \pi \ln(w/r)_{it} + \rho \ln Y_{it} \tag{4}$$

where $\eta = -(\alpha \ln \alpha - \alpha \theta)/(\alpha + \theta)$, $\nu = \kappa/(\alpha + \theta)$, $\phi = \gamma_1 \nu$, $\lambda = \gamma_2 \nu$, $\psi = \gamma_3 \nu$, $\delta = \gamma_4 \nu$, $\pi = -\alpha/(\alpha + \theta)$, $\rho = 1/(\alpha + \theta)$. Finally, allowing trade to take the form of import and export intensity (Greenaway *et al.* (1999)) yields:

$$\ln N_{it} = \eta - \delta T - \phi \ln(R\&D/Y)_{it-1} + \lambda \ln(Imports/Y)_{it} + \varphi \ln(Exports/Y)_{it}$$
$$+ \psi \ln FDI_{it} + \pi \ln(w/r)_{it} + \rho \ln Y_{it} + \Phi \mathbf{M}_{it} + \varepsilon_{it}. \tag{5}$$

R&D/Y is our measure of technology intensity, *Imports/Y* is import intensity, *Exports/Y* is export intensity, *FDI* is the measure of multinational activity in industry i (defined in Table 11.1, overleaf), η is a constant and the vector $\mathbf{M}$ contains regional controls. Equation (5) is estimated in levels by panel data techniques and also in first differences to sweep out unobserved fixed effects ω_i as follows:[1]

$$\Delta \ln N_{it} = \tilde{\eta} - \tilde{\delta} T - \tilde{\phi} \Delta \ln(R\&D/Y)_{it-1} + \tilde{\lambda} \Delta \ln(Imports/Y)_{it}$$
$$+ \tilde{\varphi} \Delta \ln(Exports/Y)_{it} + \tilde{\psi} \Delta \ln FDI_{it} + \tilde{\pi} \Delta \ln(w/r)_{it}$$
$$+ \tilde{\rho} \Delta \ln Y_{it} + \tilde{\Phi} \Delta \mathbf{M}_{it} + \omega_i + \varepsilon_{it}. \tag{6}$$

The data used to estimate equation (5) (levels) and equation (6) (differences) are based at the three-digit industry level for UK manufacturing sectors (SIC, 1980 sectors 2–4) over the period 1983 to 1992. This provides 101 industries over ten years giving 1,010 observations. All data are converted into natural logarithms and deflated to 1980 prices. Table 11.1 defines the variables used in the empirical analysis. The following section shows the results of estimating equations (5) and (6) in levels and first differences respectively. In levels the number of observations are 909 due to the lagged structure of R&D – taking one year of observations (101 sectors) out of the analysis – and in differences the number of observations are 808.

Table 11.1   Variable definitions

Variable	Definition
Y	Total industry sales by value.
$R\&D$	Research and development stock at the 3-digit level. The stock of R&D is measured as the sum of R&D expenditure for the previous 7 years, depreciated at the standard rate of 10% per annum.
Imports	The value of industry imports.
Exports	The value of industry exports.
w/r	The wages of all employees divided by rent on capital employed. This is calculated from a sample of over 3,000 firms from the Jordan's FAME company reports and accounts data base for the relevant industries over the period.
N	Total employment
K	Capital stock estimated as the sum of net capital investment of the previous 7 years, depreciated by 10% per annum.
FDI(1)	Share of total UK manufacturing employment accounted for by foreign owned multinationals.
FDI(2)	Share of net capital expenditure by foreign firms in the UK.
Region	A coefficient of variation of the regional distribution of value added in the industry, based on the 11 standard UK regions.

4   Empirical results

Table 11.2 presents the results of estimating equations (5) and (6). The table is formatted in the same manner, so that results are shown in levels by fixed and random effects (FE and RE respectively) where intercept terms are allowed to vary across sectors, capturing sector-specific time invariant effects, and first differences with heteroscedastic consistent standard errors (GLS).

Specifications 1 to 5 in Table 11.2 show the results of estimating equations (5) and (6) by including one potential demand shifter at a time. Generally the coefficients are significant, with the exception of export intensity in specification 3, and negative implying employment losses. Also, in all instances estimates in first differences are smaller than those in levels. The coefficient upon technology (R&D intensity) in specification 1 implies a maximum reduction in *aggregate* employment of over 49,000 jobs[2] (based upon fixed effects). Similarly, globalisation has also led to a fall in overall manufacturing employment, a maximum of around 23,000 jobs (based upon fixed effects, specification 2). Multinational activity under the employment definition

Table 11.2 Results of estimating equation (5) in levels by fixed and random effects, and equation (6) in first differences by generalised least squares

| | Specification 1 | | | Specification 2 | | | Specification 3 | | | Specification 4 | | |
| | Levels | | Diffs | Levels | | Diffs | Levels | | Diffs | Levels | | Diffs |
	FE	RE	GLS	FE	RE	GLS	FE	RE	GLS	FE	RE	GLS
Constant		-0.393	5.954		-0.292	6.441		-0.492	6.430		-0.525	6.326
		(2.85)	(3.48)		(2.14)	(3.81)		(3.65)	(3.80)		(4.02)	(3.76)
Output	0.289	0.531	0.279	0.289	0.524	0.281	0.289	0.542	0.280	0.301	0.562	0.283
	(11.78)	(27.99)	(10.18)	(11.74)	(27.28)	(10.16)	(11.26)	(26.78)	(10.14)	(12.29)	(30.95)	(10.29)
Wages/rent	0.084	0.077	-0.003	0.084	0.077	-0.002	0.088	0.080	-0.002	0.079	0.069	-0.003
	(4.84)	(4.55)	(0.22)	(4.83)	(4.53)	(0.15)	(5.02)	(4.72)	(0.14)	(4.59)	(4.13)	(0.24)
$(R\&D/Y)_{t-1}$	-0.029	-0.019	-0.008									
	(4.23)	(2.86)	(2.63)									
(Imports/Y)				-0.030	-0.024	$-0.126e^{-4}$						
				(4.04)	(3.34)	(0.01)						
(Exports/Y)							-0.015	-0.016	-0.001			
							(1.49)	(1.64)	(0.20)			
FDI(1)										-0.018	-0.027	-0.005
										(3.55)	(5.40)	(2.37)
FDI(2)												
Controls	Year dummies			Year dummies			Year dummies			Year dummies		
Observations	909	909	808	909	909	808	909	909	808	909	909	808
Adjusted R^2	0.992	0.741	0.306	0.992	0.739	0.302	0.992	0.760	0.302	0.992	0.782	0.306

Table 11.2 (Continued)

	Specification 5 Levels FE	Specification 5 Levels RE	Specification 5 Diffs GLS	Specification 6 Levels FE	Specification 6 Levels RE	Specification 6 Diffs GLS	Specification 7 Levels FE	Specification 7 Levels RE	Specification 7 Diffs GLS
Constant		-0.484 (3.64)	6.407 (3.79)		-0.709 (5.39)	5.649 (3.27)		-0.675 (5.08)	5.728 (3.30)
Output	0.299 (12.11)	0.559 (30.29)	0.282 (10.24)	0.282 (10.99)	0.573 (29.24)	0.278 (10.19)	0.280 (10.86)	0.572 (28.97)	0.277 (10.13)
Wages/rent	0.083 (4.74)	0.074 (4.35)	-0.002 (0.19)	0.072 (4.21)	0.066 (3.97)	-0.003 (0.25)	0.074 (4.29)	0.069 (4.13)	-0.002 (0.20)
$(R\&D/Y)_{t-1}$				-0.036 (5.01)	-0.021 (3.13)	-0.009 (2.49)	-0.037 (5.11)	-0.022 (3.29)	-0.010 (2.42)
(Imports/Y)				-0.048 (4.35)	-0.024 (2.45)	0.002 (0.42)	-0.051 (4.59)	-0.029 (2.85)	-0.001 (0.32)
(Exports/Y)				0.017 (1.17)	-0.034 (0.03)	-0.006 (0.94)	0.019 (1.32)	0.003 (0.20)	-0.006 (0.89)
FDI(1)				-0.016 (3.11)	-0.027 (5.44)	-0.005 (2.43)			
FDI(2)	-0.006 (1.40)	-0.009 (2.26)	-0.003 (1.79)				-0.006 (1.50)	-0.010 (2.45)	-0.003 (2.68)
Controls		Year dummies			Year dummies			Year dummies	
Observations		909	808		909	808		909	808
Adjusted R^2	0.992	0.769	0.304	0.993	0.789	0.309	0.993	0.778	0.307

Table 11.3 Maximum and minimum impacts under the employment definition of FDI

	Minimum	Maximum
Technology	15281	61126
Trade	12997	25995
FDI	4366	23576
Total effect	*32644*	*110697*
% of employment change	4.4	15

Table 11.4 Maximum and minimum impacts under capital expenditure definition of FDI

	Minimum	Maximum
Technology	16979	62824
Trade	15705	27619
FDI	2620	8732
Total effect	*35304*	*99175*
% of employment change	4.7	13.4

(specification 4) implies job losses of nearly 24,000 (random effects), and the
capital definition of FDI activity suggests a figure of around 6,500 jobs (random
effects, specification 5).

The final two specifications 6 and 7, shown in Table 11.2, provide estimates
of equations (5) and (6) with all potential demand shifters included. Under the
employment definition of FDI the coefficients imply the maximum and minimum impacts shown in Table 11.3.

Similarly, defining FDI by capital expenditure the coefficients imply the
maximum and minimum impacts shown in Table 11.4.

Our estimates suggest that technology, trade and multinational activity can
explain between 4.5 and 15 per cent of the total reduction in manufacturing
employment evident from our sample. Although we find no evidence that
increased exports results in employment growth, as would be expected theoretically, mostly the impact is insignificant and if anything suggests a
negative impact upon employment (as found by Greenaway *et al.* (1999)).

Under each scenario technology explains the largest proportion of the employment fall, although under the most conservative estimates there are no
statistical differences between the impact of technology and import penetration.
The fact that the results imply employment losses across each demand shifter
suggests that decomposing employment changes as follows $\Delta N = \Delta N_S + \Delta N_U$
(S and U denote skilled and unskilled), that even if the first term is positive it is
outweighed by falls in unskilled employment, so $[|N_U| > |N_S|] < 0$.

5   Conclusions

This chapter has considered how technological change, globalisation and multinational activity have influenced aggregate employment in the UK manufacturing sector. The majority of studies that have employment as their main focus have generally considered how demand changes have effected relative outcomes, such as skilled employment relative to unskilled employment. The expected outcome, that sources of technological progress are associated with an increase in the skill-premium, is often interpreted as an adverse effect, representing increased inequality and structural unemployment. Conversely, papers concerned with technological impacts, have estimated unskilled labour demand functions, with the assumption that a reduction in demand is indicative of technological progress, to the exclusion of other possibilities.

The results of this chapter show that technology intensity, import penetration and multinational activity have all contributed to the job losses witnessed in the manufacturing sector. Given the well documented shift in demand towards skilled labour this would suggest that any employment gains made by skilled workers have been outweighed by job losses amongst the lower skilled, thus consistent with a reduction in the aggregate number of jobs. At this stage, we are essentially agnostic as to the welfare implications of these results. Clearly, these results are suggestive that increased globalisation has generated a shift in demand away from unskilled labour. The literature on international spillovers, from FDI and trade, would suggest that this is indicative of technological progress, that imports and FDI have increased skill intensities in UK manufacturing. In addition, the trade effect may simply be evidence of increased specialisation of the UK economy, which can only contribute to improved revealed comparative advantage. However, it is also likely that both trade and inward investment generate a 'competitive' or crowding out effect, and clearly there are several explanations why this may occur, even in the absence of technological advantage on the part of the exporter or inward investor. It is equally likely that these effects are not mutually exclusive, and so one potential area of future research concerns the relative magnitudes and speeds with which these effects occur, and in turn the long-term response of the domestic sector to these changes. Moreover, future work should attempt to estimate the effects of technology, trade and FDI upon skilled and unskilled employment functions separately. For instance, if skilled labour has also been adversely effected, then this would be hard to reconcile with the notion of a substantial shift in demand against unskilled labour (Nickell and Bell (1995)).

Notes

1   There are advantages and disadvantages to estimating in levels. Much of the literature has sought to explain fluctuations in wage/employment by analysing data that has been first differenced or detrended. In the case of panel data an approach often

adopted to control for unobserved time invariant industry fixed effects is to first difference data. However, this type of analysis removes the trend component, where clearly the long-term persistent movements of the trend in employment is of importance. By first differencing data, researchers are only analysing year to year growth rates (Borjas and Ramey (1994)). Furthermore, estimating in levels allows an increase in a variable to influence the dependent variable in subsequent periods; this is reasonable if the effects are felt gradually over time – which is quite likely in the case of technology, trade and FDI spillovers. As stated above we also estimate all equations in first differences, as is common in the literature (Machin (1996); Machin and Van Reenen (1998); Anderton and Brenton (1999)), and a good reason for doing this is that if the data are characterised by a unit root then estimation in levels could lead to a spurious regression, thus differencing the data overcomes this problem.

Note that our definition of technology is based upon the intensity of R&D stock enabling us to estimate with all the data in either levels or first differences. Much of the literature has proxied technology intensity by the flow of R&D intensity, however under such a specification R&D intensity has to be entered in levels into an equation in changes.

2   The change in employment due to each of the potential demand shifters Z can be calculated as $\partial N = [(v \times \partial Z) \times (N \div Z)]$ where v is the estimated elasticity.

References

Anderton, B. and P. Brenton. (1999) 'Outsourcing and Low Skilled Workers in the UK', *Bulletin of Economic Research*, vol. 51, pp. 267–85.

Barrell, R. and N. Pain (1997) 'Foreign Direct Investment, Technological Change and Economic Growth within Europe', *Economic Journal*, vol. 107, pp. 1770–86.

Berman, E. and S. Machin. (2000) 'Skill Biased Technology Transfer: Evidence on the Factor Bias of Technological Change in Developing and Developed Countries', presented at the International Economic Association conference on Globalisation and Labour Markets, University of Nottingham, July 2000.

Blonigen, B. and M. Slaughter (1999) 'Foreign Affiliate Activity and US Skill Upgrading', NBER Working Paper 7040. Presented at the Annual Conference of the Royal Economic Society, St Andrews, 2000.

Borjas, G. and V. Ramey (1994) 'Time Series Evidence on the Sources of Trends in Wage Inequality', *American Economic Review, Papers and Proceedings*, vol. 84, pp. 10–16.

Conyon, M., S. Girma, S. Thompson and P. Wright. (1999) 'The Impact of Foreign Acquisition on Wages and Productivity in the UK', Centre for Research on Globalisation and Labour Markets, Research Paper 99/8.

Desjonqueres, T., S. Machin and J. Van Reenen (1999) 'Another Nail in the Coffin? Or Can the Trade Based Explanation of Changing Skill Structures be Resurrected?', *Scandinavian Journal of Economics*, vol. 101, pp. 533–54.

Driffield, N.L. (1996) *Global Competition and the Labour Market* (Reading: Harwood).

Driffield, N.L (1999) 'The Indirect Employment Effects of FDI into the UK', *Bulletin of Economic Research*, vol. 51(3), pp. 207–22.

Figini, P. and H. Gorg (1999) 'Multinational Companies and Wage Inequality in the Host Country: The Case of Ireland', *Weltwirtschaftliches Archiv*, vol. 134, pp. 594–612.

Girma, S., D. Greenaway and K. Wakelin, K. (2001) 'Wages, Productivity and Foreign Ownership in UK Manufacturing', *Scottish Journal of Political Economy*, vol. 48(2), pp. 119–33.

Gottschalk, P. and T. Smeeding. (1997) 'Cross-National Comparisons of Earnings and Income Inequality', *Journal of Economic Literature*, vol. 35, pp. 633–87.

Greenaway, D., R. Hine and P. Wright, P. (1999) 'An Empirical Assessment of the Impact of Trade on Employment in the United Kingdom', *European Journal of Political Economy*, vol. 15, pp. 485–500.

Haskel, J. (1999) 'The Trade and Labour Approaches to Wage Inequality', Queen Mary and Westfield College University of London, Working Paper no. 405.

Hine, R. and P. Wright (1998) 'Trade with Low Wage Economies, Employment and Productivity in UK Manufacturing', *Economic Journal*, vol. 108, pp. 1500–10.

Levy, F. and R. Murnane (1992) 'US Earnings Levels and Earnings Inequality: A Review of Recent Trend and Proposed Explanations', *Journal of Economic Literature*, vol. 30, pp. 1333–81.

Machin, S. (1996) 'Changes in the Demand for Skills', in A. Booth and D. Snower (eds) *Acquiring Skills: Market Failures, Their Symptoms and Policy Responses* (Cambridge: Cambridge University Press), pp. 129–46.

Machin, S. and J. Van Reenen (1998) 'Technology and Changes in Skill Structure: Evidence from Seven OECD Countries', *Quarterly Journal of Economics*, vol. 113, pp. 1215–44.

Nickell, S. and B. Bell (1995) 'The Collapse in Demand for the Unskilled and Unemployment across the OECD', *Oxford Review of Economic Policy*, vol. 11, pp. 40–62.

Pianta, M. and M. Vivarelli (2000) 'Introduction: Economic Structure, Technology and Employment', in M. Vivarelli and M. Pianta (eds) *The Employment Impact of Innovation* (London: Routledge), pp. 1–11.

Schmitt, J. (1995) 'The Changing Structure of Male Earnings in Britain 1974 to 1988', in R. Freeman and F. Katz (eds) *Differences and Changes in Wage Structure* (Chicago: Chicago University Press), pp. 177–204.

Slaughter, M. (1999) 'Globalisation and Wages: A Tale of Two Perspectives', *World Economy*, vol. 22, pp. 609–29.

Taylor, K. (1999) 'Male Earnings Dispersion over the Period 1973 to 1995 in Four Industries', Paper presented at the annual Education Employment and Economics Group, Swansea, and the annual European Association of Labour Economics, Regensburg.

Wood, A. (1994) *North–South Trade Employment and Inequality: Changing Fortunes in a Skill Driven World* (Oxford: Clarendon Press).

Wood, A. (1998) 'Globalisation and the Rise in Labour Market Inequalities', *Economic Journal*, vol. 108, pp. 1463–82.

12
The Employment and Wage Effects of Immigration: Trade and Labour Economics Perspectives*

Noel Gaston
Bond University, Australia

Doug Nelson
Tulane University, USA, and University of Nottingham, UK

1 Introduction

We may not be living in *the* age of mass migration, but we are surely living in *an* age of mass migration.[1] From 1965 through 1990 a fairly constant 2.2 per cent of the world population have been migrants.[2] However, this has involved an increasing rate of change to keep pace with the growing world population: the stock of migrants grew at 1.2 per cent from 1965 to 1975; 2.2 per cent from 1975 to 1985; and 2.6 per cent from 1985 to 1990. More importantly, for the purposes of this chapter, relative to regional population the share of migrants in the US and Canada rose from 6 per cent in 1965 to 8.6 per cent in 1990 (with the greatest growth in the 1980s and 1990s) while the share in Western Europe rose from 3.6 to 6.1 per cent over the same period. This period has also seen a substantial shift toward developing countries as source countries for this migration: in the United States this share rose from 42 per cent in 1960–64 to over 80 per cent in the 1980s and 1990s; in Canada this share rose from 12 to over 70 per cent, while this share in Australia rose from 7 to over 70 per cent. In the 1990s, Germany and Austria experienced very large flows from Eastern Europe as well.

As is well known, this period of rising immigration of unskilled workers coincides with a period of strong deterioration of the relative (and possibly the real) return to native unskilled labour in nearly all industrial countries (Levy and Murnane (1992); Davis (1992); Blackburn and Bloom (1995)). While much of the research on the causes of this phenomenon has focused on demand-side factors, with special emphasis on international trade and skill-biased technical change, unskilled immigration has received a considerable amount of attention

* The authors thank the participants at the Nottingham conference for useful comments. In particular, we thank Jonathan Haskel and Alan Kessler for useful comments on earlier drafts of this chapter, and David Greenaway for extensive substantive and editorial advice.

as a possibly relevant supply shock. However, unlike the case of the relationship between international trade and labour market outcomes, where there is considerable disagreement on the facts, the overwhelming majority of empirical studies agree that there is essentially no statistically significant effect of immigration on labour market outcomes, with the possible exception of the least skilled domestic workers (i.e. that small share of the work force that are high school dropouts).

The apparent occurrence of a largish supply shock with minimal economic effect has produced a sizeable literature, primarily among labour economists, attempting either to account for the measured smallness or to generate larger numbers. While there is fairly widespread agreement on the smallness of measurable effects of immigration, the interpretation of this fact is a matter of some considerable dispute. We will first consider accounts that attempt to retain the main structure of the labour theoretic framework involving primarily issues of internal migratory response to international migration or the labour market microstructure issues such as the possible presence of segmented labour markets. Where the inability to consistently identify significant effects from immigration was seen by some labour economists as something of a crisis, trade economists have been quick to suggest that this finding is, at least prima facie, consistent with standard trade theoretic models. We conclude the chapter with a brief discussion of the theoretical basis for this claim.

2   How labour economists have evaluated the effects of immigration

In this section we discuss some of the major findings about immigration and labour markets that have been uncovered in recent research by labour economists. As with our discussion of the impact of international trade on the labour market (Gaston and Nelson (2000a)), our primary focus here is on the contribution of immigration to the growing inequality experienced in many OECD countries during the 1980s, and the implications of that experience for future policy. In this section we consider in some detail empirical research by labour economists on the link between immigration and labour market outcomes (primarily wages). Contemporary empirical research on the labour market effects of immigration has grown quite large since its development in the early 1980s. We divide this research into two broad categories: production-function-based studies; and regression analysis in the supply-demand-institutions (SDI) framework. As we noted in the introduction, the most striking result from that research is how small are the measurable effects of what is a fairly sizeable labour market shock.

Before proceeding with this discussion we comment briefly on what may be the best-known gross distinction used to characterise this literature: area studies versus factor content studies (Borjas, Freeman and Katz (1997)). The problem is that the label is misleading. Virtually all labour theoretic frameworks apply a factor content based approach; that is, it is change in relative supply (immigration into a market) that generates the change in labour market outcomes. The issue is actually about *level of analysis*. That is: how large must the geographic unit (i.e. area) be such that observations on supplies and prices of various classes of labour are independent? As we shall see, there are good reasons for believing that geographic units such as standard metropolitan statistical areas (SMSAs) or states are linked in ways that are inconsistent with cross-sectional observations being independent draws from some distribution, but it is not at all clear that the statistically optimal level of analysis is the nation. There is considerable evidence that national borders have economic effects, but, by the same token, there is also considerable evidence that quite local labour markets take significant periods of time to fully adjust to macro shocks.[3] On balance, it is not clear to us that there is a clear reason to prefer one level of analysis to another. Level of analysis is always an important research decision, but this does not strike us as an essential distinguishing aspect in this body of research.

Production-function-based methods

The most straightforward analytical framework involves selecting a specific functional form for an aggregate production function, estimating that function on cross-sectional data, and testing hypotheses on the degree of substitutability or complementarity between inputs.[4] In addition, elasticities of derived demand can then be used to carry out policy experiments. If we start with aggregate production function $y = f(z)$, $z = \{z_1, \ldots, z_m\}$, we seek to calculate the Hicksian partial elasticities of complementarity between any two of the inputs i and k as:

$$\varsigma_{ik} = \frac{ff_{ik}}{f_i f_k}, \quad \forall i, k \in I \tag{1}$$

where we have used subscripts to denote partial derivatives. Following Hicks (1970; also see Sato and Koizumi (1973)), i and k are called *q-complements* if $\varsigma_{ik} > 0$ and *q-substitutes* if $\varsigma_{ik} < 0$.[5] Because it is easier to interpret the quantity elasticities of inverse input demand,

$$\eta_{ik} = \frac{\partial \ln w_i}{\partial \ln z_k} \tag{2}$$

these are usually calculated using the relationship:

$$\eta_{ik} = \varsigma_{ik} \theta_k \tag{3}$$

where θ_k is the distributive share of input k.

In carrying out work of this sort, investigators must select a functional form that does not prejudice the conclusion from the start. In particular, we would like the data to determine the values of the elasticities as defined. Thus, the commonly used Cobb-Douglas and CES forms will be inappropriate for any input vector with more than two arguments. As a result, investigators have generally used one or another of the flexible functional forms.[6] In addition to selecting a specific functional form, the other major choice in this body of research involves the definition of the input vector. Broadly speaking, there are two approaches: one defines the input vector in terms of observable characteristics (e.g. gender, age, immigrant status); while the other seeks to identify production-relevant characteristics (e.g. quantity of human capital).

In the first paper using this approach, Grossman (1982) used cross-sectional data for 1970 to estimate a translog function of native workers, first-generation immigrants, second-generation immigrants, and capital. She finds that both first- and second-generation immigrants substitute for native labour, but that second-generation immigrants are much closer substitutes for natives, and that new immigrants are closer substitutes for second generation immigrants than for natives. In addition, Grossman finds that capital is complementary with each type of labour, but that this complementarity is strongest with first-generation immigrants and weakest with natives. Grossman's analysis concludes with a policy simulation using the relationship in equation (3) to calculate own- and cross-elasticities to study the effect of a 10 per cent increase in the number of legal immigrants in the labour force on a short-run equilibrium in which native wages are fixed (and thus adjustment occurs on the employment margin) and a long-run equilibrium in which all wages are flexible. In the short run, native employment falls by 0.8 per cent, second-generation wages fall by 0.06 per cent, first-generation wages fall by 2.2 per cent, and the return to capital rises by 0.2 per cent. In the long run, wages are flexible, so all markets clear: native wages fall by 1 per cent, second-generation immigrant wages fall by 0.8 per cent, first-generation immigrant wages fall by 2.3 per cent, and the return to capital rises by 4.2 per cent.[7]

In an important series of papers, Borjas (1983, 1986a, 1986b, 1987) uses a number of data sets from the 1980s to study different disaggregations of labour in the context of a generalised Leontief production function. Depending on the particular breakdown of labour (e.g. by gender, race, immigration status), immigrants tend to be complements to some native labour and substitutes to others, though in all cases these effects are small – except for the effects of immigrants on other immigrants of the same type, for whom the effects can be sizeable and negative. Given Borjas' more recent position as a leading opponent of immigration and searcher for large effects, it may be worthwhile to quote his own summary of this, and other, work circa 1990:

> the methodological arsenal of modern econometrics cannot detect a single shred of evidence that immigrants have a sizable adverse impact on the earnings and employment opportunities of natives in the United States. (Borjas (1990, p. 81))

In particular, Borjas fairly consistently finds that, while immigrants may be substitutes for white native-born men, and thus increased immigration may have had a small negative effect on their labour market outcomes, immigrants are found to be complements to black native-born men who, thus, may have gained from increased immigration.

This approach is also used to examine the effects of legal Mexican immigration on labour market outcomes of Hispanic natives (King, Lowell and Bean (1986)) and illegal Mexican immigration on a wide variety of labour groups (Bean, Lowell and Taylor (1988)) with essentially the same results: the first study finds evidence of complementarity, suggesting that Mexican immigration may have a positive effect on the wages of native born Hispanics; and the second study finds effects of legal immigration like those in Borjas, and finds that illegal immigration may have a small negative effect on white, non-Hispanic workers, but essentially no effect on native Hispanic workers.

The research we have considered to this point focused on immigration status, among other things, as a production-relevant fact. Rivera-Batiz and Sechzer (1991) and Gang and Rivera-Batiz (1994), however, argue that there is no particular reason to believe that immigrant status, or race or gender, is directly production-relevant. They prefer, instead, to assume that individuals with identical bundles of production-relevant traits will receive the same wage. As a result, their strategy involves estimating a translog production function of education, experience and unskilled labour to derive the relevant Hicksian elasticities, and then using data on the skill composition of immigrants versus natives to derive distributional effects. Like Borjas and Bean *et al.*, they use individual data sorted into local market areas to estimate, like Grossman, a translog production function, and then use equation (1) to get the Hicksian elasticities of complementarity, and equation (3) to get the relevant factor demand elasticities. In the first stage they find, for both US and European data, that own supply elasticities are negative, as expected, and that the cross-elasticities imply that unskilled labour, education and skill are all complements for one another (i.e. $\varsigma_{ik} > 0$ for $i \neq k$). In addition, own elasticities are all estimated to be considerably larger than cross-elasticities. The authors then construct skill inventories of immigrant and native groups and use those, along with the estimated elasticities, to compute composite elasticities of complementarity that summarise this information. As with other work that we have reported, there are a variety of sign patterns, but 'the impact of *all* the immigrant groups on *all* the native-born groups are small in absolute magnitude' (Rivera-Batiz and Sechzer (1991, p. 106)). The largest effect is that of Mexican immigrants on Mexican-Americans, where an increase in Mexican immigration of 10 per cent will result in slightly less than an 1 per cent fall in wages of Mexican-Americans (with a similar effect on native black labour). Similarly small results are found for the European case in Gang and Rivera-Batiz (1994).

The production function approach receives its most sophisticated treatment to date in a series of papers by Michael Greenwood and Gary Hunt with a variety of colleagues. In Greenwood and Hunt (1995), the authors are interested in examining a variety of adjustment channels beyond change in wage. For input demands, they estimate a translog cost function on SMSA-level data for 1970, and find immigrant labour to be a substitute for domestic labour. In addition, they estimate labour supply functions and aggregated output demand functions for the local markets. With these results they construct a large number of simulations permitting adjustment via flexibility in native labour supply (via both variable participation rates and internal migration) and changes in demand for final output, as well as adjustment along a given isoquant. As with the previous studies, the wage, and now labour force participation, effects of immigration are uniformly small and, perhaps not surprisingly, the magnitudes of effects generally fall with the opening of additional channels of adjustment. The final output demand channel in particular seems to have a consistent effect of reducing the wage effects of immigration (or even making the effects on natives positive). These results can be seen to be closely related to the trade theoretic claim that, with multiple sectors the existence of adjustment at the output mix margin will generally lead to smaller effects (factor price insensitivity).

By the mid- and late-1980s, researchers working in applied production analysis had begun to recognise that standard flexible functional forms (including both the translog and generalised Leontief forms) could fail to satisfy concavity, but that flexibility may be destroyed if concavity is imposed globally (Diewert and Wales (1987)). Greenwood, Hunt and Kohli (1996) begin their analysis by pointing out that virtually all of the studies we have reviewed to this point present results indicating the presence of failures of concavity, in addition they estimate CES, translog and generalised Leontief cost functions on a common data set to illustrate violations. As a result, they conduct their analysis using the symmetric normalised quadratic form, developed by Diewert and Wales (1987), that permits curvature conditions to be imposed globally without endangering flexibility. The authors calculate the Hicksian elasticities of complementarity and find that native labour and immigrants are q-substitutes, while all other input pairs are q-complements. Thus, an increase in immigrants would lower the wage of native workers, and raise the wage of non-recent immigrants and capital, but these effects are quite small. For example, a 10 per cent increase in the supply of recent immigrants would reduce the wage of native-born labour by 0.96 per cent. The effect of this change on other recent immigrants, however, is quite large.

Finally, Greenwood, Hunt and Kohli (1997) mix the approaches of Grossman and Borjas with that of Rivera-Batiz by disaggregating native and immigrant labour into four skill categories each (based on earnings), as well as capital, and estimating a symmetric normalised quadratic cost function on a cross-section of SMSAs.[8] Not surprisingly, given the number of factors, there is quite a variety of q-substitutability and -complementarity, but unskilled immigrants appear to be strong q-substitutes for low- and medium-skilled native labour, and q-complements for unskilled native labour. Once again, however, the authors are unable to find any evidence that unskilled immigration leads to large changes in the income distribution or in employment opportunities, with the exception of the effect on other unskilled immigrants.

Before turning to the more widely used SDI regression approach, we briefly note a structural approach used by trade economists which could be seen as a multisectoral generalisation of the production function approach. Following original work by Burgess (1974), empirical trade economists have exploited duality theory to estimate comparative static effects of trade by treating trade as a direct argument in a GNP function.[9] The marriage of this approach to trade modelling to the production theoretic modelling of immigration seems obvious, but has only rarely been done. Wong (1988) works with an indirect trade utility function that is, itself, a function of the GNP function. This function is estimated, in translog form, on prices for home-produced durable goods, home-produced non-durable goods and services, and imported goods and services, and endowments of capital, land and labour, for a number of years between 1948 and 1983. Foreign capital and labour are taken to be perfect substitutes for the domestic factors, so the comparative statics on the indirect utility function can be used to generate the relevant elasticities. These elasticities are all small. Kohli (1993, 1999) develops this sort of analysis in considerably greater detail. Specifically, using annual Swiss data from 1950 to 1986, Kohli (1999) estimates the translog cost function associated with the primal GNP function and a z vector containing capital, home labour, immigrant labour and imports.[10] Thus, where Wong treats home and immigrant labour as perfect substitutes, Kohli is able to test this relationship. In fact, Kohli finds that home and immigrant labour are both Allen-Uzawa and Hicks q-substitutes, though not perfect substitutes. Commodity imports and immigrant labour are found to be both Allen-Uzawa and Hicks q-complements.[11] Once again, the magnitude of the estimated effect of immigration on native wages is negative, but quite small. However, Kohli simulates a short-run model in which the wage is downward inflexible, and finds the effect on home labour displacement to be large.

Overall, econometric research which explicitly exploits production theoretic structure, tends to find strong substitutability between immigrants and other immigrants of the same vintage and national origin and, otherwise, widely varying patterns of complementarity and substitutability between immigrants and natives. More importantly, the elasticities between immigrant and native labour are consistently small, and are smaller yet when other channels of adjustment than the wage are explicitly permitted.

The SDI regression approach to estimating the wage effects of immigration[12]

The labour economists' standard approach to wage inequality and income distribution is firmly rooted to an SDI analysis (Freeman (1993, pp. 44–9)). To evaluate the labour market effects of immigration, identifying how the immigration of workers with differing skills affects the relative supply of labour can be viewed as a necessary first step. In turn, the skill group characteristics of new immigrants are affected by the returns to skill as well as the distribution of earnings in both the source and host countries. Finally, labour market institutions are important because they affect the degree of wage inequality, the structure of wages and the labour market response to shocks.

Borjas *et al.* (1997) constitute a prominent example of this type of approach. What they term the 'aggregate factor proportions approach' involves regressing the ratio of skilled wages to unskilled wages in year *t*, on the relative labour supply of the two types of labour. Borjas *et al.* (1997) find that immigration affected certain groups of workers more so than others. Specifically, immigration may have been responsible for the decline in the earnings of unskilled native workers that occurred during the 1980s. Their paper has contributed to the view that, relative to the effects of growing international trade with less-developed countries, immigration may have had a proportionately larger negative impact on the earnings of unskilled US workers.

A qualitatively similar approach is used to derive estimating equations for regional unemployment or wages. For example, Altonji and Card (1991) and LaLonde and Topel (1991) estimate wage equations taking the form:

$$w_j = \gamma_\lambda \lambda_j + \beta_X X_j + v_j \tag{4}$$

where *j* indexes the local labour market, *w* is the logarithm of the wage for a particular skill group, *X* is a vector of control variables and, as above, λ is the proportion of immigrants in the local labour market. In contrast to the above study by Borjas *et al.* (1997), these studies find scant evidence that recent waves of immigration have disadvantaged US workers.

To eliminate region-specific fixed effects, due to ethnic enclave effects, for example (see Bartel (1989)), first-differencing is often used. More generally, if the immigrant share in market *j* is correlated with unobservable variables only through a time-invariant individual fixed effect, then estimating fixed effects regressions may be appropriate (e.g. Altonji and Card (1991); Topel (1994a, 1994b)). LaLonde and Topel (1991a) estimate this sort of regression in both levels and differences and find that the estimates of the effect of immigration produced by the two methods are nearly identical; that is, the wage effects are negligible.

Unfortunately, fixed effects estimation is not a cure-all for most sample selectivity and endogeneity problems. In the case of immigration and wages, the very nature of sorting on unobservable variables suggests that the migration decision of individuals may involve a process of learning about what is their correct state (i.e. industry, occupation, location, etc.). We discuss the endogeneity and sample selection further below in connection with the instrumental variables and natural experimental approaches to the study of the impact of immigration.

Of course, these regression specifications are quite general. For instance, there have been many studies using the regression framework that have focused on the importance of the large increase in the relative supply of workers during the

1970s to the increasing wage inequality that occurred throughout the late 1980s and early 1990s. The increase in the US work force caused by the labour force entry of the baby boomers easily dwarfs the increase in the labour force caused by immigration. Welch (1979), Berger (1985), Murphy, Plant and Welch (1988) and Murphy and Welch (1991) are among the better-known US studies. A common finding of these studies is that changes in cohort size associated with the Baby Boom generation did not have a significant impact on cohort earnings. Overall, supply-side changes in the United States were very quickly discounted as a candidate explanation for the increased dispersion in the income distribution in the United States during the 1980s.

Notwithstanding, the preceding findings on the effects of domestic labour supply shocks do not necessarily imply that all supply-side 'shocks' are unimportant. In the current context, some authors claim that immigration may have been responsible for the decline in the earnings of unskilled native workers that occurred during the 1980s. The immigration issue has been increasingly seen as one of 'distribution' rather than 'efficiency' (LaLonde and Topel (1997)). Freeman (1998, p. 110) argues that immigration may have had substantially larger effects on native unskilled workers than increased international trade with low-income countries. During the 1980s, a period during which wage inequality rapidly increased in the United States, immigration raised the supply of high school dropouts by approximately 25 per cent, which far exceeds the increase in the 'implicit labour supply' of such workers attributable to trade. Furthermore, Borjas *et al.* (1992, 1997) conclude that the large increase in the number of unskilled immigrants explains about one-third of the decline in the relative wage of high school *dropouts* during the 1980s. For the United States, wage inequality increased most in the west where the largest inflow of less-skilled immigrants was experienced (Topel (1994a, 1994b)).

In principle, changes in cohort quality can be analysed in the same way as changes in cohort size. Borjas (1994) considers the declining cohort quality of recent waves of immigrants to the United States to have been the result of the shift in US immigration policy, specifically the passage of the 1965 Immigration Act. However, his findings of decreasing cohort quality have recently been questioned by Butcher and DiNardo (1998) who focus on changes in the wage distribution through time. Using the methodology developed by DiNardo *et al.* (1996), they investigate the counterfactual of what the wage distribution would have looked like for new immigrants if they had faced the wage distributions from different eras. They find that earlier immigrants would have had wages much more similar to today's new arrivals, if they had faced the present-day prices for their skills.[13] Race and ethnicity, and not the changing education levels of the new immigrants, explain much of the change in comparative economic fortunes of recent immigrants once wage structure changes have been held constant. The point, as also stressed by LaLonde and Topel (1991b), is that recent cohorts of immigrants will look as if they do worse, even if they have the same set of characteristics as earlier cohorts of immigrants, if the distribution of wages has become more dispersed and if the new immigrants lie near the lower tail of the income distribution.

The use of regressions to uncover the wage effects of immigration by regressing immigrant shares and other controls on wages or relative wages poses many familiar problems. Among the more prominent concerns with multiple linear regression analysis is the omission of important right-hand-side variables. Biased estimates result if relevant characteristics or controls are not included in the regression equation. Similarly, how do various characteristics that are included in a model specification interact with one another? More generally, empirical work usually forces researchers to assume an appropriate functional form in order to reduce the problem at hand to one of estimating the parameters of interest. For example, would a linear function involve a serious mis-specification loss? As the previous section revealed, there is a wide range of functional forms from which to choose and so the robustness of parameter estimates is invariably an issue that needs to be confronted.

Variable (mis-)measurement and interpretation also pose problems. For instance, when does a migrant finally assimilate and become native? The latter problem is a particularly obvious one in those countries that are essentially composed of older generations of immigrants (e.g. Australia and the United States).[14] More formally, there is the issue of weak separability (Berndt and Christensen (1973)) of the various types of labour – not just of skilled versus unskilled labour, but also of native workers versus immigrant workers as well as first-generation migrants versus second and later generations of migrants.

One of the most important difficulties in the empirical immigration and labour market effects literature is the likely possibility that labour supply functions are not independent of wages. The problem is reminiscent of the difficulties faced by the labour economists who attempted to uncover the effects of trade liberalisation on relative wages (Gaston and Nelson (2000b)). Economic common sense suggests that the immigrant labour force share is endogenous. To make the endogeneity issue transparent, consider a simple two-equation model:

$$
\begin{aligned}
w_j &= \gamma_\lambda \lambda_j + \beta_X X_j + v_j \\
\lambda_j &= \gamma_w w_j + \beta_R R_j + v_j
\end{aligned}
\tag{5}
$$

where X and R are (exogenous) scalars and all variables are expressed in deviations from their means. As before, j indexes a local labour market. The sign of the OLS bias is given by:

$$
p \lim \gamma_\lambda^{OLS} - \gamma_\lambda = \left[\frac{\sigma_X^2}{\sigma_X^2 \sigma_w^2 - \sigma_{X\lambda}^2} \right] \cdot \left[\frac{\gamma_w \sigma_v^2 + \sigma_{vv}^2}{1 - \gamma_w \gamma_\lambda} \right].
\tag{6}
$$

It is not possible to argue *a priori* that the sign of the bias is either positive or negative. For illustration, suppose $\sigma_{X\lambda}^2 = \sigma_{vv}^2 = 0$ and that $\gamma_w > 0$ (i.e. higher relative wages are associated with higher relative supply). If the 'true' effect of a higher migrant share of unskilled workers is to depress unskilled wages (i.e. $\gamma_\lambda < 0$), then the bias is positive. That is, a failure to account for endogeneity will bias upward (i.e. toward zero) estimates of the impact of immigrants on wages.

However, note that if we are estimating some variant of the aggregate factor supply model, strictly speaking, our focus is on wage inequality. Furthermore, in many of the early studies in this literature, λ is simply taken to be the share of migrant labour in market j. Under this interpretation, it is no longer obvious that $\gamma_w > 0$. Models of immigrant worker self-selection, based on the pioneering work of Roy (1951), are extremely illuminating here.

Workers with high-earnings potential are likely to migrate from a country with an egalitarian wage structure (where they cannot easily make high earnings), while workers with low-earnings potential are especially likely to migrate from a country with great wage inequality. In terms of source country characteristics, equality of the income distribution encourages what is termed 'positive selection bias'.[15] Negative selection bias results when source countries have unequal income distributions and therefore migrants are likely to be the least skilled.[16] Recent waves to the United States tend to have been increasingly drawn from the latter group (Borjas (1994)). Immigrants are mobile, but they have tended to cluster in cities where their fellow countrymen reside. The clustering effects tend to dominate such economic incentives as differences in unemployment rates or welfare benefits across areas (Bartel (1989); Bartel and Koch (1991)). The effects of clustering are borne by the gateway cities, while the geographic concentration tends to reduce economic progress and the rate of assimilation. Of importance for the present discussion is that, given that the primary adverse wage impact of new immigrants is upon previous generations of migrants, the clustering effect may imply $\gamma_w < 0$. If the effect of clustering is sufficiently strong, then it is possible that OLS estimates are biased downwards, and not upwards.[17] Friedberg's (2001) findings are consistent with this line of argument. She studies the impact of Russian migration on occupational wages in Israel and finds that instrumental variables (IV) estimates are higher than OLS estimates. That is, rather than immigrants choosing occupations based on them offering higher wages, she finds evidence of occupational immobility (so that $\gamma_w < 0$). That is, immigrants, irrespective of their skill levels, are confined, initially at least, to low-paying occupations. Hence, OLS estimates overstate the impact of immigrants on wages.

Handling the endogeneity problem is the motivation for the use of the IV approach (e.g. Altonji and Card (1991) and Friedberg (2001)) and the quasi-experimental approach in the labour literature (e.g. Card (1990) and Hunt (1992)). Altonji and Card (1991) investigate the impact of immigrants on low-skilled native workers. They relate changes in the earnings and employment of low-skilled natives across cities to changes in the migrant population. As discussed, the problem is that the immigrant flows are likely to be correlated with current labour market conditions. Hence, Altonji and Card instrument the change in immigrants with the size of the immigrant enclave in an earlier period. They argue that the size of the immigrant enclave in the past is likely to affect immigrant flows but is not necessarily correlated with current demand shocks. In other words, the IV approach attempts to use only the variation in immigrant flows associated with variation in enclave 'pull' and not that associated with current demand shocks. Interestingly, Altonji and Card's estimate of γ_λ is one of the most negative. Notwithstanding, they conclude that immigrants and natives face little competition from one another. They find that there is some industry displacement from low-wage, immigrant-intensive industries; but still, the implied elasticities are small.[18] Despite these mobility effects, the effects on employment and unemployment rates are virtually zero.

Due to the substantial difficulties associated with choosing 'good' instruments (see Nelson and Startz (1990); Bound, Jaeger and Baker (1995)), considerably more weight in this branch of the literature has been attached to the results of the quasi- or natural experiments. Natural experiments occur when exogenous variation in independent (explanatory) variables (that determine 'treatment assignment') is created by abrupt exogenous shocks to labour markets (Meyer (1995)). For example, natural experiments can arise due to institutional peculiarities (e.g. Vietnam-era draft lotteries) or due to exogenous policy changes that affect some but not other groups (e.g. changes in policies in some states but not others).[19] In the latter case, Hanson and Spilimbergo (1999b) examine how enforcement of the US–Mexico border is affected by changes in illegal immigration. They find that the equilibrium level of border enforcement varies inversely with relative demand shocks (and consequently, demand for undocumented labour). In other words, the authorities relax border enforcement when the demand for undocumented workers is high.

Natural experiments are most useful in situations in which econometric estimates are ordinarily biased because of endogenous variables due to omitted variables or to sample selection. The basic approach involves a comparison of changes for 'treatment' and 'control' groups (i.e. differences-in-differences). This can be accomplished in a components of variance scheme (time effects, location effects, treatment group effects, interaction terms, etc.) or by using a IV approach in which one instruments for the treatment dummy variable with the natural experiment indicator variables. In this sense, the IV and natural experimental approaches are qualitatively equivalent. With IV, legitimate instruments generate a natural experiment that assigns treatment in a manner independent of the unobserved covariates. The advantage is that the source of the identifying information is transparent.

Occasionally, data are available for the time period before and after a 'treatment' (in our case, the treatment is an immigration shock) for a group that does not receive the treatment but experiences some or all of the other influences that affect the treatment group. At the very heart of the quasi-experimental approach to the immigration and labour market literature are the non-policy and non-institutional shocks that can be considered truly exogenous to existing labour market conditions in the destination country (e.g. Baby Boom, Black Death, Mariel Boatlift). That is, consider:

$$w_{jst} = \alpha + \beta D_s + \tau D_t + \gamma D_{st} + \varepsilon_{jst} \tag{7}$$

where D_t can be thought of as a time period dummy, D_s is defined as above, and $D_{st} = 1$ if $D_t = D_s = 1$, and zero otherwise. The key idea is that D_t summarises the way in which both treatment and non-treatment groups are influenced by time (e.g. macroeconomic conditions and regional growth trends). The time-invariant difference in overall means between the groups is captured by β. D_{st} indicates membership of the experimental group after it receives the treatment and γ is the true causal effect of the treatment on the outcome for this group. Again, the key identifying assumption is that $E(\varepsilon_{jst} \mid D_{st}) = 0$.

Note that γ would be zero in the absence of the treatment (i.e. the immigration shock). An unbiased estimate of γ can be obtained by the differences-in-differences estimator, that is:

$$g = (\bar{w}_{11} - \bar{w}_{01}) - (\bar{w}_{10} - \bar{w}_{00}) \tag{8}$$

where the first subscript is t and the second is for treatment s. Without question, the most cited natural experimental paper is Card (1990) that examines the impact of the Mariel Boatlift on Miami's labour market. In his paper, the first bracketed term in equation (8) represents the difference in wages for black workers in Miami before and after the Boatlift.[20] The second bracketed term is the wage difference for the same types of workers in a group of four comparison cities. The latter sites were chosen because they had relatively large populations of black and Hispanic workers and because they exhibited patterns of economic growth similar to those observed in Miami over the late 1970s and early 1980s. As is well known, despite the dramatic and sudden 7 per cent increase in the size of Miami's work force, Card is unable to detect any adverse impact on the wages or unemployment of less-skilled workers.

There are two notable quasi-experimental studies for Europe. Hunt (1992) examines the impact on wage differentials in France in 1968 of the influx of *pied noirs* from Algeria during the early 1960s; and Carrington and de Lima (1995) study the return of Portuguese colonialists from Africa and examine the wage effects across the provinces of Portugal. Consistent with Card's findings, these authors were unable to discern adverse wage effects for native workers.

Although subject to varying interpretations, the finding of small local labour market effects has been remarkably robust and in line with the findings from the econometric studies. LaLonde and Topel (1991b) estimate the elasticities of complementarity between immigrants and natives and between new immigrants and older cohorts of immigrants and find both to be very small. Taken in conjunction with their analysis of wages and earnings changes in local labour markets, they conclude that the wage effects of immigration are 'quantitatively unimportant'. Based on studies currently in print, it appears to us that such a conclusion is inevitable.

One would expect that in the face of such a huge mountain of evidence this would be the end of the story. Of course, even the briefest excursion through the recent literature reveals that the debate is far from having run its course. The attention of those intent on identifying large native labour market impacts has turned to explaining what the small statistical effect 'really means'. One explanation has highlighted the possibility that immigrants locate to areas where jobs are expanding anyway.[21] Another is that the internal migration by natives offsets the increased supply of immigrants (Filer (1992); Borjas (1994); Borjas *et al.* (1997)). The insignificant wage effects may simply be the result of factor price equalisation across US regions (see next section). In the case of the 'outwards native migration' argument, the punchline is that the small local labour market effects conceal, and may considerably understate, the negative impact of migrants on native workers. In the latter case, at least, this is now thought not to be the case. Card (2001) finds that the inter-city migration decisions of natives and older immigrants are largely unaffected by inflows of new immigrants. Moreover, Card and DiNardo (2000) find no evidence of selective out-migration by natives in response to immigrant inflows at particular locations.

Another possible reason for the insignificant cross-sectional impacts of immigration on wages relates to our discussion of dimensionality and margins of adjustment, given that the industrial composition of output may change without factor price effects. Hanson and Slaughter (2000) document the rapid growth in apparel, textiles, food products and other labour-intensive industries in California after the arrival of Mexican migrants. They focus on state-specific endowment shocks and state-specific wage responses. They show that the state output-mix changes broadly match state endowment changes and that variation in state unit factor requirements is consistent with factor price equalisation across states. States absorb regional endowment shocks through mechanisms other than changes in regional relative factor price changes. This is consistent with the findings of Blanchard and Katz (1992) that indicate that wages and income per capita converge for American states. However, Blanchard and Katz also find that employment performance diverges, that is shocks to employment grow and persist.[22] Overall, this is consistent with the view that small local labour market effects may be consistent with somewhat larger aggregate labour market effects.

The broad conclusion from the first large NBER project on immigration and trade was that immigration had a relatively smaller area impact than increased import penetration on native labour. Overall, the labour market was thought to easily adjust to migrant inflows, absorbing immigrants with little redistributive losses to natives (Abowd and Freeman (1991)). This conclusion was largely, and somewhat surprisingly, reversed by the second NBER project (Borjas and Freeman (1992)). While the wage and employment effects for natives in local labour markets are small, it was argued that certain groups of workers had been adversely affected by immigration. The augmented factor supplies of less-skilled workers, due to either the effect of trade with low-income countries or from the immigration of workers from developing countries, were thought to have contributed to the poor outcomes of less-educated American workers during the 1980s and early 1990s.

The finding that certain groups of workers may have been adversely affected by immigration is evident for some European studies as well. De New and Zimmermann (1994) find that greater concentrations of foreign workers in German industries during the 1980s were associated with small wage gains for white-collar workers, but relatively large wage losses for blue-collar workers.[23] Zimmermann (1995) attributes these findings to the greater labour market inflexibility, greater levels of unionisation and low labour mobility in Europe in comparison to the United States.[24] In the case of strong unions or wage inflexibility, the expectation is that immigration is associated with increases in native unemployment. In the case of labour immobility, equations (7) and (8) suggest that skilled wages increase and unskilled wages decrease when unskilled immigration increases.

It should, however, be noted that the results for Europe are quite mixed. Pischke and Velling (1997) find that immigration had no adverse wage or unemployment effects in German local labour markets. Similarly, Winter-Ebmer and Zweimuller (1996) using both OLS and IV estimation procedures find no detrimental immigration impact upon Austrian industry or regional wages.

Finally, a number of studies have attempted to consider trade and migration at the same time. The simplest approach to examining the effects of trade and immigration takes an agnostic position on the nature of the relationship between trade and immigration, and simply includes variables measuring both in a wage equation.[25] Freeman and Katz (1991) estimate regressions both of hourly wage and of annual hours on measures of change domestic demand, foreign demand, imports, and immigration (both stock and change), as well as a number of controls, on a cross-industry data set.[26] Changes in imports and immigration are negatively related to hourly wages and positively related to annual hours. However, the authors suggest that these regressions generate suspiciously large effects of immigration, leading to an argument that they are picking up the tendency of immigrants to move into low- and declining-wage industries (p. 246).[27] This explanation is consistent with the standard trade theoretic model, due to Mundell (1957), in which trade and factor mobility are substitutes. That is, sectors facing increasing competition from low-wage (unskilled-intensive) countries can slow the rate at which they decline by importing low-wage labour directly.[28]

Similar methodologies have been applied in the cases of Germany and Austria. Haisken-DeNew and Zimmermann (1999) use the German Socioeconomic Panel to estimate wage regressions on a variety of individual variables and region-sector-specific trade deficit and foreigner share variables, in a random effects panel model for 1984–92. In addition to carrying out the analysis on the sample of all workers, they also segment the sample by skill (under both job title and years experience definitions), by blue versus white collar. In all cases they find that trade is negatively related to wages, and immigration (in all cases but one) positively related to wages.[29] The first finding parallels that of Freeman and Katz, while the second is directly contradictory. Because the immigration results are generally larger, and more precisely estimated for high-skilled workers, the authors conclude that this is suggestive of complementarity between immigrants and high-skilled workers. Consistent with Freeman and Katz' suggestion of a substitutive relationship between trade and immigration, however, is Haisken-DeNew and Zimmermann's finding that import-competing sectors employ a larger share of immigrant workers. Winter-Ebmer and Zweimuller (1999a) examine trade and immigration in a cross-section of Austrian workers, finding that immigration increases unemployment duration by a small amount, but has no statistically significant effect of probability of unemployment. In addition, they find no effect of trade on probability of unemployment or unemployment duration. In a related study of young workers, Winter-Ebmer and Zweimuller (1999b) find exports negatively related to unemployment (though exports to the CEEC are positively related), imports having no significant effect (though those from the CEEC have a negative effect), regional stock of immigrants makes unemployment more likely, but immigrants in the sector make it less likely. Again, these effects are generally small. Finally, Winter-Ebmer and Zimmermann (1999) present results, for both Austria and Germany, for changes in overall employment growth, native employment growth, and wage growth, as a function of changes in exports (to CEEC and rest of world), imports and foreign share. In the Austrian case, immigration has essentially no effect on overall employment growth, and only small negative effects on native employment growth and wage growth. Imports also generally have a negative relationship to employment growth, with imports from the CEEC having a generally larger negative effect. For the German case there is evidence that overall immigration has a small negative effect on native employment growth and a small positive effect on wage growth, while immigration from Eastern Europe has a rather strong effect on native employment growth and a sizeable positive effect on wage growth. The effects of growth in imports and exports are uniformly small, mostly insignificant, and perversely signed. Overall, these results are consistent with results reported above that immigration effects are small, even taking into account interactions with international trade.

In this section, we focused on two of the more important 'facts' that have seemingly gained widespread acceptance. First, that immigrant flows have small local labour market effects; and second, that immigration has affected certain groups of workers more so than others. To us, the first conclusion seems inescapable. The same cannot be said for the second. In the case of the United States, such a conclusion seems an overly confident one to reach. Given the sheer size of the US labour market and the quantity of unskilled labour, more broadly defined, it is unlikely that immigration (or trade) would have contributed to the overall increase in wage inequality observed in the United States during that particular period. On the other hand, as Rodrik (1998) notes, there may have been a fundamental change in the underlying demand for unskilled labour that is attributable to the increased availability of unskilled, migrant labour. As argued by Gaston and Nelson (2000a), it may be the case that trade and immigration engender institutional responses that do leave some types of unskilled labour more vulnerable to economic shocks than others.

3 Trade theory as a guide to interpreting empirical results[30]

For some labour economists, the results reported in the previous section have an air of paradox: how can a sizeable supply shock fail to have sizeable price (i.e. wage) effects?[31] This air of paradox can be dispelled, however, with a small change in theoretical perspective. It will be recalled that both the production function and SDI approaches, explicitly or implicitly, work with the same underlying theoretical model: a many-factor × one-final output, perfectly competitive economy. The virtue of this model, from the point of view of empirical work on labour markets, is the strong identifying restrictions that it generates for empirical work. With particular reference to the study of supply shocks, like immigration, perfect competition with one final good forces all adjustment to supply shocks through the factor price. In this section, we argue: (a) that moving to a framework identical to that used by labour economists except that there are at least as many industries as factors of production, eliminates the paradox; (b) that this dimensionality assumption is more *a priori* plausible than $m \times 1$ assumption used by labour economists; and (c) that there is some systematic evidence in favour of this approach.

Given the occasionally heated disputes between trade and labour economists on this question, it is important to be clear that the issue is presumption. That is, *as a first approach* to thinking about the impact of immigration on a well-defined labour market, what is the most sensible model for generating intuition? We will argue that the only matter of substance dividing these two broad approaches (labour and trade) is dimensionality. Both take complete and perfect markets to be a plausible baseline from which to begin the analysis of immigration.[32] Somewhat less obviously, neither the presence nor absence of commodity trade, nor the exogeneity or endogeneity of labour flows, distinguishes these approaches. We will comment briefly on each of these, but first dimensionality.

In either case, we characterise production via a standard neoclassical production function:

$$y_j = f^j(z_j) \tag{9}$$

where j denotes a sector, and we drop it in the one-sector case, z_j is a vector of inputs, and $f^j(\cdot)$ is a linear homogeneous, strictly quasi-concave function.[33]

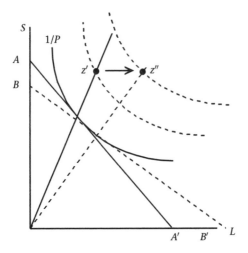

Figure 12.1   Endowment change and factor-price change in the one-sector model

A convenient representation in either case is the unit-value isoquant – the locus of all input combinations that yield €1 worth of output (i.e. letting price be P_j, this is the $1/P_j$ isoquant). In Figure 12.1 we suppose that $z' = \{S, L\}$, skilled and unskilled labour, denotes the economy's endowment, and the slope of the ray from the origin through z' identifies $s = S/L$, the equilibrium input ratio. From cost minimisation and competitive markets we know that, in equilibrium, the slope of the isoquant will be equal to $\omega = -w_u/w_s$. Thus, an increase in the relative endowment of unskilled labour (from z' to z''), a fall in s, straightforwardly leads to a fall in ω.[34] Furthermore, if we suppose that the price of the final good is fixed, this translates to a real increase in the wage of S and a real decrease in the wage of L.[35] The entire adjustment has occurred through a change in relative factor prices. As we saw in the previous section, this is the basis of the standard labour theoretic approach to determining the effect of immigration on a host economy. As we shall see in the next section, this setup provides a set of identifying assumptions that permits a very straightforward econometric analysis of the price (or, *mutatis mutandis*, employment) effects of increased immigration.

Now suppose that we make only one change in the model, we add one more good and assume that good 1 is always *S*-intensive relative to good 2. Figure 12.2 labels denote the good from Figure 12.1 'good 1' and the new good 'good 2'. Since both of the isoquants are unit-value isoquants, they must be tangent to a common €1 isocost line. As with the one-good case, the tangent gives ω, common to both industries as a result of free inter-sectoral factor mobility, and identifies s_j (the technology in use in each sector).[36] By the small-country assumption, the relative commodity price ($p = P_2/P_1$) is fixed, which fixes the

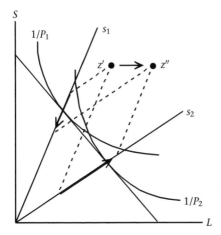

Figure 12.2 Endowment change and factor-price insensitivity in the two-sector model

unit-value isoquants, and thus fixes the common isocost, whose slope gives ω. The cone defined by the rays s_1 and s_2 is called the *cone of diversification* because any endowment in the interior of the cone involves production of both final goods at the given price, with the equilibrium technology in use. Thus, two economies, sharing the same technology sets and facing the same final good prices, but endowed with different proportions of S and L, will choose the same technologies (i.e. s_1 and s_2) and have the same ω. This is the Lerner (1952)–Samuelson (1948) *factor price equalisation theorem*. If we focus on a single country, this is easily seen as a very simple comparative static representation of immigration, with z' the initial endowment and z'' the endowment after an immigration shock consisting purely of unskilled labour.[37] It is this version of the theorem that Leamer (1995) calls the *factor price insensitivity theorem*. The mechanism that brings this factor price insensitivity about is the subject of the Rybczynski (1955) theorem. That is, with two goods, if commodity prices (and technology) are unchanged the location of the unit-value isoquants cannot change, the equilibrium isocost cannot change, which means that the ratio cannot change unless the economy specialises. Thus, the only way this economy can respond to a change in endowment, from z' to z'' (an increase in L with S fixed), is to change output mix, increasing output in the sector using L intensively (by proportionally more than the increase in L) and decreasing output in the other sector, as illustrated by the arrows. The essential point here is not that factor price insensitivity actually obtains, but that, in a world with more than one output, some of the adjustment to an endowment shock will occur via a change in the output mix, reducing the actual, and measured, costs to the competing factor (i.e. domestic unskilled labour). In the Heckscher-Ohlin-Samuelson (HOS) model illustrated here, as long as both goods are produced, the only way to generate a change in relative factor prices is to change the relative commodity prices.

From the point of view of thinking about presumption, it is important to note that factor price insensitivity is quite robust to a variety of changes in assumptions which retain the essential properties of competitive markets and at least as many traded commodities as non-traded factors of production.[38] In particular, we can introduce non-traded goods, intermediates, and even joint production.[39]

One might expect that, and some discussions seem to suggest that, the fundamental difference between the labour theoretic and trade theoretic approaches to framing empirical research relates to the explicit incorporation of international trade flows. This, however, is not the case. As we have just seen, both the labour and trade theoretic approaches tend to hold the prices of final commodities exogenously fixed. As Altonji and Card (1991) point out, one way to motivate this in the one-good case is to suppose the domestically produced good is consumed and exported in exchange for an international good which is consumed, but not produced, locally. Furthermore, the standard labour theoretic approach is to adopt a small-country assumption that fixes the relative price of the exportable and the importable goods.[40] Trade economists are fond of the small, open economy model for the same reason: analysis of the supply side of the model can be abstracted from demand considerations.

When labour economists say that their model is a 'closed economy' model, what they mean is that it is closed to immigration. That is, immigration will occur as a comparative static change in the endowment.[41] While a substantial trade theoretic literature has treated factor flows endogenously, there is no shortage of comparative static analysis.[42] Our illustration in Figure 12.2 does precisely that, and one might reasonably argue that a small-country, comparative static framework is the natural framework for empirical analysis on this question.[43] In any event, endogeneity of factor flows certainly does not distinguish between the labour and trade theoretic approaches.

Now we would like to argue for the plausibility of factor price insensitivity as a presumption. We start by recalling that the sole relevant difference between the basic frameworks in use by labour and trade economists is dimensionality. First, dimensionality is not nearly so damaging of factor price insensitivity as it is of factor price equalisation. The former is a one-economy comparative static result, while the second seeks to make a multi-country comparison, requiring both strong assumptions about internationally common technology and global univalence to make the comparisons. While Hanson and Slaughter's work suggests that technological change within a country may interfere with inference in periods of large-scale technological change, the multi-good framework seems quite appropriate as the basis of but-for analyses of immigration shocks. Second, contrary to some of the assertions by both trade and labour economists, it does not seem to us that the choice between $m \leq n$ and $m > n$, as interpretive frameworks, should rest on whether or not the framework generates income distribution effects from immigration.[44] Given the very weak evidence in favour of such income distribution effects, this seems doubtful in any event. But it seems that, on any but fairly short-term interpretations of the concepts of commodity and factor, there are massively more commodities than factors, and in this case the *logic* of factor price insensitivity holds quite straightforwardly.[45] Note that we are not arguing that factor price insensitivity actually obtains, but that, within the parameters that are commonly agreed in the basic labour and trade theoretic traditions, $m \leq n$ seems a more plausible assumption, from which factor price insensitivity follows. We should generally expect adjustment at the output-mix margin to play a considerable role in responding to factor immigration. If the mechanism breaks down, it must be as a result of deviations from those elements of the basic model that are shared between trade and labour economists, and not on dimensionality.

So far we have argued, on essentially *a priori* grounds, that the trade theoretic framework dominates the labour theoretic framework as an intuition generator for evaluating the labour market effects of immigration. We would now like to finish this section by arguing that there is evidence in favour of the adjustment mechanism asserted in the trade theoretic account. An early contribution by Horiba and Kirkpatrick (1983) examined direct and indirect (i.e. trade-embodied) flows of labour between the north and south United States in 1965–70, finding that endowment convergence was relatively small, though in the right direction (i.e. labour and labour-intensive products are southern exports), while the indirect labour flows were considerably larger and seemed to be doing most of the work in equalising factor prices between regions. More recently, Horiba (2000) finds essentially the same results for 1975–80. In particular, this work finds again that migration and trade flows are consistent with the underlying trade model, and the migration channel involves relatively small adjustment while the indirect trade in factors is considerably larger. These results are closely related to a growing body of trade research the results of which suggest that the HO model, under various plausible extensions of the model (e.g. the presence of trading costs or Hicks-neutral international differences in technology) and generalisation of the Rybczynski theorem, does a reasonably good job of accounting for production patterns, and research on growth which fails to find a link between migration and convergence.[46]

Related to this work is a pair of papers by Hanson and Slaughter (2000) and Gandal, Hanson and Slaughter (2000), the first dealing with the US, the second with Israel. These are based on a clever accounting decomposition that seeks to identify the contributions of output-mix change and technological change in adjusting to endowment shocks. In the US case, Hanson and Slaughter (2000) present results consistent with productivity-adjusted factor-price equalisation across states and, further, present evidence suggesting that states have absorbed changes in labour endowments primarily via skill-biased technological change which is common across all states and, secondarily, via changes in output mix. That there should be evidence of output-mix adjustment in a period of rapid and substantial technological change strikes us as important, especially considering Horiba's findings for a technologically less dynamic period. However, such evidence does not exist in the Israel case, where Gandal, Hanson and Slaughter (2000) find that global changes in technology were (more than) sufficient to absorb the huge, relatively skilled influx of immigrants from Russia. In addition to the finding that output-mix adjustment was playing a role, there are two important implications of this work for the discussion to follow. First, there is some suggestion that, at least among relatively developed economies, the assumption of a common technology across countries may be less of a distortion than assuming a common technology across a finite period of time (at least during a technologically dynamic period). Second, while appropriately constructed comparative static analysis will identify important forces operating at the level of the economy as a whole, dynamic forces that are not incorporated in the analysis might well overwhelm the static forces.[47] On the other hand, since these forces are both less well understood and less controllable, their relevance for policy analysis is very unclear.

4 Conclusions

As we have stressed throughout this chapter, the primary division in the literature on the labour market effects of immigration is not empirical. Unlike the related literature on the labour market effects of trade, where there are substantial differences over matters of fact, the impression one gets from the immigration literature is that there is a widely held, and fairly tight, prior on essentially zero labour market impact.[48] It is also widely agreed that there are sizeable negative effects on migrants of the same origin and vintage, and a, perhaps not quite so widely held, agreement that the small, and shrinking, group of native high school dropouts experience economically, and statistically, significant negative consequences from contemporary immigration.

To the extent that there is a dispute in the immigration case, it revolves around the framework to be used for evaluating the results of the empirical work, and here the division is very much between labour and trade economists.[49] We have argued that the sole substantive difference between labour and trade economists relates to the dimensionality of the model used to evaluate the results – with labour economists preferring an m-factor × one-final good model and trade economists preferring an $m \times n$ good model (with a modal preference for the 2×2 model). As long as $m \geq 2$ and $n \geq 2$, output-mix adjustment will play a role in adjusting to an immigration shock, and the failure to account for that role will produce overestimates of the wage (or unemployment) effects of any given shock. Furthermore, we have also argued for the fundamental plausibility of the m-factor $\leq n$-good model on essentially *a priori* grounds. If this argument is accepted, there is some presumption that output-mix adjustment fully absorbs the immigration shock. That is, if we are going to use a perfectly competitive baseline for policy evaluation, as revealed to be preferred by both labour and trade economists, our presumption should be that immigration, short of that necessary to generate a fundamental shift in production structure, has no effect on long-run labour market conditions. Factor price insensitivity holds.

As a presumption, from which to begin an evaluation of proposed immigration policy, or an evaluation of past immigration policies, this strikes us as the right presumption. And the fact that its key implication, essentially no labour market effect of immigration, is borne out by most empirical work, should strengthen our commitment to this presumption. But it is only a presumption – a point from which we should be willing to be shifted if faced with sufficient evidence in a given case. We have argued that factor price insensitivity is surprisingly robust to plausible variations on the basic model, but the model is, itself, very simple. There are obviously many relevant facts of economic and social life that are not part of the model, but might well affect our ultimate evaluation of immigration policy. Perhaps the most significant of these relates to short-run adjustment cost. It is now well established that the economic short-run can be chronologically rather a long time, and that these adjustment costs can be substantial.[50] We only make two points here. First, these considerations are essentially orthogonal to immigration *per se*. That is, if we are concerned about adjustment costs borne by citizens, whether as a result of trade, immigration, technological change, or anything else, we have tools for dealing with them, and there is no particularly good reason for worrying about the source of worker dislocation. Second, this does not distinguish the labour and trade approaches. Within either framework, using immigration policy as an instrument for dealing with redistributive concerns is an exercise in (at least) second best.

This leads us to the most difficult question: if immigration is *really* not relevant to the long-run economic life of citizens, why does it occasionally become such a large political issue? In a companion paper to this chapter (Gaston and Nelson, 2000b), we argue that the political economy of immigration policy cannot be understood as being about labour market effects and sketch an alternative account that embeds migration politics in a broader understanding of the politics of the welfare state and cultural adjustment to change.

Notes

1   Carter and Sutch (1998), Hatton and Williamson (1998) and Sassen (1999) emphasise that large-scale migration is not a new phenomenon, and was arguably quantitatively more significant in earlier periods. However, as Sassen (1999) points out, the development of democracy, nationalism and welfare states have made immigration a politically more difficult, and potentially more explosive, issue in contemporary times than in earlier times.

2   The statistics in this paragraph are drawn from Zlotnik (1998).

3   See Helliwell (1998) for a useful overview and extension of research on the economic effects of national borders. On local labour markets see Topel (1986), Blanchard and Katz (1992); and Bound and Holzer (2000). White and Mueser (1988) provide a very interesting discussion of the implications of level of analysis for studies of domestic migration.

4   Production functions can also be estimated using time series data, but in that case one must be concerned with technological change, certainly a concern in the apparently technologically-dynamic 1980s. The equivalent assumption, that all regions within the same country have access to the same technology set, seems considerably less demanding.

5   A pair of inputs (z_i, z_k) are q-complements if an increase in the endowment of k causes an increase in the wage of i, w_i; they are q-substitutes if the increase in z_k produces a fall in w_i. Hammermesh (1993) provides a clear discussion of these concepts.

6   A functional form is flexible if it can approximate any arbitrary, twice continuously differentiable function in the sense that its parameters can be chosen such that its value, gradient and Hessian equal the corresponding magnitudes for the arbitrary function at a given point. Lau (1986) provides an excellent discussion of the issues that arise in choosing functional forms for empirical analysis. Chambers (1988, ch. 5) is a somewhat more elementary discussion, with a strong emphasis on application.

7   In related studies, Bürgenmeier, Butare and Favarger (1991) estimate a translog function of immigrant labour, native labour and capital using Swiss time-series data from 1950 to 1986, while Akbari and DeVoretz (1992) estimate a translog function on an industrial cross-section based on Canadian data for 1980. In addition to finding qualitatively similar results on the pattern of complementarity between factors, the Swiss study finds evidence of a positive relationship between immigration and capital accumulation. At the economy-wide level, the Canadian study finds no significant effect of immigrants, that is all Hicksian elasticities of complementarity between immigrants and natives are insignificantly different from zero. However, when the sample is restricted to labour-intensive industries only, the Canadian study does find evidence of labour displacement as a result of immigration.

8   In a study of the impact of low-skilled migration from Mexico, Davies *et al.* (1998) estimate a symmetric normalised quadratic production function in which the arguments are: low-skilled natives divided by gender and ethnicity (Mexican, non-Mexican); native high-skilled males and females (one category); foreign-born, low-skilled Mexicans; foreign-born, low-skilled non-Mexicans; and capital. As in the previous studies, the authors find that in both 1980 and 1990 immigrants have negative effects on the native born, but that these effects were small. The effects on other immigrants were found to be large. Furthermore, whatever the effects of trade and factor mobility within the US might be, the effects are larger in areas of high immigrant concentration.

9   The underlying idea is to treat trade as an input to final GNP under the argument that virtually all goods in trade must be processed further for final sale. See Kohli (1991) for an excellent development of the theory, econometrics and results from this research.

10   Kohli (1993) directly estimates a symmetric normalised quadratic GNP function on the same Swiss data. The results are broadly the same: increased immigration reduces home wage, but only weakly; and trade and immigration are found to be complements.

11   Interestingly, imports and capital are Allen-Uzawa substitutes, but Hicks q-complements.

12 There is a parallel literature applying regression analysis to unemployment. We focus on the wage results primarily because of the close link to the theory. We simply note here that the primary conclusions of this section – that is, small to no effects, except on migrants of similar origin and vintage, and the least-skilled native workers – holds as well for unemployment.

13 With similar implications, albeit from a different perspective, Friedberg and Hunt (1995) note that 'composition problems' make it difficult to ascertain the impact of immigration on wage inequality. For example, they argue that including the newly arrived waves of less-skilled migrants in inequality calculations is likely to bias the conclusion towards finding greater inequality in the United States.

14 Zimmermann (1995) reminds readers of the literature that the European research on immigration has more to do with the effects of possessing citizenship. Unlike the US literature, which has tended to focus on the effects of newly arrived immigrants on native workers as well as on earlier generations of immigrants, the European data do not distinguish individuals as foreign-born or not.

15 In fact, a point often overlooked is that host-country labour market conditions are absolutely central to the migration decision. For example, Hanson and Spilimbergo (1999a) found that attempted illegal immigration from Mexico is *extremely* sensitive to changes in real wages in Mexico.

16 Interestingly, increasingly negative self-selection produces labour market outcomes in both the source and host countries similar to the picture of the effects of outsourcing on wage inequality painted by Feenstra and Hanson (1996, 1997). That is, if workers emigrating from Mexico are relatively high skilled from Mexico's viewpoint and unskilled from the United States' viewpoint, then wage inequality tends to rise in both countries.

17 Friedberg and Hunt (1995) make a related criticism of Goldin's (1994) findings. Using data for 1890 to 1923, Goldin found a significant negative correlation between the percentage of foreign-born residents and wages in US cities. However, this may be a 'composition' effect, that is if immigrants earn lower wages than natives, then even if immigrants have *no* effect on native wages, they tend to be clustered into cities with lower average wages.

18 Friedberg and Hunt (1995) note that Altonji and Card's 'large and negative' estimates imply that a 10 per cent increase in the percentage of foreign-born in a local labour market implies a minuscule 0.86 per cent reduction in wages.

19 Hamermesh (2000) argues that, unlike 'acts of God', treating changes in the legal environment as exogenous is rarely convincing.

20 Card conducts a similar analysis for Hispanic workers, as well. Also, in addition to wages he uses the same methodology to examine whether the Boatlift had any effect on the unemployment rates of less-skilled workers.

21 Once again, the issue is the econometric one of handling the possibility of endogeneity. If immigrants choose their destination locations or occupations based on wage growth and the growth of job opportunities, rather than on wage levels, then controlling for the endogeneity problem appropriately requires the use of panel data.

22 Decressin and Fatás (1995) have similar findings for the regions of Europe. However, they show that changes in labour-force participation rates bear proportionately more of the burden of adjustment in response to labour market disturbances.

23 Specifically, DeNew and Zimmermann find that their IV estimates were substantially more negative than their OLS estimates (in fact, 15 times larger). On one hand, this result may be seen as being consistent with Friedberg's (2001) occupational crowding finding for Israel, discussed above. On the other hand, at a more practical level there

is evidence of some instability in the coefficients of the industry-level variables in the IV model specification. (DeNew and Zimmermann use industry dummies, industry growth rates and industry-specific time trends as determinants of share of foreign workers by industry.) As the authors acknowledge, the issue of whether their instrumenting procedure has been able to fully control for the endogeneity of the foreign share of labour may have been insufficient.

24 Interestingly, Zimmermann (1995) notes that there has been little impact of immigration on unemployment rates. The research on the effects of immigration on Australian labour market outcomes has instead focused on the likelihood of adverse unemployment effects. With a heavily regulated labour market (compared to the United States, at least), the concern has been that labour market adjustments would occur through quantity (length of the dole queue) rather than through prices (wages). However, in surveying the literature, Junankar *et al.* (1998) conclude that immigration has not increased the Australian unemployment rate.

25 Borjas, Freeman and Katz (1992, 1997) simulate a partial equilibrium labour market model in which an inelastic labour supply is shifted by a direct immigration shock and an indirect labour import shock calculated via the factor contents of commodity trade. Even in this framework, which is adopted to maximise the labour market effects of globalisation, the authors conclude: 'The bottom line from our simulations is that the economic impact of immigration is mainly redistributional and primarily affects a small group of the least-educated US native workers' (Borjas *et al.* (1997, p. 66)).

26 These changes are calculated for 1958–84. As a control, the authors also estimate these models on CPS data, with essentially the same result.

27 This tendency is observed directly in a wide variety of research.

28 By the logic of the Rybczynski theorem, the import of unskilled labour results in an increase in the output of the unskilled-labour-intensive sector and a fall in the output of the skilled-labour-intensive sector. Even if the relative endowment of skilled labour is rising as a result of domestic human capital accumulation, possibly driven by increased international competition, an increasingly unskilled-labour-abundant immigration will slow down the rate of decline of the unskilled-labour-intensive sector.

29 The one exception is a statistically significant negative relationship between number of immigrants in a region/industry and the wages of low-skilled, white-collar workers, where skill is defined by level of experience.

30 Useful general surveys of the relationship between trade and immigration can be found in Ethier (1986, 1996), Wong (1995), Razin and Sadka (1997), and Venables (1999).

31 Though, we note again, even larger supply shocks (e.g. the Baby Boom) produce relatively small wage effects. See Hammermesh (1993) for evidence that the estimated elasticities in the immigration case are not particularly different from those generally estimated. This provides some support for the notion that the search for large effects was driven, at least in part, by the large political effects of immigration: in particular the politics surrounding Proposition 187 in California, and anti-immigrant politics in Europe. Our standard political economy models take it that politics is driven by economic self-interest, so the presence of extensive political activity is taken to be indirect evidence of large economic effects. See Gaston and Nelson (2000b) for a discussion of this issue.

32 In fact, neither approach diverges much from this assumption. This distinguishes the analysis of immigration from the analysis of the labour market effects of foreign direct investment and even trade.

33 Where we need a general representation we will denote the set of all factors as I and its dimensionality as m, while the set of all goods is J with dimensionality n, i will index members of I and j will index members of J.

34 An alternative representation of this is that the value marginal product curve for unskilled labour is a downward-sloping function of $1/s$. In the two-factor case, with S and P (the price of final output) fixed, this is just the demand curve for unskilled labour.

35 This follows from the standard weighted-average property of price changes (Jones (1965)): $\hat{P} = \theta_L \hat{w}_L + \theta_s \hat{w}_s$, where θ_i denotes distributive shares and a circumflex denotes proportional changes. Thus, in Figure 12.1, $\hat{w}_s > \hat{P} = 0 > \hat{w}_L$. It is also straightforward to show that the gain to domestic skilled labour exceeds the loss to domestic unskilled labour. With appropriate redistributive policy, citizens must gain. However, without such a policy it is easy to see that households deriving most of their income from unskilled labour would lose while skilled-labour-owning households would gain.

36 Our assumption of no factor-intensity reversals guarantees that $s_1 > s_2$ for all ω.

37 Interestingly, Samuelson concludes his original article of FPE with a discussion of its implications for immigration policy, though the policy in question was that of encouraging emigration from England to Australia.

38 On dimensionality generally see Jones and Scheinkman (1977) and Ethier (1984).

39 Woodland (1982, 1984) contains exceptionally clear discussions of all these issues.

40 Altonji and Card, however, adopt a version of the large-country assumption in their own framework.

41 It should be noted that a sizeable literature in labour economics is explicitly concerned with formally and econometrically modelling the migration decision; on the whole it is not particularly concerned with aggregate equilibria. Borjas (1994) and Lalonde and Topel (1997) survey much of this literature. For a survey that covers literature on migration decision-making in fields well beyond economics, as well as those in economics, see Massey *et al.* (1998).

42 Ruffin (1984) provides a very clear presentation of the trade theoretic literature on international factor mobility.

43 Once we depart from the one-sector labour theoretic framework or the 2×2 framework of the HOS model, trade and immigration may be related in a variety of ways which need to be considered in evaluating empirical results.

44 Trade economists such as Thompson and Wooton seem to make this argument as the entering wedge of a political economy argument, while labour economists make the argument to shore up the foundations of their estimating framework.

45 See Bernstein and Weinstein (1998) for a recent development of the dimensionality argument, and its implications for tests of directions of trade predictions.

46 On the subject of the endowment–output link, and the ways results vary in moving from inter-regional to international environments, see: Davis, Weinstein, Bradford and Shimpo (1997); Davis and Weinstein (1997); Bernstein and Weinstein (1998); and Kim (1999). For the lack of a relationship between migration and convergence, see Barro and Sala-i-Martin (1991) and related work by Kim (1998) suggesting an important role for industrial structure, as well as technological change, in accounting for convergence.

47 In addition to technological change, we would also consider factor accumulation to be a dynamic force of considerable significance. It should probably be noted, as Hanson and Slaughter do, that capital accumulation may be playing a large role as well.

48 People often talk about a loosely construed 'average' opinion on the labour market effects of trade, but this represents a collective prior with very fat tails. The tails in the

immigration case (e.g. Borjas, Briggs, Huddle) are visible and aggressive in asserting their opinion, but seem to have very small impact on the aggregate professional opinion.

49   It is in fact quite striking, in the trade and labour markets case, the extent to which heated disputes about interpretation take place between people who share a common model. As one example, see the papers by Leamer, Krugman, Deardorff, and Panagariya in the *Journal of International Economics* symposium (vol. 50(1), pp. 17–116).

50   That adjustment to a local labour shock may take a long time is one of the points that we take from the research on local labour markets that we have already mentioned (e.g.: Blanchard and Katz (1992); Decressin and Fatás (1995); and Topel (1986; 1994a, b). On the economic effects of worker displacement, see Topel (1991), Ruhm (1991), Kletzer (1991, 1996), and Jacobson, Lalonde and Sullivan (1993).

References

Abowd, John and Richard Freeman (1991) 'Introduction and Summary', in John Abowd and Richard Freeman (eds), *Immigration, Trade and the Labor Market* (Chicago: University of Chicago Press for NBER), pp. 1–25.

Akbari, Ather and Don DeVoretz (1992) 'The Substitutability of Foreign-born Labour in Canadian Production: Circa 1980', *Canadian Journal of Economics*, vol. 25(3), pp. 604–14.

Altonji, Joseph and David Card (1991) 'The Effects of Immigration on the Labor Market Outcomes of Less-skilled Natives', in John Abowd and Richard Freeman (eds) *Immigration, Trade and the Labor Market* (Chicago: University of Chicago Press for NBER), pp. 201–34.

Barro, Robert and Xavier Sala-i-Martin (1991) 'Convergence across States and Regions', *Brookings Papers on Economic Activity*, vol. 1, pp. 107–82.

Bartel, Anne (1989) 'Where Do the New US Immigrants Live?', *Journal of Labor Economics*, vol. 7(4), pp. 371–91.

Bartel, Anne and Marianne Koch (1991) 'Internal Migration of U.S. Immigrants', in J. Abowd and R. Freeman (eds) *Immigration, Trade, and Labor Markets* (Chicago: University of Chicago Press for NBER), pp. 121–34.

Bean, Frank, B. Lindsay Lowell and Lowell Taylor (1988) 'Undocumented Mexican Immigrants and the Earnings of Other Workers in the US', *Demography*, vol. 25(1), pp. 35–49.

Berger, Mark (1985) 'The Effect of Cohort Size on Earnings Growth: A Reexamination of the Evidence', *Journal of Political Economy*, vol. 93(3), pp. 561–73.

Berndt, Ernst and Laurits Christensen (1973) 'The Internal Structure of Functional Relationships: Separability, Substitution, and Aggregation', *Review of Economic Studies*, vol. 40(3), pp. 403–10.

Bernstein, Jeffrey and D. Weinstein (1998) 'Do Endowments Predict the Location of Production? Evidence from National and International Data', *NBER Working Paper* no. 6,815.

Blackburn, McKinley L. and David Bloom (1995) 'Changes in the Structure of Family Income Inequality in the United States and Other Industrial Nations during the 1980s', in Solomon Polachek (ed.), *Research in Labor Economics*, (Stanford, Conn.: JAI Press) vol. 14, pp. 141–70.

Blanchard, Olivier and Lawrence Katz (1992) 'Regional Evolutions', *Brookings Papers on Economic Activity*, no. 1, pp. 1–61.

Borjas, George (1983) 'The Substitutability of Black, Hispanic, and White Labor', *Economic Inquiry*, vol. 21(1), pp. 93–106.

Borjas, George (1986a) 'The Demographic Determinants of the Demand for Black Labor', in R. Freeman and H. Holzer (eds), *The Black Youth Employment Crisis* (Chicago: University of Chicago Press for NBER), pp. 191–230.

Borjas, George (1986b) 'The Sensitivity of Labor Demand Functions to Choice of Dependent Variable', *Review of Economics and Statistics*, vol. 68(1), pp. 58–66.

Borjas, George (1987) 'Immigrants, Minorities, and Labor Market Competition', *Industrial and Labor Relations Review*, vol. 40(3), pp. 382–92.

Borjas, George (1990) *Friends or Strangers: The Impact of Immigrants on the U.S. Economy* (New York: Basic Books).

Borjas, George (1994) 'The Economics of Immigration', *Journal of Economic Literature*, vol. 32(4), pp. 1,667–717.

Borjas, George (1995) 'The Economic Benefits from Immigration', *Journal of Economic Perspectives*, vol. 9(2), pp. 3–22.

Borjas, George (1999a) 'The Economic Analysis of Immigration', in Orley Ashenfelter and David Card (eds), *Handbook of Labor Economics*, vol. 3A (Amsterdam: North-Holland), pp. 1697–760.

Borjas, George (1999b) *Heaven's Door: Immigration Policy and the American Economy* (Princeton NJ: Princeton University Press).

Borjas, George and Richard Freeman (1992) 'Introduction and Summary', in G. Borjas and R. Freeman (eds), *Immigration and the Work Force* (Chicago: University of Chicago Press for NBER), pp. 1–15.

Borjas, George, Richard Freeman and Lawrence Katz (1992) 'On the Labor Market Effects of Immigration and Trade', in G. Borjas and R. Freeman (eds) *Immigration and the Work Force* (Chicago: University of Chicago Press for NBER), pp. 213–44.

Borjas, George, Richard Freeman and Lawrence Katz (1997) 'How Much Do Immigration and Trade Affect Labor Market Outcomes?', *Brookings Papers on Economic Activity*, vol. 1, pp. 1–67.

Bound, John and Harry Holzer (2000) 'Demand Shifts, Population Adjustments, and Labor Market Outcomes during the 1980s', *Journal of Labor Economics*, vol. 18(1), pp. 20-54.

Bound, John, David Jaeger and Regina Baker (1995) 'Problems with Instrumental Variables Estimation when the Correlation between the Instruments and the Endogenous Explanatory Variable Is Weak', *Journal of the American Statistical Association*, vol. 90, pp. 443–50.

Bronfenbrenner, Martin (1971) 'The Demand for Productive Inputs', *Income Distribution Theory* (New York: Aldine), pp. 120–71.

Bürgenmeier, Beat, Théo Butare and Philippe Favarger (1991) 'Effects of Foreign Labour on the Production Pattern: The Swiss Case', *Schweizerische Zeitschrift für Volkswirtschaft und Statistik*, vol. 128(2), pp. 103–24.

Burgess, David (1974) 'Production Theory and the Derived Demand for Imports', *Journal of International Economics*, vol. 4(2), pp. 103–7.

Butcher, Kristin and John DiNardo (1998) 'The Immigrant and Native Born Wage Distribution: Evidence from United States Censuses', *NBER Working Paper* no. 6,630.

Card, David (1990) 'The Impact of the Mariel Boatlift on the Miami Labor Market', *Industrial and Labor Relations Review*, vol. 43(2), pp. 245–57.

Card, David (2001) 'Immigrant Inflows, Native Outflows, and the Local Labor Market Impacts of Higher Immigration', *Journal of Labor Economics*, vol. 19(1), pp. 22–64.

Card, David and John DiNardo (2000) 'Do Immigrant Inflows Lead to Native Outflows?', *American Economic Review*, vol. 90(2), pp. 360–7.

Carrington, William and Pedro de Lima (1996) 'The Impact of 1970s Repatriates from Africa on the Portuguese Labor Market', *Industrial and Labor Relations Review*, vol. 49(2), pp. 330–47.

Carter, Susan and Richard Sutch (1998) 'Historical Background to Current Immigration Issues', in James Smith and Barry Edmonston (eds), *The Immigration Debate: Studies on the Economic, Demographic, and Fiscal Effects of Immigration* (Washington, DC: National Academy Press), pp. 289–366.

Chambers, Robert (1988) *Applied Production Analysis: A Dual Approach* (Cambridge: Cambridge University Press).

Davies, Paul, Michael Greenwood, Gary Hunt, Ulrich Kohli and Marta Tienda (1998) 'The U.S. Labor Market Impacts of Low-Skill Migration from Mexico', in Binational Study: Migration Between Mexico and the United States (Washington, DC: US Commission on Immigration Reform), pp. 1,075–116.

Davis, Donald and David Weinstein (1997) *Economic Geography and Regional Production Structure: An Empirical Investigation* (Cambridge, MA: Harvard Institute of Economic Research).

Davis, Donald, David Weinstein, Scott Bradford and Kazushige Shimpo (1997) 'Using International and Japanese Regional Data to Determine When the Factor Abundance Theory of Trade Works', *American Economic Review*, vol. 87(3), pp. 420–46.

Davis, Steven (1992) 'Cross-Country Patterns of Change in Relative Wages', in Olivier Blanchard and Stanley Fisher (eds), *NBER Macroeconomic Annual 1992* (Cambridge, MA: MIT Press), pp. 239–92.

Decressin, Jörg and Antonio Fatás (1995), 'Regional Labor Market Dynamics in Europe', *European Economic Review*, vol. 39(9), pp. 1,627–55.

DeNew, J. and Klaus Zimmerman (1994) 'Native Wage Impacts of Foreign Labor: A Random Effects Panel Analysis', *Journal of Population Economics*, vol. 7(2), pp. 177–92.

Diewert, W. Erwin and Terence Wales (1987) 'Flexible Functional Forms and Global Curvature Conditions', *Econometrica*, vol. 55(1), pp. 43–68.

DiNardo, John, Nicole Fortin and Thomas Lemieux (1996) 'Labor Market Institutions and the Distribution of Wages, 1973–1992: A Semiparametric Approach', *Econometrica*, vol. 64(5), pp. 1,001–44.

Ethier, Wilfred (1984) 'Higher Dimensional Issues in Trade Theory', in Ronald W. Jones (ed.), *Handbook of International Economics*, vol. 1, no. 3 (Amsterdam: North-Holland), pp. 131–84.

Ethier, Wilfred (1986), 'Illegal Immigration', *American Economic Review*, vol. 76, pp. 258–62.

Ethier, Wilfred (1996) 'Theories about Trade Liberalisation and Migration: Substitutes or Complements?', in P.J. Lloyd and L. Williams (eds), *International Trade and Migration in the APEC Region* (Oxford and Melbourne: Oxford University Press), pp. 50–68.

Feenstra, Robert and Gordon Hanson (1996) 'Foreign Investment, Outsourcing and Relative Wages', in R. Feenstra, G. Grossman and D. Irwin (eds), *The Political Economy of Trade Policy* (Cambridge, MA: MIT Press), pp. 89–127.

Feenstra, Robert and Gordon Hanson (1997) 'Foreign Direct Investment and Relative Wages: Evidence from Mexico's Maquiladoras', *Journal of International Economics*, vol. 42(3/4), pp. 371–93.

Filer, Randall (1992) 'The Effect of Immigrant Arrivals on Migratory Patterns of Native Workers', in G. Borjas and R. Freeman (eds), *Immigration and the Work Force* (Chicago: University of Chicago Press for NBER), pp. 245–69.

Freeman, Richard (1993) 'Immigration from Poor to Wealthy Countries: Experience of the United States', *European Economic Review*, vol. 37(2/3), pp. 443–51.

Freeman, Richard (1998) 'Will Globalization Dominate U.S. Labor Market Outcomes?', in Susan M. Collins (ed.), *Imports, Exports and the American Worker* (Washington, DC: Brookings Institution Press), pp. 101–31.

Freeman, Richard and Lawrence Katz (1991) 'Industrial Wage and Employment Determination in an Open Economy', in J. Abowd and R. Freeman (eds), *Immigration, Trade and the Labor Market* (Chicago: University of Chicago Press for NBER), pp. 235–59.

Friedberg, Rachel (2001) 'The Impact of Mass Migration on the Israeli Labor Market', *Quarterly Journal of Economics*, vol. 116, pp. 1373–1408.

Friedberg, Rachel and Jennifer Hunt (1995) 'The Impact of Immigrants on Host Country Wages, Employment and Growth', *Journal of Economic Perspectives*, vol. 9(2), pp. 23–44.

Friedberg, Rachel and Jennifer Hunt (1999) 'Immigration and the Receiving Economy', in C. Hirschman, J. DeWind, and P. Kasinitz (eds), *The Handbook of International Migration: The American Experience* (New York: Russell Sage), pp. 342–59.

Gandal, Neil, Gordon Hanson and Matthew Slaughter (2000) 'Technology, Trade and Adjustment to Immigration in Israel', mimeo, Dartmouth College.

Gang, Ira and Francisco Rivera-Batiz (1994) 'Labor Market Effects of Immigration in the United States and Europe', *Journal of Population Economics*, vol. 7(2), pp. 157–75.

Gaston, Noel and Douglas Nelson (2000a) 'Globalisation and Wages in OECD Economies: Linking Theory with Evidence', in Joseph Francois, David Roland-Holst and Dominique van der Mensbrugghe (eds), *Globalisation and Employment Patterns: Policy, Theory, and Evidence* (Oxford: Oxford University Press for OECD and CEPR).

Gaston, Noel and Douglas Nelson (2000b) 'Immigration and Labour Market Outcomes in the United States: A Political Economy Puzzle', *Oxford Review of Economic Policy*, vol. 16(3), pp. 104–14.

Goldin, Claudia (1994) 'The Political Economy of Immigration Restriction in the US', in C. Goldin and G. Liebcap (eds), *The Regulated Economy: A Historical Approach to Political Economy* (Chicago: University of Chicago Press for NBER), pp. 223–57.

Greenwood, Michael and Gary Hunt (1995) 'Economic Effects of Immigrants on Native and Workers: Complementarity, Substitutability, and Other Channels of Influence', *Southern Economic Journal*, vol. 61(4), pp. 1076–97.

Greenwood, Michael, Gary Hunt and Ulrich Kohli (1996) 'The Short-Run and Long-Run Factor-Market Consequences of Immigration to the United States', *Journal of Regional Science*, vol. 36(1), pp. 43–66.

Greenwood, Michael, Gary Hunt and Ulrich Kohli (1997) 'The Factor-Market Consequences of Unskilled Immigration to the United States', *Labour Economics*, vol. 4(1), pp. 1–28.

Grossman, Jean Baldwin (1982) 'The Substitutability of Natives and Immigrants in Production', *Review of Economics and Statistics*, vol. 64(4), pp. 596–603.

HaiskenDe New, John and Klaus Zimmermann (1999) 'Wage and Mobility Effects of Trade and Migration', in M. Dewatripont and A. Sapir (eds), *International Trade and Employment: The European Experience* (Oxford: Oxford University Press), pp. 139–60.

Hamermesh, Daniel (1993) *Labor Demand* (Princeton NJ: Princeton University Press).

Hamermesh, Daniel (2000) 'The Craft of Labormetrics', *Industrial and Labour Relations Review*, vol. 53, pp. 363–80.

Hanson, Gordon and Matthew Slaughter (2000) 'Labor-Market Adjustment in Open Economies: Evidence from U.S. States,' mimeo, Dartmouth College.

Hanson, Gordon and Antonio Spilimbergo (1999a) 'Illegal Immigration, Border Enforcement, and Relative Wages: Evidence from Apprehensions at the U.S.–Mexico Border', *American Economic Review*, vol. 89(5), pp. 1337–57.

Hanson, Gordon and Antonio Spilimbergo (1999b) 'Political Economy, Sectoral Shocks, and Border Enforcement', NBER Working Paper, no. 7,182.

Hatton, Timothy and Jeffrey Williamson (1998) *The Age of Mass Migration: An Economic Analysis* (Oxford and New York: Oxford University Press).

Helliwell, John (1998) *How Much Do National Borders Matter?* (Washington, DC: Brookings Institution Press).

Hicks, John (1970) 'Elasticity of Substitution Again: Substitutes and Complements', *Oxford Economic Papers*, vol. 22(3), pp. 289–96.

Horiba, Yutaka (2000) 'U.S. Interregional Migration and Trade', Working Paper, Tulane University.

Horiba, Yutaka and Rickey Kirkpatrick (1983) 'U.S. North–South Labor Migration and Trade', *Journal of Regional Science*, vol. 23(1), pp. 93–103.

Hunt, Jennifer (1992) 'The Impact of the 1962 Repatriates from Algeria on the French Labor Market', *Industrial and Labor Relations Review*, vol. 45(3), pp. 556–72.

Jacobson, Louis, Robert LaLonde and Daniel Sullivan (1993) *The Costs of Worker Dislocation* (Kalamazoo, MI: W.E. Upjohn Institute for Employment Research).

Jaeger, David (1996) 'Skill Differences and the Effect of Immigrants on the Wages of Natives', US Bureau of Labor Statistics Working Paper no. 273.

Johnson, George (1980) 'The Labor Market Effects of Immigrants', *Industrial and Labor Relations Review*, vol. 33(3), pp. 331–41.

Johnson, George (1998) 'The Impact of Immigration on Income Distribution Among Minorities', in Daniel Hamermesh and Frank Bean (eds), *Help or Hindrance? The Economic Implications of Immigration for African Americans* (New York: Russell Sage Foundation), pp. 17–50.

Jones, Ronald (1965) 'The Structure of Simple General Equilibrium Models', *Journal of Political Economy*, vol. 73(6), pp. 557–72.

Jones, Ronald and José Scheinkman (1977) 'The Relevance of the Two-Sector Production Model in Trade Theory', *Journal of Political Economy*, vol. 85(5), pp. 909–35.

Junankar, P.N.R., Pope, D. and Withers, G. 'Immigration and the Australian Macroeconomy: Perspective and Prospective', *Australian Economic Review*, vol. 31, pp. 435–44.

Kim, Sukkoo (1998) 'Economic Integration and Convergence: U.S. Regions, 1840–1987', *Journal of Economic History*, vol. 58(3), pp. 659–63.

Kim, Sukkoo (1999) 'Decomposing US Regional Incomes: A Reply', *Journal of Economic History*, vol. 59, pp. 779–86.

King, Allan, B. Lindsay Lowell and Frank Bean (1986) 'The Effects of Hispanic Immigrants in the Earnings of Native Hispanic Americans', *Social Science Quarterly*, vol. 67(4), pp. 673–89.

Kletzer, Lori (1991) 'Earnings after Job Displacement: Job Tenure, Industry, and Occupation', in J. Addison (ed.), *Job Displacement: Consequences and Implications for Policy* (Detroit: Wayne State University Press), pp. 107–35.

Kletzer, Lori (1996) 'The Role of Sector-Specific Skills in Post-Displacement Earnings', *Industrial Relations*, vol. 35(4), pp. 473–90.

Kohli, Ulrich (1991) *Technology, Duality, and Foreign Trade: The GNP Function Approach to Modeling Imports and Exports* (Ann Arbor: University of Michigan Press).

Kohli, Ulrich (1993) 'International Labor Mobility and the Demand for Imports', *Schweizerische Zeitschrift für Volkswirtschaft und Statistik*, vol. 129(3), pp. 547–61.

Kohli, Ulrich (1999) 'Trade and Migration: A Production-Theory Approach', in R. Faini, J. deMelo and K. Zimmermann (eds), *Migration: The Controversies and the Evidence* (Cambridge: Cambridge University Press), pp. 117–46.

Lalonde, Robert and Robert Topel (1991a) 'Immigrants in the American Labor Market: Quality, Assimilation, and Distributional Effects', *American Economic Review*, vol. 81(2), pp. 297–302.

Lalonde, Robert and Robert Topel (1991b) 'Labor Market Adjustments to Increased Migration', in J. Abowd and R. Freeman (eds), *Immigration, Trade and the Labor Market* (Chicago: University of Chicago Press for NBER), pp. 167–99.

LaLonde, Robert and Robert Topel (1997) 'Economic Impact of International Migration and the Economic Performance of Migrants', in Mark Rosenzweig and Oded Stark (eds), *Handbook of Population and Family Economics*, vol.1B (Amsterdam: North-Holland), pp. 799–850.

Lau, Lawrence (1986) 'Functional Forms in Econometric Model Building', in Z. Griliches and M. Intriligator (eds), *Handbook of Econometrics*, vol. 3 (Amsterdam: Elsevier), pp. 1515–66.

Leamer, Edward (1995) 'The Heckscher-Ohlin Model in Theory and Practice', *Princeton Studies in International Finance*, no. 77.

Lerner, Abba (1952) 'Factor-Prices in International Trade', *Economica*, vol.19, pp. 1–15.

Levy, Frank and Richard Murnane (1992) 'US Earnings Levels and Earnings Inequality: A Review of Recent Trends and Proposed Explanations', *Journal of Economic Literature*, vol. 30(3), pp. 1333–81.

Massey, Douglas, Joaquin Arango, Graeme Hugo, Ali Kouaouci, Adela Pellegrino and J. Edward Taylor (1998) *Worlds in Motion: Understanding International Migration at the End of the Millenium* (Oxford: Clarendon Press).

Meyer, Bruce (1995) 'Natural and Quasi-Experiments in Economics', *Journal of Business and Economic Statistics*, vol. 13(2), pp. 151–61.

Mundell, Robert (1957) 'International Trade and Factor Mobility', *American Economic Review*, vol. 47(3), pp. 321–35.

Murphy, Kevin, Mark Plant and Finis Welch (1988) 'Cohort Size and Earnings in the USA', in Ronald Lee, W. Brian Arthur and Gerry Rodgers (eds), *Economics of Changing Age Distributions in Developed Countries* (Oxford and New York: Oxford University Press), pp. 39–58.

Murphy, Kevin and Finis Welch (1991) 'The Role of International Trade in Wage Differentials', in M. Kosters (ed.), *Workers and Their Wages: Changing Patterns in the United States* (Washington, DC: AEI), pp. 39–69.

Nelson, Charles R. and Richard Startz (1990) 'Some Further Results on the Exact Small Sample Properties of the Instrumental Variable Estimator', *Econometrica*, vol. 58(4), pp. 967–76.

Pischke, J.S. and Velling, J. (1997) 'Employment Effects of Immigration to Germany: An Analysis Based on Local Labour Markets', *Review of Economics and Statistics*, vol. 79, pp. 594–604.

Razin, Assaf and Efraim Sadka (1997) 'International Migration and International Trade', in Mark Rosenzweig and Oded Stark (eds), *Handbook of Population and Family Economics*, vol. 1B (Amsterdam: North-Holland), pp. 851–87.

Rivera-Batiz, Francisco and Selig Sechzer (1991) 'Substitution and Complementarity between Immigrant and Native Labor in the US', in F. Rivera-Batiz, S. Sechzer and I. Gang (eds), *US Immigration Policy Reform in the 1980s* (Westport, CT: Praeger), pp. 89–116.

Rodrik, Dani (1998) 'Comment on Freeman', in Susan M. Collins (ed.), *Imports, Exports and the American Worker* (Washington, DC: Brookings Institution Press), pp. 131–3.

Roy, A.D. (1951) 'Some Thoughts on the Distribution of Earnings', *Oxford Economic Papers*, vol. 3, pp. 135–46.

Ruffin, Roy (1984) 'International Factor Movements', in Ronald Jones and Peter Kenen (eds), *Handbook of International Economics*, vol. 1 (Amsterdam: North-Holland), pp. 237–88.

Ruhm, Christopher (1991) 'Are Workers Permanently Scarred by Job Displacements?', *American Economic Review*, vol. 81(1), pp. 319–24.

Rybczynski, T.N. (1955) 'Factor Endowments and Relative Commodity Prices', *Economica*, vol. 22, pp. 336–41.

Samuelson, Paul (1948) 'International Trade and the Equalization of Factor-Prices', *Economic Journal*, vol. 58, pp. 163–84.

Sassen, Saskia (1999) *Guests and Aliens* (New York: The New Press).

Sato, Ryuzo and Tetsunori Koizumi (1973) 'On the Elasticities of Substitution and Complementarity', *Oxford Economic Papers*, vol. 25(1), pp. 44–56.

Topel, Robert (1986) 'Local Labor Markets', *Journal of Political Economy*, vol. 94(3, Part 2), pp. S111–43.

Topel, Robert (1991) 'Specific Capital, Mobility, and Wages: Wages Rise with Job Seniority', *Journal of Political Economy*, vol. 99(1), pp. 145–76.

Topel, Robert (1994a) 'Regional Labor Markets and the Determinants of Wage Inequality', *American Economic Review*, vol. 84(2), pp. 17–22.

Topel, Robert (1994b) 'Wage Inequality and Regional Labour Market Performance in the US', in T. Tachibanaki (ed.), *Labour Market and Economic Performance: Europe, Japan and the USA* (New York: St Martin's Press), pp. 93–127.

Venables, Anthony (1999) 'Trade Liberalisation and Factor Mobility: An Overview', in Riccardo Faini, Jaime deMelo and Klaus Zimmermann (eds), *Migration: The Controversies and the Evidence* (Cambridge: Cambridge University Press), pp. 23–47.

Welch, Finis (1979) 'Effects of Cohort Size on Earnings: The Baby Boom Babies' Financial Bust', *Journal of Political Economy*, vol. 87(5, Part 2), pp. S65–97.

White, Michael and Peter Mueser (1988) 'Implications of Boundary Choice for the Measurement of Residential Mobility', *Demography*, vol. 25(3), pp. 443–59.

Wildasin, David (1991) 'Income Redistribution in a Common Labor Market', *American Economic Review*, vol. 81(4), pp. 757–74.

Winter-Ebmer, Rudolf and Klaus Zimmerman (1996) 'Immigration and the Earnings of Young Native Workers', *Oxford Economic Papers*, vol. 48, pp. 473–91.

Winter-Ebmer, Rudolf and Klaus Zimmerman (1999) 'East–West Trade and Migration: The Austro-German Case', in R. Faini, J. deMelo and K. Zimmermann (eds), *Migration: The Controversies and the Evidence* (Cambridge: Cambridge University Press), pp. 296–326.

Winter-Ebmer, Rudolf and Josef Zweimuller (1996) 'Immigration and the Earnings of Young Native Workers', *Oxford Economic Papers*, vol. 48, pp. 473–91.

Winter-Ebmer, Rudolf and Josef Zweimuller (1999a) 'Immigration, Trade, and Austrian Unemployment', in M. Landesmann and K. Pichelmann (eds), *Unemployment in Europe* (New York: St Martin's Press).

Winter-Ebmer, Rudolf and Josef Zweimuller (1999b) 'Do Immigrants Displace Native Workers? The Austrian Experience', *Journal of Population Economics*, vol. 12(2), pp. 327–40.

Wong, Kar-yiu (1986) 'Are International Trade and Factor Mobility Substitutes?', *Journal of International Economics*, vol. 21(1/2), pp. 25–44.

Wong, Kar-yiu (1988) 'International Factor Mobility and the Volume of Trade: An Empirical Study', in R. Feenstra (ed.), *Empirical Methods for International Trade* (Chicago: University of Chicago Press for NBER), pp. 231–50.

Wong, Kar-yiu (1995) 'International Labor Migration', *International Trade of Goods and Factor Mobility* (Cambridge, MA: MIT Press), pp. 625–64.

Woodland, Alan (1982) *International Trade and Resource Allocation* (Amsterdam: North-Holland).

Woodland, Alan D. (1984) 'Stability, Capital Mobility and Trade', *International Economic Review*, vol. 24, pp. 475–83.

Zimmerman, Klaus (1995) 'Tackling the European Migration Problem', *Journal of Economic Perspectives*, vol. 9(2), pp. 45–62.

Zlotnik, Hania (1998) 'International Migration 1965–96: An Overview', *Population and Development Review*, vol. 24(3), pp. 429–68.

Index